Jews and French Quebecers

Two Hundred Years of Shared History

The authors of this study have met a challenge of veritable size that not only required scientific rigour, but also necessitated acute sensitivity and objectivity.
— Paul Grégoire, Archbishop of Montreal,
October 24, 1986
(translation from the French)

Jews and French Quebecers: Two Hundred Years of Shared History . . . The result is a fresh outlook on history, one that occurs when we discover it from a truly new vantage point. It should rapidly make its way into the manuals.
— Lise Bissonette, "Point of View," *Le Soleil*,
February 18, 1987
(translation from the French)

Jews & French Quebecers

Two Hundred Years of Shared History

by Jacques Langlais & David Rome

translated by Barbara Young

Wilfrid Laurier University Press

WLU

The translation and publication of
Jews and French Quebecers: Two Hundred Years of Shared History
has been made possible by funding from the Canada Council.

Canadian Cataloguing in Publication Data

Langlais, Jacques, 1921-
   Jews and French Quebecers

Translation of: Juifs et Québécois français : 200
ans d'histoire commune.
Includes bibliographical references.
ISBN 0-88920-998-7

1. Jews – Quebec (Province) – History.
2. Antisemitism – Quebec (Province) – History.
3. Quebec (Province) – Ethnic relations.   I. Rome,
David, 1910-   . II. Title.

FC2950.J5L3513 1991   971.4'004924   C91-095062-8
F1055.J5L3513 1991

© 1991
Wilfrid Laurier University Press
Waterloo, Ontario, Canada
N2L 3C5

Printed in Canada

Cover design by Connolly Art & Design

Originally published as *Juifs et Québécois français : 200 ans d'histoire commune*
(© La Corporation des Éditions Fides, Montréal, 1986).

Jews and French Quebecers: Two Hundred Years of Shared History has been typeset
from a manuscript provided by the translator and verified by the authors.

Contents

Foreword

The title of this book deserves attention.

This book grew out of a theme chosen by the authors. It is a pooling, or more precisely a combining of their knowledge, talent and judgement. And that is what each has signed — or so it seems.

The reality is quite another matter. This book was born of a double experience, that of two very different men brought together by geography. They have followed separate personal paths through an immensely complex historical period full of misunderstandings, leaving a profound mark on their lives.

One is a Catholic priest belonging to a congregation of French origin, a missiology researcher specializing in Asian religions, a Quebec nationalist and lover of French-Canadian folklore who is dedicated to the cause of cross-cultural relations.

The other is a Zionist devoted to Quebec's Jewish community and an archivist with a passion for Quebec history. He is concerned with the period of misunderstanding and hostility between Quebec and the Jews, and more broadly, with the holocausts that have marked all of Jewish history.

The two first met overseas, then in Quebec as neighbours who sincerely wished to become acquainted, as any good neighbours must. They soon realized they would be wise to avoid the pitfalls of current controversy, and to look closely instead at both their differences and their common ground. This led them to piece together a brief history of a community within a community, of Jews among Quebecers, particularly the French Quebecers by whom they were received.

The authors wished to be as fair, as relevant and as clear as possible for their readers. The two communities share many kinship ties. Both have been affected by their minority status. Each one's survival has been under threat and both are still, more or less, in a state of alert. Both are deeply imbued with religious culture, and their basic goals are humanistic. Both are nationalists, and for the Jews this means a complex form of Zionism. Both profess

---

Notes for the Foreword are found on page 161.

ideals of peace and justice. And both consider language and heritage to be of primary importance.

If each author had set out to write these pages on his own, the task would have been easy. Each would no doubt have given his own accurate and interesting version of the facts. And the result would have been two entirely different books, probably valuable and useful, but also open to controversy.

This book is quite different. It can be compared to the work of a third mind, of Siamese twins separated by the surgery of circumstances, yet deeply attached in a third being who can express itself only in terms judged acceptable by the other two. In the end, those terms are the only ones that seem possible to either one.

The project took months to complete, even longer than it seemed. The experience was fascinating, difficult, even painful on occasion, but it was always rewarding. Readers can share in it by taking a look at the book's most troublesome passages and seeing how they were resolved. They might even enjoy verifying for themselves whether the authors faced all the major questions squarely, or perhaps side-stepped certain ones.

There are quite obvious "ruptures" in the text, which are not there by coincidence. Readers can use them as points of reference in making sense of the deepest realities experienced by these two societies, whose importance goes far beyond simply cross-cultural proximity.

But even that is not the biggest challenge. Readers can personalize the authors' experience by analyzing Quebec's present ethnic and cultural plurality with someone from another culture. Not to convince or convert, and certainly not as a game, but to develop their own traditional language and discourse, to grow in the understanding of themselves and their neighbours, each reflected in the other.

Here, then, are the results of a project that has given the authors great satisfaction. The effort to make sense of Quebec's unique destiny has been an exciting challenge. And each of the authors now has yet another reason to love this young society even more deeply than before.

David Rome

My first contact with David Rome dates from the 1950s, when he spoke at Collège Brébeuf in Montreal. It was the first time I had heard an Anglophone Jew speak, in my language, about the relations between Jewish and French Quebecers. The details of his speech now escape me, but it struck me as a milestone event for the two communities.

The name of David Rome has since been associated in my mind with ideas of openness, dialogue and understanding, and with exceptional intelligence regarding our respective histories.

Our paths crossed again some thirty years later, this time at the Monchanin Intercultural Centre. The occasion was a conference for members of various ethnic and cultural communities on the theme "Who is a Quebecer?" The major presentations at this exchange were published the following year,[1] which led me to seek out David Rome for clarifications to his text. An interview with David Rome cannot be limited to an isolated question. The archivist and historian irresistably takes over the conversation and guides his interviewer through the mysteries of the past. He does so with the ease and generosity of a scholar immersed in his subject to the point of reliving the past as intensely as the present. The conversation lasted for hours, and by the end we had made a resolution: together we would write down the history of the Jews in Quebec.

Why the Jews? Because, of all the communities who have come to share the destiny of the native peoples and the "two founding nations," the Jewish community is the oldest,[2] and has also been the most deeply involved in parliamentary and legal struggles for political, economic and educational freedom in Quebec. And also — perhaps most importantly — because the decades of anti-Semitism between 1880 and 1945 still weigh heavily on the collective memory.

Why David Rome? Speaking personally, because he opened my eyes to so much about the Jews that I had seen without understanding, and to so much about Quebec and about myself, a Quebecer by birth. Because he was a dependable, inexhaustible source of accurate, detailed information. And above all, because he had the sensitivity and experience crucial to an honest yet penetrating reading of the facts, motivations and circumstances of this family history whose pages can still burn the fingers.

Our project turned out to be full of surprises, difficult at times and always fascinating. Writing with and about someone else is more than an adventure. And when that someone else has grown hypersensitive after suffering experiences to which you are inextricably linked, when each step with him and closer to him binds you more closely to his past and future, it is even more than an unforgettable experience. It is a con-version (from convertere, to turn toward the other), with everything that implies in the way of discovery, confusion, anguish and ultimately, growth.

A strange encounter, this cross-cultural encounter. It left me without a trace of what I was or thought I was, and brought me to an increasing awareness of what I am in essence: someone for whom truth is revealed through the truth of others. In this instance, it is the truth of my Jewish friends, who are also Quebecers — in the fullest sense of the term.

Jacques Langlais

Preface to the
English Translation

This book tells a saga of intense interest for the whole of Canada, let alone societies elsewhere. It deals with the merging—through alterations of close cooperation and socio-political clashes—of two Quebec ethno-cultural communities: one, the French, already rooted in the land of Quebec and its religio-cultural tradition; the other, the Jewish, migrating from Europe through the last two centuries, equally rooted in its Jewish-Yiddish tradition. Here both communities have learned to live together, and finally to share their heritages.

A most remarkable experience, 200 years of intercultural co-vivance, it is part of the epic of the building of a nation able to make experience in the living together of world cultures not only a possibility but a reality; eventually a test case for other countries in our world on the eve of the third millennium.

The huge territory north of the St. Lawrence River—New France, Lower Canada, Quebec, with its panoramic kaleidoscope of northern beauty—has been the scene of many of the major dramas of the northern hemisphere's New World. Vital door to the North American heartland, it has served as the northern approach to New England and to the American metropolitan centres, as well as the north Atlantic, the northern border with the USSR and the northern air route between America and Europe.

Above all, it is the homeland of peoples from prehistoric native settlements to European colonists who in recent centuries were sent here by the first imperialists: the French, who settled along the St. Lawrence River and the Great Lakes and travelled the continent from the Gulf of Mexico to the Prairies and the Pacific Ocean; the English, who settled what is now the United States and the Maritime provinces.

In the eighteenth century, as the conclusion of a series of world wars, Quebec's destiny was to be conquered by the British. French soldiers and administrators left New France for the old homeland. The sixty thousand civilian residents of French origin who had belonged to this land for over a century and who were already "Canadians"—and in broader terms "Americans"—

xi

remained to live together with the English who came to settle. And with the English came the Jews, both from England and from the British colonies of the eastern seaboard. They brought to Quebec a complex, neutral society with much to teach their hosts.

The transfer of imperial rule from Versailles to London in 1760 abolished French Quebec homogeneity and unity of religion and language, and introduced new dimensions of racial and cultural pluralism, and economic and political concepts and patterns. Yet Canadians of French origin had not been left in complete isolation from their European roots. Thanks to their Catholicism and French cultural traditions they were able to keep alive not only their North European traits and the Greco-Latin character of their educational system, but also their contacts with the outer world through emissaries—notably their missionaries—in both the French and the British empires.

Originally Quebec was a less than tightly governed outpost; then it became a conquered colony. During two centuries Quebecers—all Quebecers—French, English and Jews together—had to attain satisfying development, right by right and position by position, peaceably, largely by the strength of principles inherent in an alien constitution, but always by the fraternity and the ingenuity of its own sons, and by the political genius of devoted leaders.

The Jewish newcomers readily adapted to Quebec's majority and learned French. They formed an early alliance with the Catholics against the Anglican monopoly and religious hegemony, winning themselves the right to a synagogue and, soon after, to full civic rights at the hands of the French nationalist, Catholic-led legislature. No one was surprised when, before the 1837 revolt, Ezekiel Hart entertained Louis-Joseph Papineau in his Trois-Rivières home, when Dutch Jewish immigrant Levy Koffman (become Louis Marchand) fought beside the rebels, or when A. P. Hart defended the revolutionaries before martial courts; all this largely during the first century of Jewish residence in Quebec.

The expanded peoples of Quebec lived in amity under a series of constitutions which generally recognized basic freedom and equality for all under law. These arrangements established relationships with the imperial power, with the neighbouring English-language colonies and between the French and the English in the colony, culminating in the Canadian confederation of 1867.

Within the conditions of English and French duality, Quebec has witnessed the creation of a people in all dimensions of loyalty and fraternity, language, religion, literature, defence of group interests, custom, economy, institutions, music and law. Despite the occasional impingement of neighbouring jurisdictions and, at times, open violence between conflicting interests, Quebec history has generally been marked by a convention of peacefulness which can serve as a rare model. Tradition has avoided clash. Indeed, the convention of shunning conflict is a major theme of Quebec and Canadian history. Rednecks are not absent, but the people of all major groups have usually put them in their places.

During two peaceful centuries the "immigrant" peoples of Quebec developed an intense and rich life—the Anglophone as an integral part of American, Anglo-Saxon and anglo-Canadian culture; the Québécois in French, somewhat more independently of the civilization of Paris, and more recent arrivals, a mélange of other European, Asiatic, African and French Antilles origin. Each group has its own history of ethnocultural relations with the dominant English or French, yet retention of its own cultural heritage—the totality shaped rather in its own Québécois "American" way. These French Quebec centuries have seen, by and large, the recognition of its language, its church and its custom.

Moderation, discipline and a dedication to the extended family enabled Quebec society to avoid exile and assimilation; to interpret treaties and charters into minority rights and human rights and into the claims of the majority; and to translate the bloody catastrophes of the Upper and Lower Canada rebellions into the first Canadian confederation.

The apparatus of Quebec patriotism was developed largely during the birth of the colony of Canada, when its poets—French, English and Jewish—developed a vast bibliography of periodicals and a people's literature and the spokesmen for the rebels of 1837 became officials in the post-Durham governments. Québécois claimed and won moral status and even "rebellion losses" for the Anglophone street fighters who burned the parliament buildings in Montreal—all this when ironically super-loyalist Benjamin Hart was virtually driven from Canada by the Anglophone regime for protesting his imperialist loyalty.

This was to be the last time that London authorities were to intervene in Canadian crises; out of the Upper and Lower Canada rebellions emerged in 1840 a government directly responsible to the citizenry, a prelude to the Confederation of 1867.

Inevitably the wide concept of Quebec as an independent state arose. Indeed, this has become one of the poles in the range of French-Canadian nationalist self-perception and alternatives for people's fulfillment. Yet the Quebec tradition of moderation has even permitted Anglophones to participate with Francophones in the pursuit of the French tryst with fulfillment, notably as when T. S. Brown and Wolfred Nelson shared in the leadership of the French in the Rebellion of 1837-38.

The Ultramontane Influence

A score of years after the 1837-38 rebellions in Quebec and Ontario, two momentous events occurred in Quebec. From tiny Lithuania and other Slav countries came a growing stream of a new type of immigrants, Yiddish-speaking, who were to introduce a new and radically different culture to Quebec. At the same time, and also from Europe, there emanated into Canada ultramontanism, a powerful religious movement which came to be probably more influential in Quebec than in any other region on the continent. For fourscore years the church in Quebec permitted an intensive, though mostly academic, teaching of contempt and hostility towards the Jewish people. The record is so harsh that it is surprising the consequences were not more dire. The Jewish community reacted with dismay, fear and distrust, particularly as the movement was allied with developing Quebec nationalism, buttressed by the considerable talents of Monsignor Paquet (1832-1900), Canon Groulx (1878-1967), journalist J. P. Tardivel (1857-1942) and the influence of *Action sociale catholique* and *La Semaine religieuse de Québec*, not to speak of the pulpit.

Strangely enough, this bolder and more hostile "patriotism" flourished even after Confederation. A series of journalists and religious spokesmen, defenders of French Quebec provincial interests, were for decades consistently hostile to Jews and were at times more active in oppressing them than in advancing the people of Quebec. This school of patriotic education continued into the twentieth century under the more political but equally anti-Semitic leaders of Action française, Action nationale, Henri Bourrassa in his younger years and, above all, by Canon Groulx and the journalist Adrien Arcand.

The movement became increasingly involved in partisan politics; indeed some parties were formed and some political anti-Semitic campaigns were carried out with the blessing of nationalist leaders. Maurice Duplessis' Union Nationale party was so named because it was initially a merger of several such nationalist organizations. Most fatefully, Quebec activists supported the Ottawa government in keeping the gates of Canada shut to Jews fleeing Europe's fascist regimes, as Abella and Troper's *None is Too Many* records.

Such "patriotic" activities also became very closely related to church life in Quebec. As religious institutions became involved, racist teachings entered the educational system. Some clergy high in the church became supporters of the anti-Jewish groups, so that it was often difficult to distinguish among religion, language, racism and patriotism. Indeed, while the world church recognized that extremist patriotisms cloaked universal evil, menacing religion and humanity itself, the Quebec Catholic hierarchy openly disregarded Vatican warnings and opted for this unsavoury form of nationalism.

It is remarkable that during this period of hostility to Judaism, Zionist leader Louis Fitch publicly defended the Catholic system of college education, and later sat in the provincial legislature on Duplessis' ticket; that *Adler* journalist B. G. Sack presented the nationalist campaign in defence of the French language as a model to the Jews; that philosopher Yehudah Kaufman backed the nationalist minority movements in continental Europe and the United States in their struggles for their rights; and that union leader Leon Chazanovitch opposed the Jewish-Protestant partnership in the education of Jewish school children.

In spite of eighty years of harsh social tensions, the territory of Quebec remained peaceful and adopted a mode of modern pluralism. The outsider privileged to witness this tribal operation cannot but be inspired by the phenomenon, which could be particularly instructive for other provinces, states and nations.

Confederation

Even during the emergence of isolationist ultramontanism, the political leaders of Quebec, Ontario and the Maritime provinces met in Charlottetown — soon to be joined by British Columbia and the Prairie provinces — to form a confederation, a compact to govern themselves freely negotiated by Canadians and only formally enacted by the British Parliament.

Canada, like the United States, is one of the few modern nations formed by its own people with a constitution they themselves developed out of their own experience and wisdom. Its creation consisted to a large extent of French Quebec freely coming to agreement with Anglophone Ontario on many clearly understood issues. The outcome was a nation, already multicultural, largely French and English in its fabric, enjoying a level and style of living admired by all humanity, able to deal amicably with such domestic problems as arise inevitably and everywhere. Its crises, including participation in two world wars and bloodshed on complex issues, have served to weld a subdued yet profound patriotism. The creation of this Confederation was worthy of the hope of its makers; worthy of its six-score years' durability since and of the ten unequal provincial histories which came to constitute the state. Quebec's role was wisely foreseen, carefully prepared and constantly adjusted long after the colony had become a dominion, long after events had moved beyond foresight.

This speaks much for the solidarity of Quebec, but much also for the tolerance of the negotiators with Quebec. Protestant Upper Canada agreed to a British dominion where the Roman Catholic Church enjoyed status not available to Anglican archbishops, where Catholic schools were state established and charities were a church domain — until the Quebec Catholic majority in its Quiet Revolution decreed otherwise by provincial legislation, and until the same jurisdiction decided to subsidize Jewish schools, hospitals and cultural institutions, a step which is almost unique in the Western world.

Quebec has remained different, even as it shares many of the traits of its sister provinces. To note its specific cultural and familial character, we need only speak of the love that bound its citizens into a special unity: a love of the French language and of the Catholic religion and a common concern for harmonious relations between the English and the French parties.

The Quiet Revolution

Probably the most dazzling of the kaleidoscopic Canadian frames in our long history has been the sudden alteration of the Quebec scene once the Second World War came to an end. At that moment, the entire nation came to understand profoundly the meaning of the war it had just fought and the idealism which alone made sense out of its vast human cost. The fragility of human civilization, the evil significance of the enemy's teachings, the universal implications of racism to the survival of ethics, the profound falsehood at the root of anti-Semitism, the ease with which the anti-human forces had penetrated the moral foundations of nations and families, the host of enslavements which had chained mankind – all awakened a sensitivity to other cultures, never so deeply felt before.

The menace of the racist horror had developed and grown over the entire world for some eighty years, and not least in Canada and in Quebec. The awakening here was therefore particularly significant – and painful. It was a spontaneous, unanimous experience, as the nation decided to root out the enslaving forces and to transform itself into the most democratic and just nation which its citizenry could conceive and implant.

The Quebec counterpart of the world's liberation was particularly radical, if only because in its pre-war state it had been ultramontane in denomination and Duplessist politically. The "quiet" revolution was nevertheless resounding – in education, in civil liberties, in democracy, in multiculturalism and, radically, in regard to anti-Semitism. The teachings of Canon Groulx and Tardivel were virtually forgotten; André Laurendeau repeated his renunciation of Jeune Canada. The ecumenical movement led by the archbishop of Montreal, and by such pioneers in good will as Jesuit Stéphane Valiquette and Sister Marie-Noëlle de Baillehache, has been able to alter the religious climate of Quebec, as have institutions as the Intercultural Institute of Montreal and other private and governmental initiatives.

Under Premier Jean Lesage, nationalistic teaching was modernized and economic programmes were intensified. The anti-clericalism of the new generation and the broader democratization of post-ultramontanism expanded public interest in the new patriotism. The welcoming hand extended by the Quiet Revolution to minorities such as Jews and to immigrants, who became important, full-fledged components of Quebec society, altered all perceptions. The views of those of the ancient Québécois root, of the Québécois by choice and of those brought here by the new workings of fate on the world scale, coalesced.

Quebec learned to identify itself with language and culture both within its border and on the world scale of commerce, diplomacy, education, citizenship and rights. With a sense of pride and love of province came impatience with the humiliatingly outdated perception of Quebec retained by other Canadians. Some were simply ignorant of the Québécois' changed society.

Others seemed deliberately to refuse to develop, through their ministries of cultural affairs, an appreciation of their own substantial regional culture or cultures, let alone of multilingualism and multiculturalism. There appeared a culture gap, at least in the area of national self-perception, between Quebec and the other provinces.

This psychological indifference to the new Quebec served to aggravate dissatisfactions to the point of crisis, as much as had the older objective situations, the inequalities and injustices in the intersocial condition. This climate encouraged a bold Quebec patriotism, ever more assertive, daring, often defensive. The rooted society of French Quebec has developed with no parallel for thousands of miles; a cultural island for a few million, speaking a world language which no one else this side of the North Atlantic Ocean speaks; descendants of a mere sixty thousand only two centuries ago; cosmopolitan in traditions and achievements to match the great American and European centres, yet so close to their linguistic, folkloric, rural heritage that each treasures the family heritage. All believe in a unique religious culture; range socially from proletarian to the rarest worldly refinement; are ready to absorb foreigners within rural society and urban centres, yet losing few by assimilation within their Quebec. Premiers to policemen, cardinals to laymen, judges, ministers, professors, bank presidents, novelists, editors, cinéastes, opera singers, poets, mining engineers, historians, diplomats, they govern themselves — yet without an army.

The consequences are writ in recent annals, in the passionate and as-yet-incomplete emotional history, in the perceptions of the course of life of every resident of the province and the country. Each has reached his or her own conclusions about the nation's fate. In this complex of questions all Canadians — Québécois, Jews and millions of others — continue to live in democracy, in complexity of religions and of cultures. They have learned to appreciate their respective as well as their common heritage and ultimately, to meet their unique historical challenge: to live in peace and harmony.

Preface to the
Original French Version

This book is addressed first and foremost to French Quebecers.[1]

Descendants of the first French colonists cannot ignore the native people who preceded them by several millennia. Neither can they forget the first immigrants who came here by choice, the Jews. They cannot forget that these groundbreakers, along with the native people and the English, were their original partners in building Quebec.

It is unthinkable that French Quebecers in particular should forget, because they share so much in common with the Jewish community: related religions, political experiences and minority status which unite them in the same historical process. By choosing Quebec as a refuge, Jews signalled their confidence in the laws and institutions of the land and the openness of its people. Five thousand years of history has taught them to recognize a hospitable environment, and their migrations constitute a veritable barometer of the social climate prevailing in different parts of the world.

Compared to many other peoples, the Jewish people is few in numbers. It is fragmented into a multitude of communities scattered among the major Western cities and many different countries. Its dispersion did not end when the state of Israel was created. Today there are just half as many Jews there (3,062,000 in 1971) as in the United States, and the same number as in New York. This diaspora forms a unique network of economic and cultural exchange throughout the West and especially in North America, which has effectively served the interests of certain empires.

This book is also addressed to other communities who have chosen Quebec as their adopted land. Just as French Quebecers are a minority in Canada, these Quebecers are a minority in Quebec. Each generation faces a range of choices from ghettoization to assimilation, including various forms of sharing that embody a respect for other cultural identities. Some of these have not yet been explored. Jews were the first group in Quebec to make this choice. On

Notes for the Preface are found on page 161.

the whole, they have responded in much the same way as others in their situation, opting for integration which leaves their cultural heritage intact. They have created all the institutions of a society within a society: congregations, synagogues, cemeteries, schools, recreation and immigrant aid centres. Their refusal of assimilation implies a confidence that Quebec, as host society, agrees to respect the differences that exist in its ethnic and cultural communities. They stand before Quebec as a people jealous of its identity, but also as brothers, sisters and equals who want to build a new type of society.

Today, there are 6 million men and women living in Quebec. The majority (80%) is defined as belonging to the French culture, although ethnic diversity is growing steadily within this group. It includes, for example, over 20,000 Sephardic Jews. Until recently, the Anglophone community in Quebec has been virtually alone in representing North America's cultural and religious plurality. It includes some 80,000 Jews, most of them Ashkenazim.

Together, these 100,000 Quebec Jews, Ashkenazi and Sephardic, Anglophone and Francophone, form one of the largest diasporas after that of New York.[2] And what is more important, their history is that of the nation's first immigrants.

Relatives, Partners and Neighbours

In fact, Jews have been part of the Quebec constellation since the time of the French settlers. Although they were forbidden to settle in the colony, their capital contributed to the economy of New France, and to its resistance against attacks by the British navy. On a deeper level, they have occupied a unique place in the "Canadian" religious universe. Jews and Christians share a spiritual kingship in Abraham, father of the believers, and above all in Christianity's Judaic roots.

With the 1760 conquest, the Jews became partners and neighbours as well as spiritual kin. They fought beside Canadians to win civil and religious freedoms for Quebec. And they helped put Montreal on the world commercial and industrial map.

In many respects, today's Ashkenazim and Sephardim form the most representative bilingual, and predominantly bicultural community in Quebec society. Theirs is a milieu of astonishing cultural wealth, a society within a society formed by successive waves of immigration from Europe, North Africa and the Near East. Anglophone Sephardim arrived after the Conquest, bringing with them remarkable skills in such key fields as politics, administration, industry, commerce and international trade.

The great Yiddish migration from Eastern Europe took place between 1880 and the second half of the twentieth century. It was the first migration from the Old World of people whose mother tongue was neither English nor French. The scientific and literary work of these Yiddish-speaking people burst upon the scene with amazing energy, transforming Montreal into one of the world capitals of Jewish culture, and dominating the ethnic patchwork that was Saint Lawrence Boulevard.

The Jewish community and its neighbour (sometimes also its partner) the Francophone community, had a common destiny and a shared history. They lived it without ever really understanding or even recognizing one another. Both groups knew what it meant to be uprooted, one from the Ukraine, Poland and Romania, the other from the Laurentian soil. They had also felt the negative effects of early industrialization. Mothers and daughters worked and suffered side by side in the sweat shops and lived in the same quarters. Both communities found themselves facing the same complex question of Canadian and American trade unionism. And they waged a parallel battle to preserve their language, faith, literature and customs.

Two little-understood nationalisms, widely analyzed, proclaimed and passionately played out, often just a few streets apart. Two societies that crowded into the same building on Saint Lawrence Boulevard during the finest hours of their collective life, the Monument National, meeting ground for some of the most illustrious representatives of each culture: orators, poets, writers, intellectuals, theatre people.

Decades of Rupture

Proximity and kinship never prevent misunderstanding and prejudice from erecting walls of mistrust and hostility between communities that, in many cases, share a common destiny. Certain chapters of this work recall the decades of antisemitism which tore Quebec apart between 1880 and 1940, part of an epidemic that originated in Europe and spread across the West, culminating in the Nazi horror.

Those years of terror had a profound effect on the generations that lived through them. The culmination of the Second World War would awaken people to the unbelievable reality of racism. Quebec discovered it at Dachau, the day after the victory, through the eyes of a respected journalist, René Lévesque.

Post-War Liberations

The end of the war greatly affected the 1950s. Communities and individuals throughout the world sought freedom from oppression, however they could. French Quebec was shaken to the core by the Quiet Revolution, which had its equivalent in Jewish society.

Once the Francophone milieu had opened the doors to modernism and pluralism, Anglophone Jews adopted a more realistic attitude toward the deeply rooted aspirations of French Quebecers: increased use of French in business, a political presence in the Cabinet, organizations for religious and cultural dialogue, hospitals open to the general public, media outlets. From this point of view, the works of Naïm Kattan, and films such as *Lies My Father Told Me*,[3] offered unique opportunities for mutual discovery.

The arrival of Sephardic Jews from North Africa after 1958, deeply affected French Quebecers. It was during this period that Gérard Pelletier launched his call, "Feu l'unanimité" (Unanimity is dead) in *Cité libre*. The substantial influx of Francophones from another culture vividly confirmed Pelletier's diagnosis. At the same time, it revealed the tragic lack of immigrant services in the Francophone milieu. But most important of all, it changed French Quebecer's image of Jewish Quebecers. They had previously been perceived as business-oriented Anglophones forever absent from French society and culture. North African Jews, however, permeated the French milieu: in industry and commerce, at the universities, in hospitals and recreation centres, and even in the families of French Quebecers.

The promise of dialogue among Quebecers of all cultures, and thus between French Quebecers and their Jewish partners, will only develop in the crucible of rigorous self-criticism that answers one fundamental question: Who is this Other that so intrigues me, upsets me or leaves me indifferent? Someone I have constructed from my own ideas about history, the prejudices of my community, my cultural presuppositions? Or someone close at hand who has been living in a different but legitimate reality for hundreds and thousands of years? This is a fundamental issue, for dialogue should lead to a meeting of minds, which is not achieved through self-created images or mirror-gazing but rather, through mutual discovery of our respective realities.

This book emerged from dialogue. It is a movement toward in-depth communication between two communities that are at once separated and united by sister traditions. Our goal is not to repond to the many questions posed concerning the respective cultures, but to raise others that make a direct appeal to reality, to the facts. This implies a process of self-criticism, and, above all, a willingness to listen.

Extending our own horizons to discover that Other reality, while at the same time catching a glimpse of our own situation in the openness of mutual communication: this is our ambition in the pages that follow.

CHAPTER I

Early Jewish Presence in Quebec, 1627-1882

The history of relations between today's Jewish and French-Canadian communities in Quebec seems paradoxical at times. One key to understanding why is that neither Jews nor Protestants were present during the French settlement of the St. Lawrence and Mississippi River valleys. The full impact of this situation has never been measured. Several years ago, the Portuguese ambassador in Canada, Eduardo Brazao, observed that his country could have written an important chapter in the early history of the New World had it not made the mistake of exiling its Jewish nationals. Lisbon was then the centre of a huge commercial empire.

By expelling the Jews in 1496, the Portuguese had deprived themselves of a social class that held the levers of the domestic economy, and had severed its ties with the international network of European Jews who influenced European finance and trade.

The ambassador could just as easily have been talking about Colbert's France. If that country had been more powerful and could have mobilized Jewish commercial interests in its trade with Canada and the Caribbean, its history might have taken quite a different course. But anti-Semitism prevailed despite Colbert's realism. He refused to listen to mutterings against the Jews, adding that France should ignore the jealousy shown by Catholic merchants toward Jews and Protestants: "It is important to take a balanced view of whether the trade they control, through contacts all over the world with other Jews, could benefit the state."[1]

It is certainly not easy to evaluate the economic impact of their absence, but one fact does support the Portuguese ambassador's position. The French empire took a more open attitude and welcomed a Jewish family expelled from Portugal, the Gradis of Bordeaux. They in turn played a major role in the economy and defence of France's North American colony, which faced competition from British establishments on the Atlantic coast. But the Jewish

---

absence can be seen most clearly in terms of the social and cultural repercussions it had on the history of Quebec's early settlement by the French.

Travel in New France Prohibited

The settlement process took place according to principles of strict homogeneity. The planners of New France had a clear purpose: to establish a colony in America where Catholics alone would have the right to emigrate after 1627. The companies responsible for the process "pledged, in the name of the King, to help fund the church and support its ministers."[2]

Catholic and French: that was the French-Canadian community's point of departure and remains its traditional definition even today. During 400 years of history, homogeneity has been elevated to the status of a national myth. Textbooks have routinely overlooked the ethnic and cultural diversity that has enriched Quebec society from the very beginning. The earliest contributors were the province's native peoples, although European groups were also present, often in smaller numbers: Scottish, Irish, German, Swiss, as well as English and later Italian. The Blacks had made an early contribution to the history of the French regime[3] which should not be overlooked and the most recent input has come from Quebec's Asian and North African newcomers.

The "other," then, took on such dramatic significance that it had to be excluded so that the community could define itself. The "other" first referred to the "savage" living in the forest on the edges of "civilization," then to the English, with their different language and religion and finally to the immigrant, the outsider, the uprooted.

The Jews presented something of a paradox. On one hand, they were officially banished from the colony[4] – no surprise to the colonists, who knew they had been legal outsiders since the Middle Ages. They were perceived as wandering Jews, cut off from the peasant class because they were forbidden to own property and excluded from public office because they were often not permitted to dwell in the capital. All forms of stability were denied them, so they had to invest in movable goods that could be easily carried and traded: money, gold and precious gems. They were active in business and trade on a broad scale, quickly specialized in certain occupations and became involved in the money traffic through lending and banking. This mobility led them to cultivate an international solidarity that favoured strong ties of family and friendship throughout the diaspora, proving essential to their survival in times of persecution.[5]

Despite the prohibition that weighed on them, Jews maintained a twofold presence in New France. They joined in the colonial administration from their base in the old country by investing in companies instructed by the king with developing his American possessions. They were also present in Quebec religious life, though in rather ambiguous terms. The Jews represented the best and the worst to Christians. The best was expressed by everything the Church held most sacred: the Holy Family, the apostles, the first Christian communities and, as a backdrop, the grand Old Testament figures who prepared the way for their own Golden Age. The worst was summoned up constantly in the liturgy, expressed by the confrontation between Jesus and the Jewish leaders and especially by the tragic outcome of the Passion. This tangible absence in the colony was evoked in rituals that reiterated the pious curses of medieval thought. In fact, those same curses echoed down through the years in Quebec churches until Vatican II.

The Jews, then, left a double impression on the new, yet-to-be-constructed world: a mythical presence in the Scriptures and a total absence in the New World itself. This had a profound effect on the image formulated by French Quebecers of themselves and of others. Quebec was their chosen land, essentially a homogeneous culture and their mission was to remain faithful to its Catholic and French origins.

In reality, the integration process proved more difficult for those who had lived along the St. Lawrence since Champlain's day than it did for the new arrivals themselves. To the Jews, it represented the latest episode in a story that went back 3,000 years, a history which had led them from their ancient homeland to the four corners of the world. But the Canadiens of the time had to learn to live with others, starting with the Amerindians and then with the British, who enjoyed definite economic, political and in a sense social and cultural advantages. This situation fuelled their drive to cultivate an identity and to struggle for their survival and rights. They counted not only on their own French Catholic tradition to help them succeed, but on British law and precedent as well. They even created the myth of a Golden Age; an idyllic era prior to the Conquest whose people were exclusively Catholic and French, and descended from a host of founding saints. Out of this myth grew a kind of nationalism with racist overtones, used by a partisan and self-proclaimed patriotic political party to benefit interests that were supposedly religious, but in fact readily extremist.

French Quebec internalized this myth of a homogeneous society. It made no effort to associate others with its dreams and vision of the future and found no means of giving them cultural space in which to flourish.

In this sense, the absence of Protestants and Jews during the country's first wave of European settlement posed a historic challenge to French Quebecers, to which no satisfactory response was found.

The Jewish community is an early case in point. When the moment of truth finally came and a number of concrete questions were asked; such as the welcome given to immigrants and their place in Quebec's collective life, the reaction was predictably swift. A group of French Quebecers made up of intellectuals in the Catholic Church as well as in political and patriotic organizations, expressed fierce opposition to educational autonomy and economic emancipation for the newcomers. They faced lively opposition, for the newcomers were equally determined to preserve their own religious and cultural heritage.

The First Jewish Families

There was no confrontation in the early days. When the first Jewish immigrants arrived, French Quebecers seemed to view them as intermediaries, or more precisely as a buffer between themselves and the new power. The Jews and Canadiens, then, enjoyed a sort of honeymoon that lasted over a century, from 1760 to 1870. Nowhere else, it has been said, did Jews experience, during that period, the same kind of welcome, freedom and security.

The year 1760 marked the end of New France and the departure of the French elite, leaving the common folk to face the conquerors on their own. More significantly, it was the signal that they were entering a new universe: the English-speaking world. From then on, North America was English from north to south and its political and economic centre was London. The port of Montreal quickly became integrated into the massive trading network of the British Empire, which extended over all five continents.

Needless to say, the new administrators exercised absolute control over the major sources of public wealth: the fur trade, agriculture and manufacturing production. Most important, they controlled imports and exports, which were limited to England and its colonies after the enactment of British legislation in 1763. As historians of the day observed, the people who benefited most from the new regime were the "few hundred English adventurers who flocked to the country so they could exploit its resources."[6]

The handful of Jewish families associated with the new regime arrived during this period of economic change. The analysis of B. K. Sandwell is useful in understanding the full impact of the transformation:

> It was a transition from an economy in which money and credit were unimportant, and a feudal relationship existed between the tillers of the soil and the lords of the manor, to an economy in which everything was regulated by market price. The lords had no skill in this sort of economy and were speedily worsted by the "business men" — among whom the few Jews then in America were pre-eminent for their exceptional energy, judgment and cash resources.[7]

England and France saw to it that Jews were excluded from land ownership and even simple military service. English Jews, therefore, entered into business, forging an essential link between the colonial administration or large companies and the Canadiens.

This was especially true of the army. The Franks[8] of New York, for example, played an important role as British troop suppliers during the military operations that led to the conquest of New France.

The first Jewish families, bearing the names Hart, Joseph, Frank, David, Judah, Hays, Solomons, Mayers, Lyon and Abraham, settled in Quebec City, Montreal, Trois-Rivières, Berthier, Rivière-du-Loup (now Louiseville), Yamachiche and Saint-Denis, and played a low-key but essential role during the occupation and reorganization of the territory.

Almost all of them had brought capital with them. They were merchants, importers, army suppliers, wheat exporters, money lenders, wholesalers, bankers, pioneers in shipping and later in telephone, telegraph and water works.[9]

In short, they were one of the first generations of Jews in 2,000 years who were recognized as full-fledged human beings, entirely free. Elsewhere in the world, they were still bound by the medieval heritage of bondage, ghettos and extortion. Several decades still separated them from the French Revolution and the Napoleonic era. Their free status, already implicit in the 1763 Treaty of Paris,[10] was soon to be codified in Quebec's constitution. This was prior to the 1774 Act of Quebec, which recognized the right of all groups to exist, regardless of language, legal tradition or religion. As Hilda Neatby observed, "The Québec Act can be cited as an example of those most precious human liberties, freedom of conscience and freedom of worship."[11] It was, she added, "the first comprehensive charter of religious liberty" in the West.

The few Jewish families who settled on the banks of the St. Lawrence had close ties with relatives in New York and other large centres outside Quebec, importing books and other goods and sending their children away from home to be educated. This friendly exchange foreshadowed the distant future; the time of the great migration from Central Europe when the Jewish communities in New York and Montreal would maintain steady commercial and cultural relations.

These families already formed what some historians have termed a third society, or intergroup. From the outset, they were not identified with the English. They were not part of the administration because they did not participate in the political life, privileges and benefits of the colony as did the shareholders of the Hudson Bay or transportation companies. They were not part of British society through shared lineage, religion or interests. In the eyes of the Canadiens, they went to their own synagogue in their own part of Montreal and were related to one another by marriage.

Their cultural affinity with the occupiers dates from their migration to England in the seventeenth century from Lithuania, Poland and Germany. They had roots in London, Portsmouth and Plymouth, the cities from which their ancestors had embarked for America. Some, such as the Calnecks and Clements, had settled in Nova Scotia even before the fall of Quebec.

The Harts

These founding families made a lasting impression on Canadian society. The Hart family stands out for its impressive family expansion and thorough integration into French Quebec history.

Aaron Hart (1724?-1800) was born in London to parents who had come from Germany bearing the name Hirsch, which in English is hart. After a stay in Jamaica, Aaron Hart went to New York to live with relatives. The year was

1756. He was soon joined by his brothers Harmon and Bernard; his brother Leman stayed in London to supervise the organization of a distillery.

A Jacobs and a Levy accompanied the military in its march to Montreal. The first settled in Quebec City and then Saint-Denis, the second chose New York and Aaron Hart opted for Trois-Rivières in 1761. This decision may have been influenced by his friendship with Haldimand, the governor of the region, but it was also probably based on the site, which he saw as a prime location for the fur trade. He did in fact prosper, putting pressure on his competitors in Quebec City and Montreal. He developed contacts with merchants in London and Liverpool, trading fur for arms, furniture, clothing, draperies, jewellery and other items which he sold to the local and native population.

With Aarons' move to Trois-Rivières, the family found itself firmly established in three key North Atlantic areas of the British Empire: England, New England and Canada.

In 1768, Aaron wed his cousin Dorothy Catherine Judah in Portsmouth, England. The marriage brought his cousins and brothers-in-law Uriah and Samuel to Trois-Rivières and formed the nucleus of a large family which included four sons—Moses, Ezekiel, Benjamin and Alexander—and five daughters educated by the Ursulines in Trois-Rivières. One daughter, Chavah, married a Judah and two others, Sarah and Charlotte, married Samuel and Moses David respectively, sons of Montreal's Lazarus David.

Aaron Hart achieved fame and fortune before his death in 1800. His will contained an impressive list of bequests to his wife and children.[12] He left a seigneury to his sons, as well as land and a house in the centre of Trois-Rivières. This man of initiative, who had endured and conquered early hardship, left his family a thriving business and assets that his children would go on to expand.

First Generation of Quebec-Born Jews

Of all the Jewish families who settled in Quebec during the early years of the British regime—the Davids, Franks, Josephs, Judahs and Solomons—the Harts truly excelled at adapting to local realities and contributing to the rise of the young colony.

Aaron's two eldest sons, Moses and Ezekiel, stayed in Trois-Rivières and consolidated their father's business, the former concentrating on the beer industry and the latter on the fur trade. Moses acquired several seigneuries including Grondine and Gaspé, and worked to promote steam navigation. He launched two ships, the *Hart* and the *Toronto*. Ezekiel became interested in politics and was elected as the member for Trois-Rivières on April 11, 1806 with the support of both the Protestant and Roman Catholic clergy. Despite his apparent failure in Quebec's parliamentary arena, he broke important new ground in helping the Jewish community achieve full recognition of its civil rights. He was essentially a business leader, however, and became one of the founders of the Bank of Montreal in 1817.

Benjamin and Alexander settled in Montreal and set up several prosperous concerns there. Both were shipowners. Alexander eventually returned to England while Benjamin laid the foundations of the Shearith Israel congregation, building a synagogue to this end. Like Ezekiel, he set out on a political career that was destined to founder. He threw his energies behind a movement that favoured annexation to the United States, a popular notion among some English-speaking Montrealers at the time. He so alienated the government that he was forced into exile in New York, where he remained until his death.

From the very beginning, the Hart family, or clan, entrenched its roots deep into the heart of French-speaking Quebec. Its members helped transform Montreal into a hub of national and international trade, yet they remained most closely identified with Trois-Rivières. It was there that Aaron had revived the fur trade, having faced, at the time, what seemed to be stiff competition from the Hudson's Bay Company. Business interests led him to use his family ties with the Levys and Judahs to establish trading relations between his city, New York and especially Liverpool. He introduced new economic concepts: public markets, debt collection according to the principles of British commercial legislation and weight regulation for gold coin.[13] Moses went on to found a bank in Trois-Rivières.

But perhaps the most interesting aspect of this family was its astonishing creativity. Ezekiel cherished a dream: "To establish an international bank, with branches and commercial outlets in all of the world's major centres."[14] Moses Hart also harboured a dream: to found a universal religion inspired by the writings of American political economists Thomas Payne and Andrew Dean. This passion for movements of universalist salvation can be found throughout Jewish history, from Isaiah to Karl Marx.

The efforts of a few Jewish families such as the Harts prompted the children of the 60,000 habitants, who remained after 1760, more quickly into the era of profound social and economic change that characterized the nineteenth century: industrialization, international trade and soon afterward, the trade union and socialist movements that paved the way for the labour struggles of the twentieth century.

Within a few generations, Aaron Hart's descendants had travelled beyond the borders of the province and settled throughout North America. The Harts who now live in Quebec are Protestant and Catholic, Anglophone and more often Francophone, not unlike the Smiths, Ryans and O'Learys. Their roots penetrate deep into the past and are intertwined with the very roots of the Quebec people. That, among other factors, makes the Hart clan an integral part of their heritage.

The First English Sephardic Community

The survival of the Jewish people through the centuries and up to the present can be traced to an instinctive understanding that its network of communities, tiny islands afloat on the seas of the world, must be kept alive at all costs. Jewish communities have woven an organic web of astonishing strength, with family, economic, cultural and religious ties crisscrossing from one country to another. The Jews are certainly not the only people to live in a diaspora: the Chinese, Indians, Armenians, Gypsies and other less well-known groups do the same. But what makes their case unique is that they have had to learn to survive in hostile, often unbearable conditions, and have been doing so since the time of Egypt and Mesopotamia, despite exodus, ghettos, the Inquisition, immigration prohibitions, the pogroms of Eastern Europe and, more recently, the Nazi Holocaust.

Just what is the Jewish community? A small group of Jewish people that has expanded and flourished with the help of a whole range of social structures: first the synagogue, then the school, the associations and for those who leave this world, the "house of life" or cemetery as it is known in the West.

If there is one other nation especially well placed to understand the strength of the Jewish community, it is undoubtedly the French-speaking people of Quebec. Not only does their religion share a spiritual heritage with Judaism, but the history of their survival and the occupation of their lands offer analogies with the history of the Jews in America. French Quebecers, too, are grouped into communities which they call parishes, forming a tightly-knit network of kinship ties, neighbourly relations and socio-economic activities. The more isolated groups, scattered in a diaspora including northern Quebec, Ontario, the United States and western Canada maintained close ties with the original Quebec communities, at least during the early generations.

What was the parish? A community dominated by a steeple, with its priest, respected citizens, school, associations and its deceased as well, resting in the shadow of the church. The parishes were so closely knit that whole communities were known to pull up stakes and follow their priest to settle in the United States or western Canada, in Abitibi or northern Ontario.

The Jewish "parish" is the congregation. Once a number of families had settled in a particular place (ten was enough), they gathered together naturally into a congregation. The first initiative was usually to build a synagogue and invite a teacher, a minister or a rabbi. To this nucleus was soon added the school, where students learned about their religious tradition, then the various associations that met the cultural and social needs of the community and finally, the cemetery.

But Jewish and French Quebecers share more than simply a parallel structure. The two communities have shown a remarkable facility for both resisting and adapting to environments that are erosive and often hostile to their culture; in short, they share a similar ability to survive. If French-Canadian survival, after just two centuries of cultural isolation, had been called a miracle; what word, then, can be used to describe Jewish survival during the nineteen centuries separating today's diaspora from the final resistance at Massada?

History linked these two communities from 1760 onward. Both are minorities aware of the threat to their social and cultural identities; side by side they have evolved on the parcel of land known as Quebec. This historical "convivance" has led them, at various intervals, to fight together for their rights, or to face off over issues such as the Jewish school question. In the end, however, they have always managed to arrive at a fundamental reconciliation that draws them closer and makes them more accessible to one another.

The year 1760 clearly did not have the same meaning for the French and the Jews. Whether they liked it or not, the French were forced to change their allegiances. Important decisions were subsequently made in London instead of Paris. The official powers spoke English and were Protestant by religion. They mistrusted any cultural attachment to France, especially with the approach of the French Revolution. They even hoped to "anglicize" this tiny population of 60,000 peasants stripped of its political intelligentsia. They also mistrusted its religious allegiance to the Church of Rome.

The Jews, on the other hand, came in with a new British administration that supported them and was confident of their loyalty, the basis for excellent relations. But they were far from enjoying the equal rights they would soon fight for alongside the Canadiens. Jews were traditionally dependent on a system of privilege that enabled them to hold certain public officers without, however, allowing them to reach the pinnacle of the power structure that ruled the colony. They were intermediaries between the British and the Canadiens, the link between Quebec's power elite and its grassroots base.

The Mother Congregation: Shearith Israel

Very soon after the first families settled in the colony's major centres, the Jewish community was born and began to expand. In 1768, Montreal became home to the first Canadian congregation, Shearith Israel (Remnants of Israel). In fact, the original Jewish community was made up of immigrants arriving from England and the British colonies, whose forebears were German Ashkenazim (Ashkenazi means German in Hebrew) but who had adopted the Sephardic rite (from the medieval Hebrew word Sefarad, meaning Spain). Naturally, they affiliated their Montreal congregation with the Sephardic[15] congregation in London, an affiliation still honoured at their synagogue on Lemieux Street.

In 1777, the Montreal congregation was in a position to build a synagogue, the first in Canada, at the corner of Notre-Dame and St. Jacques streets. It was indispensable to a community that was growing and passing on its Jewish traditions from generation to generation. There was soon another pressing need—the need for a "house of life"—and it was met by the congregation in 1781. This acquisition resulted in a remarkable document involving the seigneurs of Montreal and the *messieurs* of Saint-Sulpice. It was entitled *Declaration of the Fief and Seigneury of Montreal at the Register of Landed Properties of the Domain of His Majesty in the Province of Quebec in Canada, written on February, 1781 by Jean Brassier, surveyer*. It concluded with the following paragraph: "The remainder of the property, measuring four arpents seven rods wide by approximately four arpents deep, entirely vacant and without buildings, is owned by the Décarris heirs who have sold off thirty square feet for the Jewish Cemetery."[16]

The Jews call their last resting place the "house of life," a euphemistic expression of their faith. It indicates the value they ascribe to the great continuity of the community beyond death. In 1882, a Hebrew maskil[17] recorded the views of a group of European immigrants, educated and isolated in the Canadian prairies. Their words give us an idea of the plight and horror felt by Jews at the prospect of death not followed by a tradition burial:

> We wanted to come here in order to honestly earn our livelihood in a land where we would not be exposed to the mockery and ridicule of our Gentile neighbours because of our faith and looks. . . . It is evident that under such circumstances no one can think of anything of a higher order, such as the reading of a newspaper or of a book, as we were accustomed to do at home. Nor have we enough time to do our daily prayers. We come home at night and, wearied and exhausted, sleep overtakes us before we have even eaten. We shall all perish here and not have so much as a Jewish burial. The child of an immigrant died here today and there is no burial ground for it.[18]

These immigrants attributed such importance to burial rites that they often acquired a "house of life" before they organized a congregation. Although their attachment to the synagogue was voluntary, it was also necessary if they were to be assured a proper burial.

The original group was soon dispersed, through mixed marriages and emigration to New York, Philadelphia and Newport. Most of the families who stayed were of Ashkenazic origin. This first Canadian congregation thus displayed a cultural ambivalence that made it fragile, yet more open to diversity within the budding Jewish community. It was fragile because, while the rite was strictly Sephardic, the only language these people spoke other than English was usually Yiddish. Though their ministers had Spanish names such as de Lara, Piza and de Sola, their writings do not include a single syllable of ladino. In addition, they identified themselves with the Yiddish term for a synagogue, Shool. This ambivalence was exactly what made it possible to unite the disparate elements of the young community and maintain links with the two great spiritual poles of the North American diaspora: London and New York.

The Montreal congregation saw to the needs of the colony's Jewish community for many years. It was tiny: sixty-five years after the Conquest, in 1825, it still numbered a mere 90 people in Lower Canada.

Two major events soon changed the life and face of the community: the law of 1831 and the influx of immigrants from Germany and Eastern Europe during the 1840s.

Early Contributions to Political History

Jews participated in Quebec political life as an infinitesimal minority of the overall population (the Jewish community never exceeded 2%). However, this minority played a political role that far surpassed its numbers, especially in the early days. One wellspring of its energy may have been that it always considered itself a third society operating within a distinct social and cultural universe.

Aside from the Amerindians, this society consisted mostly of merchants, and from the outset it charted a path between the two "white" majorities: the English establishment and the two-century old French settlement. More specifically, it was and remained an ally to the English and a neighbour to the French. It was the original, and for a long time the only immigrant community in Quebec.

The Jews came to Canada not as the first settlers of the French empire or as British colonists, but as immigrants seeking freedom in the New World and a new social context where they could struggle for equality and human rights. They arrived at the time when the first settlers, conquered in 1760, were also being forced to fight for their rights, religion and equality before the law.

In retrospect, the Jewish contribution to Quebec political life seems even richer for its remarkably diverse social and cultural roots. In the early days the community was quite homogeneous but, in many ways, its development was a highly accelerated version of the path followed by the French-speaking community in Quebec. The Jews of Lower Canada, having come from various Western countries, appeared to share common religious and cultural characteristics as long as only one congregation existed in Montreal. Theirs was a Sephardic Judaism, well-assimilated into the English-speaking world. Their Francophone neighbours also displayed a degree of ethnic and cultural diversity. The majority were French and some were Amerindian, but almost all professed the Roman Catholic faith.

The founding of the German Ashkenazic congregation in 1846 was another indication of increasing pluralism within the Jewish community. It foreshadowed the changes wrought by the flood of Yiddish-speaking immigrants who arrived from the *shtetl* between 1860 and 1880, bringing with them a different rite and a culture characterized by the immense ethnic and linguistic diversity of Eastern Europe.

The French-speaking population did not achieve this kind of cultural diversity until much later. This phenomenon would first occur with the arrival of Protestants from France and Switzerland, to be followed by the Francophone immigration of the 1950s and 1960s, which included Jews and Muslims from north Africa, Christians and indigenous people from Black Africa and the Caribbean, and Buddhists from southeast Asia.

Politically speaking, this cultural diversity gave the Jewish community a range of political options unparalleled in the history of the two majorities, the English and French. Thus, its role in Quebec political history was often to bring fresh ideas to the French community, long marginalized by political and economic structures, and for that reason often engaged in similar struggles.

The Constitutional Battles (1763-1832)

In 1763 Jewish signatures began to appear on petitions sent from the colony to London. The first was that of Eleazer Levy, reminding the king that "the majority of us were established in this colony at the time of cession to Your Majesty's arms" and requesting that the colony be granted a Legislative Assembly. The petitioners made a fresh attempt in 1770, joined by Aaron Hart. The year 1773 brought yet another petition, this time from the residents of Montreal, including Samuel Jacobs, Levy Solomons and Ezekiel Solomons. The same signatories took action again some months later.

Though it aroused discontent among the Canadiens, the Quebec Act of 1774 gave Canada a Legislative Council and was thus a step toward full civil liberties, especially in the area of religion. That same year, the petitioners asked that the king repeal the act and create an elected parliament. Some fifteen Jewish leaders were among the signatories, including new names: Lazarus David, Simon Levy, Andrew Hays, David Salesby Frank and Isaac Judah.

The American Revolution (1775-83) put a halt to the movement, but in 1784 a new petition was sent to London asking for a constitution and government founded on sound liberal principles. This time, the list of 25 Jews who signed included more new names: Elias Solomons, Hyam Myers, David Jacobs, Abraham Hart, Moses Hart, Ezekiel Hart, John Franks, David David, Isaac Abrams and Uriah Judah.

These men pleaded the cause of political freedom from the mother country, side by side with their British and Canadien colleagues. They reappear at various crucial points in the economic, social, political and religious life of the colony.[19] Their tenacity in petitioning London finally bore fruit. The 1791 Constitutional Act gave the colony a constitutional government and a Legislative Assembly. They had won the first round.

The Fight for Equality

The noble ideas that led to the French Revolution and its slogan "liberty, equality, fraternity" had been in the air for some time. France issued a declaration of the rights of man and citizens, and the civil and political rights of Jews (1791). That same year, the United States adopted its own bill of rights and in 1808, Napoleon declared Judaism to be an accepted religion.

"From the outset," writes historian Sack, "the old Province of Quebec was destined to play an outstanding part in the life of the Jews in British North America. For here it was that they gained a measure of recognition and here that they made their greatest contribution to the country. Consequently, it was here, too, that the 'Jewish question' arose for the first time in any form in Canada."[20]

The person who brought it into the spotlight was none other than Ezekiel Hart, the son of well-known Trois-Rivières citizen Aaron Hart. The people of Trois-Rivières, led by their priest, elected Ezekiel Hart as a member of the Legislative Assembly in the by-election of April 17, 1807. The West had never before seen this type of political involvement by a Jew. His election in Trois-Rivières is a clear sign of how the Jews were well-integrated in the French-Canadian society of the day. But Hart's experience soon became a political and social test case of considerable historical importance.

To put this event in the proper perspective, it is important to remember that in 1808 the House of Assembly was the site of a battle waged between the Parti canadien and the governor's party. Ezekiel Hart was a personal friend of the governor, Sir James Henry Craig, and was godfather to one of his children, Ira James Craig. He was thus a prime target for Parti canadien leader Pierre Bédard. On January 29, 1808, Hart was sworn into office on the Bible in the usual fashion, but with his head covered in keeping with Jewish tradition. A motion was immediately tabled in the legislature pointing out that the new member had not taken his oath "in the customary manner." But Bédard went further. He objected to Hart's admission to the House on the grounds that members of the Jewish religion were excluded from the British Parliament. In the end, Hart was expelled from the House by a vote of 21 to 5.

He was re-elected by his supporters in Trois-Rivières and once again took the oath of office, this time in the Christian manner, but to no avail. A long debate ensued in the House, which once again ended in Ezekiel Hart's expulsion on May 5 for being a Jew. But one fact remains: the motion—largely a political manoeuvre—was overturned by the Executive Council, which responded to questions by the governor about the eligibility of members of the Jewish religion to sit in the House of Assembly: "The Committee is of the opinion that a Jew may be elected to the House of Assembly of this Province and may sit and vote upon taking the Oaths required by Law in the customary manner."[21] The idea of equality before the law, regardless of culture or religion, was beginning to gain ground.

French Canadians thus rejected the choice made by their fellow citizens in Trois-Rivières, basing their decision on an argument taken straight from the Middle Ages ("Cujus regio, ejus religio").[22] In other words, since Canada was a Christian country it could only be governed by Christians and members of other religions could therefore not claim the same rights.

Curiously enough, this argument from another era would be used again a century later by both Protestant and Catholic opponents of Jewish separate schools. Society was soon prepared to grant Jews a kind of visitor status and English-speaking Protestants even considered them privileged visitors whose children were welcome in their schools. But that was a far cry from recognizing their claim to equal rights and giving their parents access to school boards as administrators. The social and political concepts of a people would have to be completely revolutionized for that to occur.

Nonetheless, the Hart affair did have positive repercussions. For the French, it revealed a wide range of opinions on the issue of Jewish emancipation and for the Jews, it represented a step in the struggle by French Canadians for a more just and open society, where all people could become fullfledged members. From that time on, the Jews made steady progress.

A First for Britain: The 1832 "Emancipation"

Twenty years later, the issue of Jewish religious rights appeared before the House again. This time, the tone of the debate was completely different and Jews found valuable allies in the Canadiens and their parliamentary leader, Louis-Joseph Papineau.

Up to then, Jews had not been permitted to legally keep their own birth, marriage and death records. This sometimes caused serious problems in settling succession claims and real estate transactions.

Well before the world's other nations—except France in 1791 with its declaration of human rights—Quebec's Legislative Council took on the task of drafting a bill designed to establish the principle of religious equality for Jewish citizens. It granted them the same rights as members of the two officially recognized Christian denominations, Anglicanism and Catholicism. The law was adopted during the 1830 session and was ratified in London on January 13, 1831. This success led immediately to the same legal freedoms for other Christian groups such as Wesleyans and Presbyterians.

Important though this step was toward complete emancipation, it was up to the Jews and their allies to explore all the practical implications of the new law. A liberal movement was filtering into Quebec political circles from France and the United States, and spokespersons for the Jewish community took advantage of it to step up their petitions demanding the same civil rights as all other citizens.

On January 31, 1831 Mr. Neilson, member of the House and director of the *Quebec Gazette,* presented a petition supporting the Jews before the House. It demanded that Jews be granted the right to accept and perform any public office available in the province, on the grounds that being Jewish did not constitute grounds for denying this right. A petition was filed on February 7 of the same year by Samuel Bécancourt Hart, a grandson of Aaron Hart, asking the House to lift the legal incapacity which was imposed by the Colonial Executive Office, and which victimized him and other Jews. He was not permitted to be a justice of the peace on the pretext that as a Jew, he was unable to take the legally required oath. The petition was supported by none other than Louis-Joseph Papineau, then Speaker of the House, and was warmly received in both Houses.

As a result of the petitions, the two Houses adopted a second bill without debate[23] on March 16, 1831. It stipulated that "persons professing the Jewish religion are entitled to all the rights and privileges of the other Subjects of His Majesty in this Province."[24]

The law was ratified in London on April 12, 1832 — twenty-seven years before England adopted similar legislation for its own citizens. Canadian Jews regarded it as the great charter for their emancipation. As historian Joseph Tassé observed in 1870:

> Ezekiel Hart lived long enough to see the Bill adopted, and to witness just how far thinking had progressed since the days when Parliament had closed its doors in his face and forced him to withdraw from political life. By granting political emancipation to Jews, Canada moved far ahead of England in matters of justice and liberality; in fact, in 1847, 1850, 1857 and 1858 the question of whether to grant Jews political rights was still being discussed at Westminster.[25]

Once the basic principle of legal equality had been accepted, its advocates were left to explore the practical consequences of the legislation. One of the first opportunities arose when two Jews, Moses J. Hayes and Benjamin Hart, were nominated to be justices of the peace. The oath of office had not been revised to comply with the 1832 legislation, however, and a House committee had decided to maintain the text of the law as a clear expression of the will of the legislators. They therefore had to refuse the offer and wait until 1837, when Queen Victoria herself named them to the Magisterial Bench, confirmation that from then on, Canadian Jews would enjoy all the rights of other British subjects.

The 1832 law is a measure of how much ground had been gained since the Quebec Act of 1774, which has been cited as the first charter in Canada, and perhaps the entire West, to guarantee complete religious freedom and civil equality to the two great Christian traditions.[26] The law was clearly aimed at the Canadiens, but it could not help but benefit the other community that was also fighting for its fundamental rights — the Jewish community. Thus, even when the Jews were deprived of legal status, they had been able to build Canada's first synagogue in 1777 and live in peace, tolerated by the powers of the day.

This legislation was already far ahead of British laws of the same period. For the Jews, it represented civil and political emancipation and the end to a state of inequality that stretched back to the Middle Ages. Thus, they were fully within their legal rights in 1838, when they replaced the Saint-Jacques Street synagogue, which had disappeared around 1820, with a new one on Chenneville Street near La Gauchetière. It was the only synagogue in North America at the time. From then on, the future of the tiny community rested on a solid legal framework that helped it rise and meet the challenges to come.

When looking back, it is clear that these events virtually juxtaposed the two major steps that occur in any cross-cultural progress; specifically, the expulsion of Ezekiel Hart in 1807 and again in 1808 from the Legislative Assembly by Parti canadien members and the unanimous and quite natural adoption in 1831 of the principle of equal rights for Jews in Lower Canada by members of the same nationalist party. Such a dramatic about-face, within just twenty years, only confirms that opposition and confrontation, lively and impassioned though they may be, can lead to reconciliation between groups and communities. Past opponents can indeed revise their attitudes, spurred on by the bitter memory of the absurdity and sometimes outright injustice of their original attitudes.

The Jews and the War in Quebec

Quebec was perhaps the first place in the world where the Jews were induce to take up arms in an international conflict, something they have rarely done during their history. Never in fifteen centuries of living in a diaspora had they been welcomed into the military. As a result, they were unfamiliar with military traditions and knowledge, with the possible exception of logistics.

During the eighteenth century, military thinking did not consider logistics to be an important aspect of overall strategy. Therefore, civilians were given the responsibility of supplying the army with men, provisions and arms. For this reason, important merchants accompanied the army and sometimes even preceded it into enemy territory in order to set up supply lines. Thus, in 1758 Samuel Jacobs followed the British from Fort Cumberland to Quebec City aboard his ship the *Betsy*, which was loaded with provisions and flying the British flag. During the siege of Quebec in 1759, Wolfe himself bought the vessel and its cargo.

A Historic Duo: The Gradis and the Franks

During the decades before the fall of New France, this type of participation was widespread. Jews could be found on both sides of the barricades. France had the Gradis of Bourdeaux, a family of shipowners made famous by Abraham Gradis, who according to French historian Camille Jullian, "appeared to protect and represent France more than the royalty itself."[27]

His involvement in Quebec history is a blend of patriotism, business initiative, high finance and even political strategies, a saga documented in the archives of the Gradis family, the French navy and the province of Quebec. It provides a lively example of how finance became interwoven with foreign politics and wars during that period.

Abraham Gradis' first business and military operation involved Louisbourg, the key to the whole defense system protecting France's North American possessions. In 1744, Gradis chartered the *Fort-Louis* so he could join the Duke of Anville's expedition against the fortress, which had recently fallen to the English. He then sent the *David* and the *Superbe* (1748) to consolidate the defence of Ile Royale, today Cape Breton. From 1748 on, however, New France became his major preoccupation. He formed a trading company, the Société du Canada, to keep the lines of communication open between Bordeaux and Quebec. He was thus able to save the colony from famine in 1752 by sending a load of flour aboard the *Benjamin* at the request of Paris.

Warned by Louis XV's advisors as to how grave the situation was, the ship-owner decided to charter all the vessels he could find. He suffered serious financial difficulties, but won the sea battle despite harassment from the British. He even dreamed of extending his network of sea links to Louisiana and the Caribbean; however, the Seven Years War (1756-63) ruined his plans. He realized that only a desperate effort could save New France. Paris entrusted him with the role of agent to the King's Navy. He was invested with all the powers and privileges of the position, and stood second only to De Rostan as the nation's major authority in naval matters.

He hastily armed a fleet and added his own best ship, the *Robuste*, which had already proven a good match for the vessels of the British fleet, and the *Prince Noir* which belonged to a relative, David Alexander of Bayonne. Throughout the war, Gradis could count on the cooperation of other Jews, often family members, to organize his expeditions to Canada.

When Paris began to have difficulty finding recruits for Montcalm's army, Gradis once again came to the rescue.[28] He set to work finding troops and then outfitting and transporting them. He managed to ship 400 soldiers and their officers in 1757, which cost him the loss of the *David* on the return leg of its journey.

A new expedition was mounted in 1758, consisting this time of fourteen vessels. Gradis chartered ships belonging to two other Jewish shipowners, Raphaël Klende and Benjamin Gradis. The flotilla was attacked by the British on its way back, and only one vessel returned to Bordeaux. The venture cost Gradis his own eight ships, yet he remained undeterred by the catastrophe.

As communications between Quebec and France became more precarious, there were times when Gradis was Montcalm's only reliable supplier of men, provisions and arms. He owed his victory over General Abercrombie at Ticonderoga to reinforcements sent by Gradis. Several times, he mentions the assistance he received from the person he considered his right hand man in Bordeaux. The British blockade soon tightened, and Gradis provided him the only help he received from France and his only contact with homeland and family.

By November 1758 the situation was desperate. Gradis wrote to Marin de la Guadeloupe: "Nothing has happened for 20 months now, except that we have let our navy be destroyed. We have just lost Ile Royale and now Canada is threatened. We have only one warship left . . . and it is impossible to send a single vessel to the colonies."[29]

Nonetheless, the shipowner continued to cooperate with the French Naval Office, finding it several vessels, looking after French prisoners in England and carrying out missions assigned to him by Montcalm.

The cession of New France to England with the signing of the Treaty of Paris (1763) cut the Gradis family ties with Quebec. But its contribution had been enormous — according to historian Benjamin G. Sack, Gradis prolonged the life of the French regime on the banks of the St. Lawrence by several years. Many French Canadians were never aware of his role though, perhaps partly because of extortion by the intendant Bigot, who diverted goods arriving from Bordeaux for his own purposes. In France, however, David Gradis and his son Abraham received unequivocal recognition from Louis XVI in 1779 for the services they provided from the time they were "charged with the procurement of all supplies for Canada and Ile Royale from 1748 until the time those vast lands suffered the misfortune of falling under British domination."[30] They were granted all the rights and privileges of other French citizens, including the right to own property in the colonies.

In the British camp, Jewish traders were also at the forefront of the action. Frank was to Wolfe what Gradis had been to Montcalm.

Moses Frank of New York, his father Jacob and his brother David, in cooperation with Isaac Levy, were major suppliers for the British army. During the Seven Years War, Frank established an association with Arnold Nesbitt and the brothers James and George Colebrook. Their company became one of the main suppliers for the British army in North America.

Some may find it strange that there were Jews at work on both sides of the line of fire. One of the Franks was even accused of disloyalty. But that attitude overlooks the many wars that have occurred between peoples of the same language in Europe itself: in Germany, France, England and, closer to home, in Ireland. Even the Seven Years War, which changed the course of Western history, was essentially a conflict involving Westerners who shared the same religious and cultural heritage. Why, then, does it surprise us that the Jews were divided in their "national" allegiances? We know that the Jews of France and Germany proclaimed Napoleon as the champion of their emancipation, while those who lived in England saw in him a tyrant to be overthrown. When Nelson was victorious at Trafalgar, Montreal Jews joined in the official celebrations arranged by the government. This conflict between Jews of British and French background is a clear indication of each group's national loyalties.

Comrades in Arms for the First Time: 1812

At the time of the British conquest, war appeared to face off the earliest Jewish arrivals against the French of New France, but soon after, war rallied these same communities around a common cause: resistance to the American invasion of 1812. The governor hastily rounded up volunteer troops to drive back the three armies. French Canadians thus found themselves fighting side by side with Jews, most of whom had been born in Quebec: David David, Henry Joseph, Benjamin Hart, Alexander Hart, Isaac Phineas, Jacob Frank, Benjamin Frank, Benjamin Solomons and Myers Michael. Ezekiel Hart, who had distinguished himself as a militia officer, was promoted to lieutenant in the 8th Batallion of Trois-Rivières. Samuel David was captain, then major of the 2nd Batallion (Volunteer) of Montreal, a mostly French-Canadian unit. All took part in the battle of Chateauguay beside Salaberry and his light infantry and helped save Canada from annexation to the United States.[31]

This represented a new social phenomenon in European Jewish history: considerable numbers of Jews fighting side by side with Christian soldiers in a military campaign. It implied a far-reaching evolution in the interpersonal relations at the heart of society, expressed by a broad acceptance of different religious observances: Sunday mass for some and Saturday Sabbath or kosher laws for others. The common life of these soldiers from different traditions never created problems in Quebec, even in 1812, just three years after the Ezekiel Hart affair and a full twenty years before the great charter of 1832.

The Rebellion of 1837-38

Louis-Joseph Papineau was a man of liberal ideals who openly supported Jewish rights and had the backing of his French-Canadian followers. But not all Jews were able to accept his revolutionary approach, or share his dream of political emancipation for Canada. The American Revolution had had a tremendous impact on Papineau and he found William Lyon Mackenzie of Upper Canada to be a powerful ally in his drive to install an American-style republic on the banks of the St. Lawrence. They faced two major obstacles: opposition by the Catholic Church in the Francophone community of Lower Canada and loyalist sentiments among the English, shared by the majority of Jews. Centuries of persecution had taught the Jews to mistrust nationalist tendencies and to value the stability and freedom guaranteed by the British regime. Their sympathies were once again divided when the Patriote Movement began to grow. Most remained loyalists, but a minority fell in line with Papineau.

In Trois-Rivières, Moses Hart and Henry Judah, friends of Papineau, gave impassioned speeches against the abuses of the regime. Ezekiel Hart opened his Trois-Rivières home to the leaders of the rebellion, Papineau, Viger and Roy de Portelance. In Montreal, lawyer Adolph Mordecai Hart joined the ranks of their supporters by defending the rebels in court after their arrest. Mention should also be made of Louis Marchand, originally Levi Koopman, a Jewish immigrant from Holland. He settled in Saint-Mathias-sur-Richelieu and embraced the cause of the Patriotes. He frequently gave speeches at their assemblies and was a regional delegate at the meeting of six counties held at Saint-Charles on October 23 and 24, 1837. He eventually joined the fighting on November 11, participating in an attack on a cavalry and artillery division at Saint-Jean. He was thought of as an agitator and forced to leave the country, living in exile until Durham's amnesty, in 1838. Once back, he settled in Montreal and became an enterprising business person. He was a close associate of Louis-Hyppolyte Lafontaine and pursued a political career, holding important positions within the Saint-Jean-Baptiste Society.

Although only a minority of Jews supported the cause of the Patriotes, that does not diminish the symbolic value of their action. It represented the traditional openness of Jews to radical ideas of social and political change, and embodied the positive relations that existed between Canadiens and Jews during the first century of British rule.

Growth of the First Congregation: The de Solas

The arrival of Abraham de Sola in 1847 also took on symbolic significance. He belonged to an old rabbinical family from London; was learned, cultivated and a gifted orator. He was probably the first Sephardi to settle in the country. He not only served his congregation for 35 years, but also produced scholarly works on Judaism, taught Religious Studies, Oriental languages and Spanish at McGill University and devoted himself to cultural and scientific activities.

The presence of this major figure put Montreal on the intellectual map of the Jewish world. He was the first of many world-class, creative thinkers to live there. In subsequent decades many more would settle in Montreal: Yiddish poet J. I. Segal, and writers A. Robaek, Melech Rawitch and Rachel Korn, folklorist and rabbi J. L. Zlotnik, Anglophone poet A. M. Klein, poet and singer Leonard Cohen, Hebrew scholar Reuben Brainin, painter Jan Menses, novelist Saul Bellow, musicologist Israel Rabinowitch, demographer Louis Rosenberg, Francophone writer Naïm Kattan, Talmudist Simchah Petrushko and educator Shloimeh Wiseman.

Abraham de Sola had two sons: Meldola, who succeeded him as rabbi of the synagogue for forty years and Clarence, who was a business person, leader of the Canadian Jewish community, founder of Zionism in the country and as such, president of the first national Jewish institution, the Canadian Zionist Federation. The prestige conferred by this family on Jews in Quebec and elsewhere in Canada confirmed the leading role held by Montreal's Jewish community in Canadian society.

Just when the Shearith Israel congregation was establishing its reputation, a German-Polish community was taking root in Montreal, signalling a radical change in Jewish community life. Benjamin Hart had foreseen the shift a decade earlier, when a group of Ashkenazim had appeared on the Quebec scene. He viewed them as a threat to the London Sephardic tradition. Gradually, the number of Ashkenazim had increased and he feared that soon Montreal's English-speaking Sephardim would be outnumbered, even at the synagogue. To ward off this danger, Hart had established the legal framework for an Ashkenazic congregation in 1847. It remained inactive for ten years, but provided a structural setting for the German-Polish congregation, which adopted the name Shaar Hashomayim.

But Benjamin Hart could not predict the great Ashkenazic migration from Eastern Europe that swept across America between 1870 and 1960. Montreal was one port of entry and a major hub of activity after New York. This migration soon overwhelmed the original Montreal community and eventually marginalized it. Problems of language, class,[32] custom and numbers, would lead the new arrivals to gather in particular working-class neighbourhoods. The English-speaking Sephardim were cool toward the newcomers. As late as

1859, Abraham de Sola, enlightened though he was, refused to take part in laying the cornerstone of their Ashkenazic synagogue.

It may seem surprising that, during this period, there were two synagogues in a city as small as Montreal where the Jewish population numbered scarcely 150. But each group was deeply attached to its own traditions and Judaism has always accommodated this kind of pluralism. Christians can understand the situation, for they too share different forms of faith which can be deeply divisive, as was the case among certain members of the same church in Canada, particularly the French and Irish Catholics.

The 1882 Reform

Montreal's small Jewish community, divided by the two tendencies, would succumb to yet another divisive event in 1882 with the formation of the first reform congregation. The founding of the reform congregation preceded by over eighty years (directly after Vatican II) a similar reform which Quebec Catholics called their "aggiornamento." More than one analogy can be drawn between it and the Jewish reform;[33] both communities experienced a kind of social and religious revolution.

The pioneers of the Jewish reform introduced by Mendelssohn (1729-86) presented their ideas as a legitimate form of Judaism, in keeping with tradition rather than breaking from it. In actual fact, the differences between the traditionalists and innovators revolved around their theological approaches, which were given the (Christian) terms Orthodox and Reform. These differences diminished in time.

In Canada, the young reform movement emerged from the more liberal and less conformist Sephardic congregation, which had long been acculturated to the English-speaking world.[34] Not that the congregation had German, much less Mendelssohnian inclinations; the early immigrants who founded it came out of an orthodox, western European tradition. It had shown flexibility in adapting its traditions to the North American context, and was therefore able to welcome Jews of all outlooks. The venerable institution responded to the reform with adaptations and concessions. For a long time the reformers managed to put up with them, though they had difficulty accepting the emphasis on decorum (a sensitive issue for Mendelssohn's disciples), omission, sabbath days, the celebration of mussaf prayer and sermons in English.

The first reform congregation was not founded in Canada until 1882, with the formation of Temple Emanu-El. It had about sixty members, who met in a former church on Beaver Hall Hill. They used family benches and the organ, unlike the orthodox synagogues, but did not go so far as to pray with heads uncovered as they would later do.

To understand the impact of these innovations, it is important to remember that one principle of the Mendelssohnian reform went far beyond structural organization; it redefined the relation between religion and society. Jewish life should blend in with the dominant culture, at least on the surface. Jews should pray in churches rather than in their own distinct places of worship and in the street they should be indistinguishable from other citizens.

At the heart of this movement lay a secular view of society. While religion permeated Jewish life to the very core in the orthodox, Eastern European tradition, it was simply one aspect of existence for the reformers. They envisaged a world of parallel religions, all distinctly separate from political, social, cultural and economic life. This idea was clearly reflected in the religious education of children, which reduced the *cheder* (Jewish elementary school), *Yeshivah* (school of Talmudic study) and *chevrah* (study circle) to a Sunday school based on the Protestant model. It would be also reflected in the acceptance of birth control and a less committed version of Judaism, at least religious Judaism.

The two original congregations, Shearith Israel and Shaar Hashomayim, raised no legal objection to the new synagogue. The *Star, Gazette* and *Witness*, however, published letters by their orthodox readers railing against allusions by one reform rabbi to the ignorance that sometimes clouded Jewish vision. For him, the reform represented liberation from the narrow-mindedness of meaningless prayer rituals and pagan doctrines, primitive vestiges of the past.[35]

Again in 1897, during the national meeting of the Central Conference of American Rabbis in Montreal, the *Witness* described the delegates as people who had forgotten the stone from which they were hewn, adding that their celebrations differed very little from Methodist services.[36]

The Jewish reform found no support in the Yiddish fortress, where the only ideological rival to orthodoxy was atheism. It thus took on a western European character and developed close ties to the class of Jews who first arrived from England and Germany. This identification with a particular social class remains today.

Paradoxically, opposition raised by the orthodox community indirectly helped promoters of the reform in Montreal, who looked to the Gentile community for recognition and acceptance. They soon began inviting Christian ministers, Francophones and government officials to speak to their congregation. This phenomenon was particular to the reform group in Montreal, which came to distance itself from the rest of the Jewish community. It rejected the orthodox Judaism practised by the *shtetl* immigrants in no uncertain terms.[37]

In time, however, the vast majority of orthodox Jews recognized the importance and thus the canonical possibility of adapting their lifestyles and synagogues to the outside world, at least superficially. This was true of all but a minority of strict believers who are still present in the streets of Montreal. The reformers, in turn, had to acknowledge the socio-economic rise of the orthodox immigrants and grant them social acceptance.[38]

Thus, Quebec's Jewish community was torn apart by a religious and cultural crisis perhaps even more acute than the one that divided the Catholic community over half a century later. Immigrants newly arrived from the ghettos of the *shtetl* instinctively strove to reproduce the type of society they had always known. Both orthodox and secular Jews recognized the importance of their effort. Orthodox thinkers considered it essential to perpetuating the Jewish religion in the New World; secular reformers felt it was invaluable to the survival of the Jewish culture, its nationalism, cohesion and languages: Hebrew and Yiddish. The newcomers pursued their goals with even greater energy, faced as they were with a culture obsessed by the liberalism and budding secularism of North American society.

So began the difficult but inevitable cross-cultural encounter between traditional Judaism (steeped in Yiddish culture of the *shtetl*) and Western ideals represented by a young, aggressively liberal and emerging English-speaking America.

The Associations: Emergence of a New Judaism

With the many new synagogues in the Montreal area arose a whole new vocabulary. The terms "immigration" and "migration of the impoverished" became associated with the terms "philanthropy" and "organization," two innovations that attracted an increasing number of Jews in Quebec and elsewhere to make a commitment that went beyond their traditional beliefs.

Montreal Jews divided along congregational lines thus came together in associations that were launched in response to the growing needs of their immigrants. The Hebrew Philanthropic Society (*Chevrah Ezrat Evioné Israel*), for instance, was founded in Montreal in 1847 by the young Abraham de Sola, who had just arrived from England to take over the Sephardic congregation. That summer, about thirty impoverished immigrants, most from Germany and some with families, received assistance from the charitable society.[39]

We must remember that Jewish emigrants to North America, unlike those who left for Palestine, did not receive guidance from selection agencies at their point of origin or assistance from support groups on arrival. Jewish agencies limited themselves to obtaining boat or train tickets for the impoverished and attending to emergency situations.

The Montreal community, still fairly small, was soon overwhelmed by the flood of human misery that continued to swell. The following statistics deserve reflection. In 1871, there were 1,300 Jews in Canada. Thirty years later there were 16,401. Taking into account the births and deaths during the crossings, this increase of 15,000 people represents a minimum of 20,000 immigrants, or an average of 700 each year. Communities in various parts of Canada, led by Montreal, had to welcome and provide for them on a short-term basis and help them set up community institutions such as schools for the long term. Of the thousands of immigrants who came to settle in centres such as Montreal, only a small fraction received or requested aid. The annual budget designated for this purpose by the community amounted to about $1,000 in the early days and $2,000 by the end of the century.

The immigrants somehow managed on their own and, if miracles are to enter the discussion, their perseverance wrought the miracle of a thriving Jewish community in America. One effort which might seem insignificant at first, displays the spirit of honesty and self-help that inspired these modest people. In 1883, a loan system was established in Montreal to aid Russian refugees settling in Montreal, which provided between $10 and $30 per person. The records show that the loans were quickly repaid and the charitable organization could therefore assist other impoverished newcomers more effectively.

Even so the role of the immigrant aid associations should by no means be underestimated. Each one dealt with specific needs. The Young Men's Hebrew Benevolent Society (YMHBS) was founded in 1863 and welcomed Jewish refugees from the United States, which was then fighting its War of Secession (1861-65). This society became the Baron de Hirsch Institute (1890). The Jewish Colonization Association, also founded by Baron de Hirsch in both London and Paris, fostered the migration of immigrants to the Canadian prairies.

With the launching of these organizations, Montreal's Jewish community entered a new phase of development. It was no longer restricted to one or two synagogues, a school and the women's associations. Its horizons broadened to take in the city, the country and the entire world. It reached all Jewish citizens, whatever their personal choices, offering them the chance to service its members, participate as volunteers in its programmes and express their opinions about its collective life.

This breaking down of barriers marked the advent of a new Judaism, a twentieth-century form of Judaism unprecedented in Jewish history.

The founding of the YMHBS seems to have changed the way Canadian Jewry perceived itself. For the first time, Canadian Judaism was defined by something other than religion. Its members now had a new frame of reference for belonging to the Jewish community and it went beyond their political or ideological differences. No organization or structure, even the synagogue, had priority over the others. Each represented one aspect of Jewish reality and a way of identifying with Jewry as a whole. From then on, Judaism was the sum of all those disparate groups. In time the sum multiplied and the horizons of Judaism broadened accordingly.

Nineteenth-century Montreal was the birthplace of this evolution. Its "philanthropic" associations soon served as models and often provided the framework for other Jewish associations in Canada. They also established and maintained contacts with the Jewish community worldwide.

CHAPTER II

The Great Yiddish Migration, 1880-1940

From Shtetl to America

The story begins in Eastern Europe—Russia, Poland and Romania—where Jews from the West had been building a rich cultural heritage since the Middle Ages, in the form of the *shtetl*.[1] They spoke Yiddish, originally a Middle Rhine dialect adopted by their ancestors as they travelled eastward after being driven from England (1290), Germany and other lands.

Yiddish-speaking Jewry thus straddled three empires: the Russian, German and Austro-Hungarian. For seven centuries, they survived adversity as only such a minority could—a minority which had persevered for thousands of years and refused to die. They suffered pogroms and child abductions; as treaties were formed between Moscow, Berlin and Vienna, they were shunted back and forth from Polish to Russian administrations and watched as their nationalities changed from Austrian to Romanian or German. They finally found a niche in this mosaic of young nations, making up about ten percent of the total population. Instinctively, they turned to the imperial authority and acted as intermediaries between the various oppressed minorities. On average, they were better educated than their fellow Ukrainian, Polish, Estonian and Moravian counterparts and, therefore, acted as their interpreters, scribes and spokespersons. Having always been barred from the capitals and from owning landed property, which excluded them from agriculture, they responded by forming a class of artisans, tailors, cobblers, small merchants, peddlers and moneylenders scattered throughout the countryside and small towns.

The Westward Exodus

Suddenly, for no obvious reason, these people struck out for the West. The most popularly-cited starting date for the exodus is 1880, a time of pogroms similar to those of the early 1900s (1903, 1905, 1917 and more recently 1938,

---

Notes for Chapter II are found on pages 164-66.

1942 and up to the present). Anti-Semitic campaigns were waged against the Jews periodically with the complicity of the Orthodox Church synod and Tsar and they shook Europe's conscience to its very foundations.

Jews from the *shtetl* surged forth spontaneously in their thousands and tens of thousands in a desperate flight to the West, with neither voice nor leaders. Once begun, the migration never slowed, except during World Wars I and II. It expressed an instinctive mass reaction to a brand of intolerance that foreshadowed the darker horror brewing on the horizon.

Historians have since analyzed this latest exodus and traced its causes to the French Revolution, which rocked the secular pillars of monarchical, hierarchical societies the world over. The cry for "liberty, equality, fraternity" echoed to the very depths of the European countryside. Napoleon's victorious march to Moscow brought Eastern Europe out of the Middle Ages and into a historical process that awakened ethnic groups to ideas of self-determination and nationalism. Through the Napoleonic breach in the medieval dam flooded an irreversible current of modernism, with its science, universalism, technical knowledge and urbanization. From Rousseau to Schopenhauer, Hegel and Marx, the revolutionary concept of a new humanity was capturing the minds of European youth.

This concept was accompanied by a new brand of anti-Semitism, racist in nature and more destructive and bitter than the religious anti-Semitism of medieval times. It emerged as ultramontanism in the West, while in Eastern Europe it took the form of lightning-quick premeditated pogroms, which no one knew where or when they would stop.

The myth of an American paradise—the Eldorado, Golden America and American Frontier—took shape against this background, fascinating the imagination of an impoverished people for whom the old country was now full of despair.

This historical situation, along with spiritualist movements such as Hasidism[2] and Zionism,[3] stirred up an unprecedented ferment of thought and action among these people, to the point that the traditional leaders of their society found themselves, literally, left far behind.

Shtetl *in Turmoil*

For the first time in Jewish history, the social fabric of the Yiddish-speaking world was torn apart by a conflict between generations. Young people—creative minds and revolutionaries as well as fugitives and desperadoes—began to dream of America and an Americanized world. Families discussed Judaism, Zionism and industrialization; Hebrew and Yiddish art and literature, science; Jewish trade unionism, anti-Tsarist revolution, social democracy and socialism; migration, modern Jewish education, Jewish sciences and international Jewish organizations; community planning and philanthropy; Jewish assimilation, art, music and theatre; reform and the press; the nature of the Jewries of western Europe and of the Americas.

In the eyes of traditionalists, conservatives and the devout, there was no historical link between the ancient diaspora and the new ideas, which were thus
considered worthless. Their people had survived for seventeen centuries
under intolerable conditions, and they did not believe that the new approach
offered any solution to Jewish problems. They clung to traditional forms of
Jewish resistance as they would once again react before the spectre of
Auschwitz: turning away from evil—even the evil embodied in pogroms and
holocausts—and focussing on God, his Torah and his People. For them, turning away from evil removed it from all its practical manifestations. Evil was
thereby reduced to *bitul* (nothingness) or ridiculed as the Yiddish *mik-
lomersht* (self-proclaiming). When used to describe high-ranking positions,
the term suggests that those holding such positions had no real authority.
From this perspective, the forces of apparent power in the world wield no
real authority over those they oppress.

In the *shtetl*, centuries of Ashkenazic religious tradition inspired by Rashi[4]
fostered a Jewish culture and society quite different from the world built by
their Mediterranean predecessors of the Gaonic[5] period or their Sephardic
contemporaries of the Maimonides school. Rashi focussed his teachings on
the Talmud. He developed an original pedagogy, a Talmudic study method,
Yiddish linguistics, folklore that drew on Talmudic science and sociology
based on the primacy of Talmudic scholars. His system complemented an
ancient tradition that regulated life's every moment and every act. It was codified in the Ashkenazic version of the *Chulchan Aruch*, which had survived in a
dialectical body of work called the *Sheolot u'Tshuvot*. Ashkenazic life was
imbued with religion and centred around the traditional interpretation of
God's word. Jews immersed themselves in the sacred texts and the oral heritage of commentaries and subtleties enunciated by various schools: the Talmud, folklore, Yiddish, Hebrew and Aramaic. Study went hand in hand with
prayer, another devout exploration of the divine will. This led to the science
of casuistry, needed to establish the value of actions, good or bad, and gave
rise to the standards and structures of Yiddish orthodoxy.

To combat the "Revolutionaries of the Light" (*Haskalah*), this tradition
froze the morphology of the law, stiffened its resistance to any adaptation and
ultimately, wove a sacred cloak around the orthodox way of life.

Such was the religion of the *shtetl* when the great migration began. It was
traditionalist and opposed to the Mendelssohnian reforms being adopted in
Germany and America; it was the religion of the devout who came to Montreal. Their religious leaders showed little interest in the history of Zionism,
new science, the Canadian Jewish Congress, Yiddish or Hebrew literature,
journalism, urbanization, politics, philanthropy or the struggle against anti-
Semitism.

Yet almost all the activists who made modern Jewish history were deeply
infused with traditional culture and science. Quebec's Yiddish-speaking community was no exception. It included scholars such as the grandfather of Mordecai Richler, the father of Leah Rosenberg, rebbe Judah Rosenberg, as well as

Irving Layton's father and countless people who met in the streets, small synagogues or prayer chapels.

Yiddish-Speaking Immigrants

These were the people who initiated the migration at the end of the nineteenth century, following in the footsteps of the 50,000 precursors who had
left for Germany between 1830 and 1870. They marched toward America, the
promised land, the "last great hope of humanity." In 1880 *Hovèvé Zion*
("Those who cherish Zion") was founded. A few years later *Bilui* ("House of
Jacob, rise and go forth"), the organization that sent the first Jewish colonists
from Russia to Palestine was formed.

D. Juresco, a Romanian observer at the time tried to understand the spontaneous reaction of these destitute wayfarers who left their homes by the thousands to seek asylum in unknown lands, including Canada:

> What could possibly possess all these Jews, young and old, to rise
> and flee the country without knowing where they were going, like
> Loth from Gomorrah?
> These people, models of patience and resignation before the inevi-
> table force of circumstances, would never have left the lands of their
> birth if they had not lost all hope of improving their lot here.
> The sinister anti-Semitic propaganda spread by government offi-
> cials, backed by political influence and indifference among our best
> Romanian citizens, foments hatred against us. Jews are deprived of
> all the necessities of life and their misery continues to grow. It could
> grow much worse, judging by the words of the barbarians who live
> here: exterminating the Jews has become one of the ideals of the
> new century.
> The instinct for personal survival is at the root of this migration.[6]

In fact, the migration laid the foundation of the Jewish community in Montreal as we know it today, much as it did in New York, London, Paris, Buenos
Aires, Chicago, Johannesburg and Jerusalem. It saved millions of Jews from
extermination in the *shtetl* and in Nazi Europe. It recreated the human fabric
and fundamental character of Judaism on this side of the Atlantic.

Among the immigrants who streamed toward America, some decided to settle in the countries they were crossing or in European ports of departure,
while others reached Latin America, Australia and South Africa. But most
obtained a ticket for North America, the land of their dreams. For decades, the
United States and Canada were one and the same in their minds. Some
landed in Halifax or Montreal and took the train to join relatives in Milwaukee
or Chicago, while others arrived in New York and continued to Montreal or
Toronto. Quebecers were becoming acquainted with the *shtetl* refugees,
witnesses and victims of the horrors wrought by the new anti-Semitism.

What did these immigrants have in common? What would they do in America? How would they adapt?

At first glance, they could be confused with the mass of Russians, Poles, Romanians, Italians, Ukrainians and Galicians flooding into American and Canadian immigration offices. They too were from Europe, after all, and often spoke one or more European languages. Nonetheless, they had one clear disadvantage in relation to the other travellers: they were already set apart by the weight of their past, heavy with the rejection and brutality of anti-Semitism.

However, they possessed one unique asset: their Jewish culture, expressed in Yiddish and Hebrew. Founded on religious and folk traditions, drawing from the common history of the Hebrew people and above all, professing an unconquerable and irrepressible faith in the future. Jewish hope had endured over the centuries despite exile, conquest, inquisitions, pogroms and genocide. It went on to survive Auschwitz and Dachau.

These men and women embarked upon America as if it were the Promised Land, the "land of milk and honey." They tackled it with the boldness of people who have nothing to lose, materially or psychologically. Most who arrived during the first wave were poor and had no aging relatives to support, so it was easier for them to disregard tradition. They were best-prepared to meet the challenge of being integrated into an unknown, uncivilized, sometimes brutal land offering unlimited freedom, where only the strongest were likely to survive.

These early immigrants did not benefit from immigrant aid organizations which would appear in the twentieth century. They went from ship to labour market not knowing how to speak English. Many were sent to the American west, where they found a landscape that recalled the *shtetl*, and many of the same ethnic communities as well: Ukrainian, Lithuanian and Polish. But most had to manage in the urban ghetto, starting at the bottom of the ladder in sweatshops, the small manufacturing businesses where working conditions were atrocious and salaries unimaginable by today's standards.[7]

They were a people who successfully rose to a challenge of immense scope, motivated by deep-seated and fundamental aspirations. It is no surprise, then, that individuals of exceptional talent emerged from their ranks. If anything is surprising, it is not their quality but their sheer numbers. An entire constellation of remarkable thinkers and leaders led the way as educational, cultural and social institutions were formed from within by the Yiddish-speaking communities of the New World.

Insertion into Quebec

These were the people who came to Quebec in search of a place in the sun. Some stopped off in Canada by chance after taking the first available boat for America. Growing numbers arrived from England, where they had heard about the Dominion and its Ukraine-like prairie from writers such as Israel Zangwill (1864-1926), an English writer of Russian origin, known as the Jewish Dickens. He wrote of his vision of *ITO-Land* (Jewish Territorial Organization), which he founded and located in the Canadian prairies.

In Quebec, they found a land ill-prepared by history for such an influx. Not only were they the first non-Anglophone migration to arrive since the Conquest, but they were totally impoverished, divided, disorganized, ignorant of the economic and industrial realities of the New World and cut off from their new milieu because of language. Often they could not even name their adopted homeland, though they loved it passionately from the moment they arrived, as it represented a new found freedom

As elsewhere in North America, the immigrants were naturally drawn to certain parts of the city. Until 1914, the Montreal community adopted the older Crémazie neighbourhood south of Ontario Street on either side of what is now St. Lawrence Boulevard. Decade after decade they moved northward along this commercial artery, the backbone of the city, spilling out between Park Avenue on the west and Saint-Denis Street on the east. By 1921 they had reached St. Louis Square and in 1931 Mount Royal, forging ahead of the next wave of immigrants who would arrive from Greece and Portugal.[8]

But the fundamental reason they drew together is that none of these people dreamed for a moment of denying their Jewishness — no matter how it was defined by their own intellectuals. Throughout their history in Quebec, material survival took second place to the task of perpetuating tradition, which was also the driving force behind their collective experience of migration and hope. They were doing as their ancestors had done since the time of Abraham. And unlike other immigrants, they did not have the option of returning to their native land after several years in order to resume their former lives. Quebec was the Promised Land. It was bilingual and welcomed many ethnic groups. It did not ask them to assimilate and disappear into the homogeneity of another culture, Francophone or Anglophone, Catholic, Protestant or atheist. It was a land where they felt free to be themselves.

Montreal's Remarkable Yiddish Working Class

These immigrants were hiding a cultural treasure house beneath their material poverty: an ancient faith, national tradition and burgeoning literature, a universal and mandatory education system for their sons, something the Quebec government would take another half-century to implement, to say nothing of seventeen centuries of collective life in diaspora.

A strong sense of organization had not developed within the traditional society of the *shtetl* as it had in the neighbouring German community. However, the *shtetl* was characterized by powerful family ties, perhaps stronger than in the other groups who migrated to Quebec. Men and women toiled from dawn to dusk so that their sons could live a free and happy life in the new land, or so that a brother, brother-in-law or aging relatives could join them.

But pressing needs created daily emergencies for everyone, from the new arrival seeking shelter to the impromptu boss of a small garment factory whose workers depended upon him to survive. Initiatives sprang up from all directions.

Social Institutions

Despite difficult beginnings, Montreal's Yiddish-speaking society quickly developed its own network of cultural, social and economic institutions dedicated to ethnic and cultural survival in the face of potential obliteration by the steamroller of North American civilization. All were much more than simply practical responses to immediate crises. They gave the country a generation of scholars, doctors, sociologists, historians, journalists, lawyers, rabbis, poets, thinkers, business people and social revolutionaries. In just two generations, they led the community out of the run-down neighbourhood along St. Lawrence Boulevard and into the residential areas northwest of the city.

This mass of impoverished and exploited immigrants created cultural institutions such as the Jewish Public Library and the daily newspaper *Canader Adler (Canadian Eagle)*, as well as a whole network of volunteer associations and mutual aid societies. Several of them have survived, either with their original name and structure intact or in the same spirit that created them. They multiplied and performed miracles in Montreal, much the same as the French Quebecers did with Caisses Populaires Desjardins. One such institution was the Debt of Honour Association, which gave out interest-free loans, even to non-Jews. The borrower was left to decide on the generosity of the interest payments. Another was a small neighbourhood travel agency that advanced money enabling people to bring over other family members. Yet others were the *landsmannschafften* or mutual aid societies, where often a handclasp sufficed when formalizing an agreement. These social organizations brought together immigrants from the same regions — Poles, Romanians, Ukrainians, Russians — and later became the mutual societies which remain to this day.[9] They organized cemeteries, prayer centres, life and health insurance and health care networks for their members. They represented an effort to reconstitute the extended family of the *shtetl*. Their members went to the same synagogues, joined the same unions or the Jewish Public Library and played in the same chess clubs.

With increased organization, more people than ever were able to carve out their niche. Some worked in the garment industry, still at the primitive stage of sweatshop production. The half of the community that earned a living in such hellish conditions was made up of unskilled labourers who could not speak the language. The other half formed the multitude of peddlers, small shopkeepers, restaurant owners, insurance and real estate agents and teachers who conducted business in the neighbouring streets of St. Lawrence Boulevard.

The many popular movements that had sprung up in Yiddish-speaking Montreal served as a way of reaching the larger immigrant community and soliciting support, if necessary. There were May Day demonstrations and new programmes to discuss: convening the Canadian Jewish Congress, taking trade union action, setting up a community council, library or school. Consultation among the "societies," as the intellectuals called them somewhat disdainfully, was an ongoing part of community life as the immigrant society found its footing.

Educational Institutions

The Yiddish-speaking community continued to grant children a privileged place at the heart of this immense integration process and to put the emphasis on their education. The expectations and demands that weighed on Jewish children were enormous: a complex tradition, pressure by the community to ensure its continuity, two distinct lives — one at home and another in the street, as well as two forms of education — one introducing them to Quebec life and another, the *cheder*,[10] preparing them for Jewish life. All young Jews attended primary as well as secondary school, an unprecedented phenomenon in Quebec at the time. This was in keeping with the dictates of their religious tradition, which ranked study higher than any other duty. Even today, an impressive proportion of Jews attend colleges, universities and institutes of higher learning in Quebec.

So firmly anchored was this tradition that even the revolutionaries who had broken away from the ghettos of the *shtetl* still respected the *cheder*, its symbol in both content and effectiveness. They waited a long time before proposing alternatives, an indication of how difficult it was to separate culture and religion in Judaism.

The Yiddish-speaking community was soon guided by its thinkers and leaders in setting up progressive educational institutions. During the Montreal convention of the Labour Zionists of North America in 1910, a network of modern Yiddish, socialist and Zionist schools was created which stood among the top schools of their kind. They were run by philosophers such as Shloimeh Wiseman, Samson Dunsky, Jacob Zipper, Leon Rubenstein, H. Noveck and W. Chaitman, who ranked among the best-known Jewish educators in the world. In the years to follow, these men would also be the first in the West to develop a school system based on American Catholic parish schools, with one administration offering both general and religious education. Their initiatives would be adopted in foreign lands and instituted in other areas of Jewish education as well.

And so, a people who had once lived in chronic anarchy came to Montreal and elevated "the organization" to a quasi-religion, as its instrument of national salvation. The height of this movement was undoubtedly the establishment of an umbrella organization in 1919, the Canadian Jewish Congress.

The creation of the Canadian Jewish Congress stands as a unique achievement. The ideal of total comprehensive and fraternal unity, of a Jewish democratic organization freely accepted by the entire *kehillah*, was born in the beginning of this century. The annals of the Congress reveal the achievements of men such as: Ruben Brainin, Leib Zuker, Moishe Dickstein, Simon Belkin, Michael Garber, H. M. Caiserman, Louis Rosenberg, A. B. Bennett and Mark Selchen. The high-mindedness and sensitivity they demonstrated is part of the current, continuing agenda of Canadian Jewry and its educational curriculum.

In February 1909, the editor of the *Adler* urged that the legislative committee of the Baron de Hirsch Institute, which had proved effective in dealing with the Federal Government, Parliament, the Legislative Assembly and municipal bodies, be reorganized to include all organizations in the community, but the suggestion was to no avail. Efforts were made in several countries to bring such an institution into being, but only in Canada was it realized, first in 1919 and again in 1934.

There is no parallel to the Canadian Jewish Congress. Today, the Canadian Jewish Congress is seen as the most extensive, nation-wide Jewish organization responsible for a wide programme of action on behalf of the community, representing every Jewish citizen in the country. This is the one assembly where women, men, the young and the aged can discuss and resolve (under one roof) the Jewish problems that concern them: Soviet Jewry, singles, Yiddish, Canadian anti-Semitism, theatres, women's issues, arms control, the aged, terrorism, cults, immigration, religious matters, history and archives, Christian-Jewish relations, the disabled, students, small communities, Nazi war criminals, Israel, the Holocaust, charity funding, constitutional questions and other matters which they may wish to place on the agenda in the presence of the entire community. There is no other nation-wide Jewish institution in the world in which a congress unites all the Jews in the country to deal with the many interests of the entire citizenry.

The Battle over Yiddish in Montreal

The relationship between French Quebecers and the language and culture of France has been described as a passionate one. But another linguistic passion burns in Quebec: the love of Yiddish felt by Montreal Jews from the *shtetl*.

The Yiddish language evolved in a peculiar manner. For centuries, it had no name. It was considered German, "Judeo-German" and even jargon. Its introduction to Montreal coincided with a period in the last century when the people of the *shtetl* first identified with it and simply called it Yiddish, or "Jewish," as if Hebrew, Aramaic and Ladino had ceased to exist; as if nothing had happened from Abraham to Maimonides.

Yiddish language and literature belong to popular culture. Whereas Hebrew is the language of science, religion, university research, scholarship, antiquity and archaeology, Yiddish had slipped between the fingers of academics and universities, including the Hebrew University in Jerusalem. It was literally "invented" according to the haphazard rules of human interchange. When the time came to structure the language and base it on a rigidly-controlled academic foundation, the task was not entrusted to the universities. Instead, a popular world institute was created in Vilnius, Lithuania[11] and named the Yiddish Scientific Institute (YIVO). Its identity was centred around Yiddish traditions and was run by committed laymen. The institute became a cultural hub, generating powerful ideas and actions that enriched Jewish science for more than half a century.

In this social and cultural context, it is no surprise that Yiddish writers were widely read. Thousands of ordinary people were familiar with them and talked to them, for the writers were often neighbours, fellow workers or teachers as well. And it was no surprise that Montreal became one of the cultural capitals of the Yiddish-speaking world.

Today, Yiddish has lost the language war in the Jewish universe to Hebrew and the country's official languages. But at the time of the great migration, it fought impressively in Quebec against Hebrew and English, winning a privileged position in the annals of Jewish literature with novelists such as M. Shmuelson; poets such as J. I. Segal, one of the great writers of Jewish millennial history, as well as Rachel Korn, Melech Rawitch and Mordecai Husid, all of Montreal. The city's spoken Yiddish has its own local colour as well, which can be clearly felt in its rhythm and expressions.

Cultural Institutions

The Jewish Public Library must be one of Montreal's truest reflections of the Yiddish spirit. When it opened on St. Urbain Street, it pinned to its functions the title of the People's University. This unusual title appears on the Quebec government charter it received in 1914. As the name indicates; it did far more than loan books. It was a popular lay temple of Jewish culture right from the start and probably more highly respected than any other in the world — despite the fact that its leaders had to beg for fuel in the winter to keep the coal fires burning. A whole succession of great thinkers were needed to plan the project and keep it alive for so many decades: Reuben Brainin, a scholar of modern Hebrew language and literature; Yehudah Kaufman, a historian of Jewish philosophy and Hebrew poetry and Melech Rawitch, a guiding spirit of Jewish literature in Poland and one of the great poets of the Yiddish language. A small army of tireless volunteers was also required to keep this unique institution alive for three-quarters of a century, during a period when most people had little use for public libraries and people's universities.

Montreal's Yiddish society was many-faceted. It was populist, intellectual, religious, politicized, anarchic, Zionist, revolutionary, institutionalized, impassioned and responsive to the arts. It provided a forum for discussion, reflection, action and reaction in its newspaper, the *Canader Adler*, which appeared for over seventy years. This great Yiddish daily was run by an impressive team. H. Wolofsky was its publisher and musicologist Israel Rabinovitch the editor. It also received input from historian B. G. Sack; fabulist and journalist H. Hirsch; Hebrew scholar and activist R. Brainin, who also published his own newspaper *Der Veg* (*The Path*) and was a founder of the Canadian Jewish Congress; theatre critic J. B. Goldstein; Zionist theoretician

S. Schneour; Maimonides specialist H. Kruger, in addition to a host of other writers, theoreticians, educators, social activists and rabbis. The microfilms[12] of this newspaper, which appeared from 1907 until recently, represent an archive of a very important period in Quebec history, when today's Jewish reality in the province was just taking shape.

Thus, an unexpected shift in the course of history led a group of extraordinary individuals to transform Montreal into a cultural centre of world renown, a unique testing ground where creative thinkers inspired by the great concepts of modern Jewish idealism gave shape to social institutions; where writers worked as factory labourers, bakers, tram drivers or teachers. The people talked with them at work, in the street and at home. The community rallied to help them publish their books. Grocers and merchants read them in the back rooms of their shops, from copies bearing warm wishes from writers who were considered for the Nobel Prize. A conversation with any of these personalities on Clark of Fairmount Streets—Segal or Petrushko, for example—was not just the small talk of a passing moment, though that may be how it appeared. The personal accounts of many in the community tell us that these special contacts left their mark. They were a legacy buried in the innermost soul; like an indescribable dream best kept secret, even at home, but which nonetheless contributed to the creative ambience that characterized Yiddish-speaking Montreal for decades.

From time to time, these writers travelled. A visit by J. I. Segal to Toronto or Winnipeg was cause for great celebration in those Yiddish communities. The festivities carried on long after the speeches were over at the school or community centre and all the books were sold. The unique place of Yiddish and its popular spirit were reaffirmed as a source of inspiration for a community whose basic values were at risk.

In Montreal, on the other hand, there were Yiddish "summits" where the community assembled to hear writers and thinkers from New York and Europe. Even after sixty years, vivid memories remain of visits by Sholem Aleichem, Sholem Asch, Reuben Brainin, Chaim Zhitlovsky, Chaim Greenberg, Baruch Zukerman, Yehudah Kaufman, Shneur Zalman Shazar or H. Masliansky. They left still-visible traces in the history of the young Quebec community. Their signatures and thoughts can be read in the book of honour at the Jewish Public Library in Montreal. They expressed their admiration for the essential character of the institution and the central place it occupied in the cultural history of Quebec Jewry.[13]

One symbolic detail deserves mention: for the most part, these significant encounters took place at the Monument national on St. Lawrence Boulevard, the cultural hub for both the French and Jewish communities. It could just as easily be called the Monument to Nations.

This historical process gave birth to a new cultural phenomenon. At the end of World War II, a final wave of Yiddish-speaking Jews disembarked in Canada by the tens of thousands—most of them from Eastern Europe. They were alive with the spirit of their Polish, Romanian and Russian communities, all "selected" and motivated by the experience of having escaped the Holocaust. They included some immensely talented men and women active in the art world and in social and political circles, as well as a number of the most famous names in Jewish literature. They became immersed in Montreal's Yiddish society and felt at home there. Suddenly, Montreal began to attract Jews from Jerusalem, New York, Buenos Aires and Johannesburg; pilgrims flocked to Quebec to visit Rachel Korn and Melech Rawitch as they had in the past to see Segal, Wiseman, Dunsky and Petrushko. The Jewish Public Library found its second wind — it had moved to the corner of Mount Royal and Esplanade Streets.[14] Literary prizes began to pour into Montreal, where an impressive number of new works appeared by Mordecai Husid, Rawitch, Korn, Yehudah Elberg, Shaffir and others.

This outburst of energy gave birth to a truly Québécois school of Yiddish literature, culminating in the dominant figure of Jacob Isaac Segal. It also included many others: educator S. Wiseman, who translated Greek, Latin and American works into Hebrew; J.Zipper, who immortalized the spirit of the *shtetl*; Husid, the impressionist poet of the concept of Holocaust; Dunsky, who translated the classic text by Midrash Rabbah on the books of the Bible; moralist painter Aleksander Bercovitch; folklorist Zlotnik and painter-philosopher Jan Menses, whose work is preserved at the Vatican and in a dozen other world-famous collections. These people lived in the small streets off St. Lawrence Boulevard between Saint-Denis Street and Park Avenue. No wonder, then, that they had a profound impact on the perceptive soul of a young man who was to become one of Canada's great writers, Abraham M. Klein, and that he expressed his impressions in intensely Québécois English poetry and in his remarkable novel concerning the cosmic significance of the restoration of Israel: *The Second Scroll*.

Reaction of the Original Jewish Community

The influx of Yiddish speakers into the Jewish society of the day could not help but create turmoil, not so much for Quebec society at large, as for the community itself.

Montreal's Jewish community, established for a hundred years in 1870, had put down deep roots in Quebec. It had won the respect of its neighbours and even developed a social philosophy resembling British-style philanthropy.

As thousands of fellow Jews arrived from the *shtetl* at the turn of the century, the tiny community — numbering just 518 people in 1871 — agreed to come to their aid. The task far surpassed its own means. None of its members was particularly rich. Fortunately, a European philanthropist, Baron Maurice de Hirsch,[15] held some original opinions about the fate of Eastern Europe's poor and about ways of helping them become more useful to society. His convictions led him to establish the Jewish Colonization Association in 1890, which he funded generously.

He was particularly interested in Montreal's problems and admired the philanthropists in the Quebec community. He joined forces with them to launch a charitable organization that earned the city of Montreal international respect in the area of social welfare. It is now known as the Allied Jewish Community Services.

The baron and baroness made Montreal one of their preferred beneficiaries, thereby ranking the young city among the major international centres in the worldwide migration and reintegration that occurred as Judaism was transformed. The institutions they supported eventually grew into the Jewish community as it is structured now: Jewish schools and hospitals, the Combined Jewish Appeal, the Canadian Jewish Congress and the Allied Jewish Community Services. Several of these institutions bear the baron's name and keep his memory alive in contemporary Montreal.

Until the end of the nineteenth century, when the community was suddenly submerged by the Yiddish migration, the original Jewish community had conducted its philanthropic activity through the Young Men's Hebrew Benevolent Society, which became the Baron de Hirsch Institute in 1890. In just a few decades, it was subject to a massive injection of new ideas, analyses, discussions, organizations and platforms, where ideas clashed with particular intensity because the protagonists enjoyed a kind of freedom unheard of in the Old World.

The battles fought by the new Yiddish-speaking community were not directed toward Quebec society, despite its integrationist passion and the proselytizing of certain Protestant missionaries. They were rather internal, ideological conflicts, first with the small middle-class community (*Yahudim*) that received them: Anglophile, disdainful of Yiddish, ignorant of the Talmud and Jewish folklore, strangers to *shtetl* life, seen as lukewarm in terms of religion, "philanthropic" in its social action and concerned more with the efficiency of its institutions than the mutual aid being organized by its beneficiaries.

Still more fundamental was the conflict that tore it apart from within. The devout opposed the agnostics and atheists and among non-believers, those who were in the Yiddish camp confronted Hebraists, each elevating its language to the status of a religion for personal and national salvation. Traditionalists faced iconoclasts, and Zionists who looked to Jerusalem took issue with Zionists who dreamed of a Jewish nation in Libya, Santo Domingo or British Columbia. All were opposed by the socialists and later the communists, democratic humanists and others who rejected a Jewish territorial solution altogether. Instead they proposed a global approach focussing on a solution for all human problems.

This ideological pluralism within Jewish society could not help but highlight the astonishing diversity of the Jewish community as a whole. A Jewish gathering during that period would bring together Jews who had been educated for generations in the purest of British traditions and understood not a word of Yiddish, German Jews who understood slightly more of this language and Jews who spoke Yiddish as their mother tongue and traced their origins to Russia, Estonia, Poland, Hungary, Austria, Romania and the Ukraine. Other differences often added complexity to the class tension between the new arrivals (*Yiddishè gass*) and the establishment (*yahudim*). Immigrants from Eastern Europe considered themselves Russian by geography but Jewish by culture, while their forerunners in North America saw themselves as Canadian by geography, British by culture and Jewish by religion alone, a dramatically new distinction in terms of the orthodox tradition.[16] In the words of Nathan Glazer,[17] while the first saw themselves as a "people or nation," the second defined themselves as a "religious group."

Early Challenges

A migration such as that of the *shtetl* Jews poses endless problems. Unlike other immigrants, they left no homeland behind to safeguard their traditions, religion, language, lifestyle and the thousand-and-one other facets of their culture; no place where these could be passed on from generation to generation. They had no cultural wellspring, whether in France, England, China or India, to which they could turn for replenishment.

There were no support structures to welcome the Yiddish-speaking immigrants. Their community was ill-prepared for integration into America, with its sweatshops and growing trade unionism, and it was torn from within by opposing schools of thought. It therefore rallied around one obsession: to perpetuate itself and resist the disintegration of its cultural and community identity in the North American melting pot. Its members shared the feeling that in order to perpetuate tradition, each individual first had to exercise his or her personal will to survive. They also understood that keeping their culture alive was a collective challenge. Their task was complicated by the fact that in the *shtetl*, they had long suffered from chronic anarchy in most areas of collective life, from rabbis and synagogues right down to supplies of kosher meat.

Their society was in upheaval. A new and enterprising generation suggested objectives that went far beyond internal restructuring. They dreamed of sweeping changes, often based on avant-garde political or social philosophies, and they counted on the grass roots to help them achieve their goals. This gave rise to a great outburst of ideas, analyses and experimentation, of projects that meshed or clashed. It also created a new mystique, the advent of the "organization" as the "sacrament" of collective salvation in a culture that knew nothing of such a concept until the advent of Hasidism.[18] The capitulation and downfall of the ancient Yiddish-speaking world was signalled by the adoption of this social survival technique and of "development by political movements" such as *Aufklärung*, and later, in self-defence, by ultraconservative orthodoxy itself.

Under the circumstances, it is no surprise that Montreal became a meeting-ground for intellectuals and activists who had migrated from the *shtetl* with others from their community and shared their ideologies. There were Poale Zion workers, territorial Zionists, tiny groups of disciplines of individual "rebbes," Bundist workers,[19] anarchists, Zionists and those who held on to traditions associated with Yiddish; there were people attracted to the writers, artists and journalists of the city or concerned with the gasp and confusion in religious circles. All were heard and respected in Montreal.

Such an avalanche of questions and answers occurs only rarely in the history of a people. The Yiddish-speaking immigrants and local Jewish communities who welcomed them had never before experienced anything of this scope. The new arrivals found themselves living in conditions of unimagined freedom: freedom of conscience, freedom of expression and a democratic environment. They also experienced the disappearance of ancient institutions that had always acted to restrict or reject their questioning. They had an unlimited opportunity to plan and act, to launch their own institutions in a free society — Quebec society.

Confusion? Anarchy? Wasted energy? Futile initiatives? Probably. But above all, an experience that left its mark on the Jewish community then and for the future, perhaps more than its members imagined.

Quebec provided an ideal setting for a community dedicated to defending its identity, precisely because of its bicultural and even multi-ethnic fabric, especially in the Anglophone milieu. Quebec society also upheld the political and legal traditions inherited from eighteenth-century England. This became evident during the Plamondon affair, for example, and the Jewish separate school debate. Despite the anti-Semitic activity of some Quebec intellectuals, the Jewish community could generally turn to the courts of the government and win its case.

Some leading members of the Jewish community recognized this in retrospect. Toronto lawyer J. L. Cohen wrote to a Montreal rabbi in 1923:

> Is it not true that the Jews find themselves, if anything, better situated there than in any other section of the Dominion? . . . The majority of Quebec professes or practises no desire to impose its character on others who reside within its boundaries. On the contrary, they assert merely their desire to retain their own individuality, and indicate their willingness that others follow for themselves a like course.[20]

And in 1959, historian and journalist Ben Kayfetz wrote from Toronto that:

> Montreal's French Catholic-English Protestant polarity may be the key to its Jewish development. It has given the impetus perhaps to a day-school system that encompasses fully half of all Jewish children who get any Jewish education, to large institutions like a Jewish Public Library, a Jewish General Hospital, and a Young Men's Hebrew Association.[21]

Basically, the people of the *shtetl* had an intuitive sense from the time they arrived that their survival was virtually assured in Quebec. They were prepared to meet the challenges of living side by side with other communities in Quebec and Canadian society.

The Jews and the Industrial Revolution

The Quebec experience during the last two centuries cannot be fully appreciated without a thorough understanding of the strong ethnic and cultural forces that contributed to building the province as we know it.

The unwritten and almost forgotten history of the Yiddish community provides a case in point: this Jewish society, or rather civilization, left its mark on Montreal's economic and cultural life from 1870 onward. It would be fascinating to compare the community with others in New York, Toronto, Buenos Aires or anywhere else that the Jews from the *shtetl* sought refuge. It actually stood out among these mini-societies scattered throughout the world, with an influence that far surpassed its numbers, probably because of the unique conditions that prevailed in Quebec society.

Industrial Quebec in the Late Nineteenth Century

The arrival of mechanization, factories and salaried labour prepared the way for the "Industrial Revolution" in Quebec during the early nineteenth century as it did in other Western countries.[22] A whole process of social and economic change was thus set in motion, culminating in a growth crisis at the end of the century comparable to that of the 1960s.

Early industrialization deeply affected a whole population of emigrants who had recently settled in the Quebec countryside. Their rural, agricultural lifestyle, patriarchal and parochial in structure, was abruptly transformed. They entered an existence shattered by chaotic urbanization and dominated by industry, which was swept up in a savage form of capitalism that the early trade union movement was trying to tame. The union movement propagated new ideas aimed at bringing fundamental reform to industrial society. During the 1880s, in the Noble Order of the Knights of Labour for example,[23] there was talk of abolishing salaried labour, creating cooperatives and even overhauling the entire economic system. During that period, unions acted as pressure groups with respect to government. After 1899, "international" trade unionism from outside Canada became firmly established in Quebec. There were 74 international trade unions in 1901, and by 1921 the number had risen to 334.

The Shtetl Immigrants

The people of the *shtetl* arrived in throngs after 1880 against this backdrop of exhausting, backbreaking labour, still bearing the imprint of the semi-feudal society that had been their home in nineteenth-century Eastern Europe.

Theirs was the first and largest immigration in Quebec history of people who spoke neither English nor French. This human tidal wave expanded the pool of unskilled labour already fed by the flow of Francophones arriving from rural areas. The two peoples forged a shared destiny, especially in their neighbourhoods and trade unions.

But the immigrants brought more than mere vestiges of the past with them. Their intellectuals read Hegel and Marx. Their union leaders were trained in the ranks of the Bund, the general association of Jewish workers from Lithuania, Poland and Romania. It was formed in 1897, inspired by the revolutionary trends of the period. Until 1903, it was affiliated with the Russian Social-Democratic Workers Party. Its visionaries and their predecessors had been crushed for centuries by the ostracism of the Eastern European states, but were also imbued with the ideals of social justice found in the Bible and the Talmud. They listened closely to the messages of hope coming from the West: distant messages from the French Revolution, the Napoleonic crusades against empires that oppressed their people, and the liberalism of the Christian West. Other echoes came from close at hand: the Russian revolutionaries and workers who longed for the end of Tsarism. They became aware of growing trade unionism in Switzerland, Spain and France, and before long, the Marxist critique of industrial capitalism and its apocalyptic dream of a classless, stateless society.

For the time being, the *shtetl* Jews brought with them various qualities that influenced the future of Quebec industry: the energy and mobility that carried them across the seas to Quebec; technical skills as craftsmen in wood, iron and leather; the creative, enterprising spirit that made them famous as shopkeepers, peddlers and owners of small businesses; and above all, the new ideas of their intellectuals, quickly dubbed revolutionaries by a milieu that was still blind to the new set of social, economic and political problems facing the New World.

From then on, this sub-group developed along parallel lines to the path taken by Quebec society, already in the throes of urban and industrial growth. A new class of large and small entrepreneurs gradually took over the garment industry, the largest industry in Quebec during that period. At the same time, a Jewish working class quickly began to form, made up of people who were highly sensitive to the cultural, social and economic issues related to trade unionism. This working class was particularly volatile because it fell victim to the inhumane exploitation of industrial capitalism, still in its most brutal phase.

In those two classes, owner and worker, lay the paradox of the Yiddish-speaking sub-group. It led anti-Semites of the 1930s to contradict themselves as they stirred up popular sentiment against the Jews, identifying them as unscrupulous capitalists one moment and accusing them of being socialists and dangerous activists the next.

The Flourishing of Small Business

The *shtetl* immigrants had fled a world where all avenues were closed to them, and landed in the Promised Land of their dreams. It did not disappoint them as far as freedom was concerned, including the freedom to be involved in small business. The continuous wave of migration was the best proof of that. They arrived without friends, money and in many cases without a trade. Tailors and even small merchants from the Russian or Polish villages had no preparation for taking on Canadian-style competition other than their general knowledge, family traditions and determination.

These people became the merchants of downtown Montreal, the peddlers who toured the countryside and some even became small-scale manufacturers. This is how H. Vineberg describes the Montreal of the 1870s in his "Memories of a Jewish Old Timer":

> Jews lived by trade, in small stores. There were several large Jewish firms and two Jewish cigar manufacturers; no doctors or lawyers. After coming to Canada, they would spend the first several months peddling in the countryside.[24]

The Sweatshops

Jews became identified with the garment industry more than any other. The firm of Moss Brothers was founded in Montreal in 1836 with an initial capital of £60,000. It employed 800 men and women and its annual production rose as high as £90,000, of which 11/12 was exported. Australia alone purchased goods worth £40,000.

The textile industry had provided an early case of commercial concentration and monopolization, unlike the garment industry that followed. At the time of its rise in th 1860s, it was still "not very concentrated, but there were many firms and competition was lively."[25] It was characterized by the sweatshop system, in which sewing was done at home by women[26] who were paid on a piecework basis at scandalously low rates. The industry was dominated by Jewish manufacturers by the turn of the century, and it became the biggest exploiter of *shtetl* immigrants.[27] The system was in fact an ingenious form of labour organization, requiring minimum space from the owner and maximum productivity from the workers. The highest possible efficiency was extracted by the sub-contractors, who became veritable slave drivers to the basic workers.

Here is a description published in the Montreal *Herald* of February 3, 1897:

> Much has been written about the miseries which this system entails to thousands of unfortunate beings in such large cities as London and New York; but perhaps few Montrealers are aware that the system is proportionately as great in Montreal, and that it is fast spreading. . . . The operators and the victims of this system are mostly Hebrews, the number of whom is continually increasing. It is estimated by men who have made special enquiries that there are now over a thousand of them in the square bounded by Craig, Sanguinet, St. Catharine and Bleury Streets. Nearly all of them live in old, dark tenements. The overcrowding is general, there being cases where families have only one room each in order to save rent.

Occupied as they are from early morning until night, they have little time, even if they had the inclination, to give a thought to the sanitary condition of their surroundings, which are often simply vile. The combination living-room and workshop offers one of the saddest spectacles which can be sought by any humanly disposed person, who seeks light on the subject of human misery.

The head of the factory inspectors, Mr. Lessard, asserts that the ordinary week's work of these people is from 75 to 80 hours. Men and women who do not work at home bring work home on Sunday.[28]

Jules Helbronner (1844-1921), another Jewish observer, was a journalist at *La Presse*. He considered piecework and subcontracting the two scourges of the sweatshop system. He wrote:

The divisions and subdivisions caused by the general practice of working by the piece reduces the position of a worker to that of a simple machine, and of a useless machine, when some new invention improves the machinery of which he is the only complement.

From the working by the piece comes the real sweating process, and its true operator is the sub-contractor. Workmen protest strongly against the introduction of this intermediary, whom the masters have imposed on them, and whose profits are necessarily obtained from the price of their handiwork.[29]

That was the sweating system, with its endless round of poverty and illness, an undeniable product of the industrial nineteenth century. For many years, working in the sweatshops was the fate of Jewish immigrants belonging to the generation that sacrificed itself to lay the human and financial bases of today's Jewish community.

This mass of lowly workers and craftspeople, exploited and exhausted, provided fertile ground for discussions of freedom. Paradoxically, they were also the unrecognized avant-garde of the union movement. The result was that a few decades later, they had much better working conditions than other Quebecers, who thus had to reckon with them.

The Labour Movement and Trade Unionism

The origins of Quebec trade unionism can be traced to 1827, when a printers' union was formed in Quebec City. It was followed by several other trade unions, but not until 1860-70 did an organized labour movement begin to emerge. This long gestation period provides little for the historian to study. There are few dates and scanty information about how the organizations functioned and what they did, though certain strikes did make the newspaper headlines.

The Jewish labour movement experienced the same difficult beginnings. Jewish trade unions were scattered, lasted a short time and disappeared without a trace. Some were affiliated with larger organizations, but there is little documentation in this area, either.

Tailors' unions or garment workers' unions appeared from time to time. During one of the early May Day celebrations, there were men, women, French Quebecers, Italian musicians and Jewish workers from the sweatshops parading together, carrying banners.

Three interwoven phenomena characterized Quebec during the 1870s: Jewish and other immigrants arrived on the labour market, industry underwent strong growth and workers began to assert their solidarity. British and American workers brought their trade union experience to Quebec and encouraged the Knights of Labour (1881) and international unions affiliated with the American Federation of Labour (1886) to enter the country as well.[30] At the same time, the first group of affiliated trade unions was formed in Quebec, the Canadian Trades and Labour Council (1883 and 1886). Strikes were soon better organized and workers' demands were more precise and better articulated. At *La Presse*, Jules Helbronner wrote a courageous worker's column under the pseudonym of Jean-Baptiste Gagnepetit, but he rarely made reference to Jewish trade unionism in Montreal.

There seems to have been a lack of communication between the Jewish union movement and the other works' organizations in the province. Nonetheless, Jewish trade unions made their presence felt here and there with strikes such as the one held in June 1883, by the United Cigar Makers, local 658, at Samuel Davis and Sons. Born in London, Samuel Davis founded his company in 1861 and eventually became one of the biggest employers in the tobacco industry, with 457 employees. We know that about fifty percent of his workers were unionized in 1888, and that this percentage was higher than the industry average.[31]

But the union movement was especially active in the garment industry. At the 1895 Labour Congress, garment workers asked for an inquiry into the sweating system in Canada. Its demands received mention in the annual report on strikes and lockouts prepared by the Canadian Department of Labour:

> Around issues such as abolition of sweat shops, child labour, and work at home, the clothing workers began to unionize. Unions in the field then included the Journeymen Tailors Union (a fore-runner of the Amalgamated Clothing Workers of America), the United Garment Workers of America and the United Hat and Cap Workers. The National Trades and Labour Congress also tried its hand at organization. In 1904 it was considering hiring "two Hebrew organizers to better organize the Jewish working people." . . . In their battle to improve conditions, the clothing workers fought many strikes. Between 1900 and 1914, 40,000 of them took part in 158 strikes. The time lost in these strikes was 10% of total time lost for all strikes in Canadian industry between 1901 and 1915. In 1913, 4,500 cloth-

ing workers at Montreal were involved in a 6 weeks strike . . . and at Montreal, 1,000 were on strike for 7 months.[32]

As in other countries, the struggles of organized labour carried over into the political arena. The ranks of the Jewish workers included unionists trained in many different schools of thought, from Karl Marx and the British socialists to Mediterranean anarchism, with input from the American Knights of Labour as well.[33]

Because of their cultural background, these unionists could not limit their focus to labour relations and legislation; they also took an interest in working conditions in Russia, Poland and Romania. Some had been part of the Second and even the Third International. Others had established kibbutzim in Israel and helped Jewish workers in Palestine create the State of Israel. Golda Meir once stayed on St. Joseph Boulevard in Montreal as a guest of H. M. Caiserman, a unionist who was also president of the Jewish Public Library, a historian of Jewish literature in Quebec, the man who initiated the Canadian Jewish Congress.

Because of many factors including numbers, ideology and culture, Jewish trade unions played a much more prominent role in the new Jewish subgroup than the parallel Christian unions did in the society of French Quebec. Jews, for example, were involved in founding both a labour party in 1889 and a socialist party in 1906. At the fifth national (continental) Congress of Labour Zionists[34] in Montreal, there was even mention of collaborating with the Socialist Party of Canada, founded in 1904.[35]

The project did not go forward, mainly because of opposition by one of the party's great thinkers, S. Schneour. He deplored the anti-Semitic attitude of the Socialist Party, particularly in the area of immigration.[36]

This active contact between Jewish trade unionists and Canadian socialists sowed panic in the Quebec press. A report in *Action sociale catholique* of January 30, 1911 described Montreal as a hotbed of Russian anarchists who were veterans of the mutiny on the battleship *Potemkin*. These anarchists were seen as the most dangerous elements of Russian Jewish nihilism. The Montreal reporter quotes the Toronto *World* as saying that Montreal was home to a wing of the International that was directing the world anarchist movement.

May Day demonstrations, held every year from 1906 on, were closely watched by the press. On May 2, 1910, *Le Devoir* noted that the previous day's demonstration at Champ de Mars was divided into three sections, English, French and Jewish, and that evening speeches by the socialist leaders were delivered in English, French and Yiddish. In *Le Devoir* of May 2, 1913 two details of the "socialist" demonstration attracted the reporter's attention: a young women dressed in red and carrying the red flag, and the Semitic aspect of the demonstrators.

The following year, *La Presse* of May 2, 1914 estimated the number of "socialist" demonstrators at 3,000. Among the groups carrying banners were the Jewish clothing and tailors' unions. May Day demonstrations continued to be organized throughout the 1920s by the labour left, which included Jewish unions and socialists.

Jewish trade unionists tried unsuccessfully to convince Francophone workers to join their struggles. They ran into opposition from the clergy and later the Catholic trade unions, which fought cooperation between workers of different religions on the same work site, and closed their doors to non-Catholic workers.

In time, however, more non-Catholic workers joined the international unions (those with links to parallel unions outside Quebec and Canada). The Jews were pioneers in this movement, but in time their numbers dropped, their income grew and they became concentrated in increasingly specialized locals. Other groups such as the French Canadians, Greeks and Portuguese then succeeded them in a typically Québécois procession of ethnic and cultural communities rising to economic security.

This social and economic mobility was later felt more strongly because Canada only admitted a few Jewish immigrants between 1925 and 1947. The government's action was based on the sinister principle of *None is Too Many*.[37] A void soon began to appear in the Jewish working class, a group diminished by aging, death and retraining, as well as by the unwillingness of young people to follow in their parents' footsteps and become industrial workers.

The Symbolic Career of David Lewis

The life of David Lewis (1909-81) bridged the two generations that built Montreal's Yiddish community: the immigrants, and their children and grandchildren who were born in Quebec. His meteoric rise is thus a symbol of the challenges his community had to overcome when it first came to Quebec. It also demonstrates the vitality, initiative and tenacity of the community as it moved from the ghetto, during the early decades.

The story of this political figure from Montreal is particularly useful because it is familiar to Quebecers. His political career began in Montreal before the war with the CCF (Cooperative Commonwealth Federation), which later became the NDP (New Democratic Party). He later returned to a career in politics after years on the sidelines, this time as national leader of the NDP from 1971 to 1975.[38]

David Lewis' background throws light on his success. He was born in the *shtetl*, in the village of Svisloshch (Swislocz in Polish), then located in Poland but now part of the Soviet Republic of Byelorussia. His father was an active member of a leather workers union and the Bund. The Losh (Losz in Polish) household was a meeting place for a group of workers who held lively discussions about the problems of the day. Such was the environment in which young David experienced the German occupation of 1915, the communist revolution of 1917, Polish independence in 1918 and the final battles in 1919 and 1920 between the Polish forces and the Red Army for control of the frontier region.

Disillusioned with both the Pilsudski regime in Warsaw and the Soviet regime in Moscow (he was a Menshevik), Moische Losh decided to leave for Montreal with his brother-in-law Max. Their plan was to join an uncle who had moved there at the turn of the century and managed to get a foothold in the clothing industry.

Throughout his youth, David shared in the lives of Montreal workers. During the holidays, he worked at his Uncle Eli's factory with his father and Uncle Max, both members of the Amalgamated Clothing Workers of America. His father, "a democratic socialist," he later wrote, took him to meetings such as one held in the early 1920s, when a celebrated menshevik by the name of Abramovich (a disgraced ex-member of the Soviet government) gave a speech in Yiddish at the National Monument Theatre on St. Lawrence Boulevard. The speaker's status did not prevent him from being roundly booed by the communists in the audience.

David Lewis' career, then, comes as no surprise. From the time he entered McGill University, he focused on political science. In 1932, he participated in founding the League for Social Reconstruction (LSR) in Toronto, an organization that was instrumental in forming the CCF. He became a member of the Quebec Labour Party executive and secretary of the Montreal Labour Party, as well as belonging to student associations concerned with workers issues. During his university days, then, David Lewis emerged as the militant socialist he would remain for the rest of his life. When he was at Oxford as a Rhodes scholar, he built up contacts with various European socialist leaders. When he returned to Canada in 1935, LSR leader J. S. Woodsworth, founder of the CCF, invited him to join in the struggle.

David Lewis' career signals and symbolizes the social and cultural revolution experienced by most Jews who immigrated to America and to Quebec in particular. This young Polish immigrant was one of the first Canadian Jews to become a Rhodes scholar. After launching his political career in Montreal's labour and Bundist circles, he left his home and moved to Toronto. There he became a labour relations lawyer.

His career would no doubt have levelled out at this stage had it not been for World War II and the demise of Fascism with Hitler's death. The irresistible breath of freedom that cleared away the last vestiges of old-world intolerance also swept David Lewis, like so many other leading figures of his community, to new and unimagined heights. In 1971, he was invited to preside over the destiny of his party, now called the NDP. This he did successfully until 1975.

Breaking with Europe

Of all the challenges that awaited the Yiddish-speaking people of North America, one was particularly agonizing, for it meant renouncing their cultural allegiances and personal emotions: that challenge was to break away from Eastern Europe, the land that had been the cradle of Yiddish tradition since the Middle Ages.

Dilemma of World War I

Unlike previous military campaigns involving Canada,[40] the 1914-18 war deeply disturbed the Jewish diaspora on both sides of the Canada-U.S. border. The community consisted mostly of new immigrants, refugees in today's terms, who felt boundless gratitude toward the country that welcomed them.

But this war placed them in a crucial dilemma. They had fled Tsarist Russia, a land hostile to Jews, where human rights were flouted and their socialist defenders massacred, exiled or sent to Siberia. They were constantly receiving news of how Jews were being deported from the border regions of Russia to the interior, setting off a whole series of the usual calamities: families separated, communities dismembered, synagogues and cemeteries desecrated, art treasures scattered, sickness, famine and refugee camps a way of life. This was the first real step in destroying the Central-European Jewish world, a process that culminated in the Holocaust.

They had no sooner turned their backs on Russia, which loomed between them and their troubled families, than it became Canada's ally in a war against Germany, the land that had given them much of their Yiddish heritage and many of their notions about the Western world. Such was the dilemma of the Russian and Polish immigrants. Their adopted country, Canada, invited and soon conscripted their sons to join an alliance with their traditional enemy to fight a people for whom they felt nothing but admiration.

The Jewish people's millennial aversion to war was finally overcome by news from Turkey that wrenched their hearts. In 1916, the Western press reported that the Turks were trying to destroy the Jewish colony in their province of Palestine. Herzl's dream and the entire Zionist project seemed to be on the verge of collapse. Canada's Zionist organizations soon received a telegram from Copenhagen, worded as follows: "Do everything to prevent more Palestinian evacuations, guarantee evacuees humane treatment, protect Jewish property, concerning outrages, contradictory declarations; Urgent need, fifteen thousand francs/aid evacuees. Begin fund-raising immediately."[41]

Without hesitation, the Jewish community shifted into action. Recent immigrants and Jews from the old Montreal community succeeded in sending some two million dollars in financial aid overseas in the middle of the war. More significant still, there was a breakthrough in the Jews' millennian aversion to war. About 4,700 young people enlisted in the Canadian Armed Forces between 1914 and 1918. The principle of military chaplaincy was also accepted, and that same year, Rabbi Herman Abramowitz of Montreal assumed the role of chaplain to the Jewish soldiers in the Canadian army.

In 1916, there was talk in some Jewish circles of creating a special Jewish unit similar to the Scottish-Canadian Black Watch and the French-Canadian 22nd Battalion. The idea never materialized, though, because it met with resistance from the community in general and the Canadian Federation of Zionist Societies in particular. It was discarded for the same reason separate schools were later rejected: fear of falling back into the trap of segregation, whether in the classrooms or the barracks.

One important detail should be noted in passing. Canada never expected to have to integrate various ethnic groups such as Italians, Serbs and Poles into its army. It simply sent them back to the armed forces of their respective countries or transferred them to the British army where they were put into special units for "foreign allies of various origins." The imperial government chose another option for the Jews: the Zionists levied a Jewish legion to liberate Palestine from the yoke of the Turks. A number of important names were involved from the beginning, including David Ben Gurion, Vladimir Jabotinsky and Itzhak Ben Zvi. The British government set up a recruitment office in New York for Jews exempt from compulsory service and opened branches in Montreal and Toronto. Canadian and American recruits were trained at Windsor, Nova Scotia, and then placed in the charge of the British Army. Canadian Zionist President Clarence de Sola supported the project wholeheartedly in Montreal. He obtained an interview with none other than Arthur James Balfour when he was visiting Ottawa in May 1917. Lord Balfour expressed happiness at being able to discuss Zionism with a Jew of irrefutable orthodoxy who was recognized as a leader of the movement. The meeting lasted three hours. He had come to understand that the British could be instrumental in fulfilling the Biblical prophecy of a return to Zion by the Jewish people. He made assurances that he would defend Zionist objectives before his Cabinet colleagues, confirming that these objectives were fully in keeping with the British foreign policy in Palestine.[42] Clarence de Sola was later informed that the British government intended to declare its official support for the principle of a Jewish homeland in Palestine. This declaration was made official on November 2, and is now known as the "Balfour Declaration."

With the momentum of the Zionist movement and encouragement from the Canadian government, Jewish troop recruitment went well. The first recruits were sent to training camp on May 23, 1918 from Toronto and Montreal. A total of about 300 Canadian Jews joined the legion before the New York office was closed on July 18, 1918. These soldiers were sent overseas to fight and thus established yet another link between Canada and the Jewish world.

The Jewish community emerged from this first collective war experience identifying more closely with its newly-adopted homeland and, also more aware of its ties with Europe and particularly Palestine. Jewish Quebecers had a history of military service that went back to the Harts and Davids. They had always seen it as a measure of their integration and their practical acceptance of Canadian reality. This reality included one characteristic of immense importance which totally escaped the immigrants who arrived during the late nineteenth and early twentieth centuries: the presence and participation of Francophones in the history, geography, development and administration of Canada, particularly in Quebec. This duality was felt more strongly than ever when French Quebecers united in turning their backs on the conscription proposed by Prime Minister Borden in 1917. This dissidence must have been difficult for the Jews to interpret.

The 1917 Russian Revolution: An Immense Disappointment

A whole generation of young Jews inspired by Poale Zion, the Bund and the noble ideas of western Europe's revolutionaries had dreamt of the Tsar's fall and the installation of a democratic regime in Russia.

The anti-Tsarist revolution led by Kerensky and the fall of Tsar Nicholas II in 1917 fulfilled these dreams. A new era was dawning, and with it came a broad shift in allegiances. The persecuted of yesteryear were suddenly enthusiastic citizens of the new Russia.

A few months passed before the communist counter-revolution destroyed this attempt at Western-style democracy. The new regime did not immediately reveal its true totalitarian, anti-religious and anti-Semitic character.

In Canada and elsewhere, a well-orchestrated propaganda campaign came to the defense of the new regime. Thus, during the final year of the war, confusion reigned in the Jewish community over the value and allegiances of the younger generation. A number of Canadian Jews welcomed these events and the world communist strategy, as did many of their fellow citizens who had roots in central Europe. Some aligned themselves with the Communist Party of Canada, but the overwhelming majority regarded this movement with serious reservations. They recalled that it was Kerensky and his moderates who had toppled the Tsar while the Bolshevik leaders were not even in Russia. They also remembered that since communism had achieved power, it had sought to destroy Judaism, Hebrew, Zionism, Jewish cultural and educational institutions, as well as community links with parents and friends living in other countries.

In Quebec, the communists fought against projects and efforts launched by the Jewish community to establish institutions designed to perpetuate Jewish religious and cultural traditions. The community was highly sensitive to the danger communism represented to the synagogue, Hebrew school and Canadian Jewish Congress. Reaction was particularly strong among the radical workers, who had paid dearly for participating in international activities centred on Moscow. They pointed out that red trade unionism had willingly sacrificed the unity of the labour movement and workers' interests to advance the cause of world revolution.

The Communist Party of Canada carried on its public activities under the banner of the Canadian Labour Party.[43] In 1924, when the Labour Party included 200 members of Jewish origin (in 1928, the number remained 200 out of 4,400 members), it chose an Eastern European Jew, Michael Buhay, as its candidate in the federal riding of Cartier. A considerable portion of Montreal's Jewish community lived in that riding and Buhay managed to win 600 votes.[44] The following year, Buhay replaced M. Spector as editor of the Communist newspaper *The Worker*, and in 1929 replaced John MacDonald on the central committee.

This episode involved only a tiny fraction of the Jewish community, those who praised the Trotskyist/Stalinist ideology for Jews and Quebecers. The community regarded them as enemies of religion, nationalism, traditions and institutions in Canada, of Zionism and the Hebrew language, of efforts to perpetuate Judaism and defend the rights of Jews living under anti-Semitic regimes.

In the eyes of the Soviet sympathizers, messianic Russia would solve the world's problems by international revolution. They organized a series of political and cultural institutions: newspapers, theatres, mutual aid organizations and study groups. They agitated for a Jewish state in Siberia and went so far as to organize a fund-raising campaign in 1929 for Arabs who were killing Jewish colonists in Hebron. And in 1939, during the war with Hitler, they supported Germany's alliance with Russia and tried to slow the Canadian war effort.

This tiny but very active group achieved a major victory by electing Fred Rose to the House of Commons in 1943. Their triumph ended a few years later, however, when Rose was convicted of treason. The Canadian Labour Party disappeared from the Canadian scene after Stalin's death, when Nikita Khrushchev told his Soviet colleagues that they could not deny the murderous actions perpetuated by the Stalin regime against Communists, Jews and others, actions which the Canadian party had always denied.

Canada still harbours a few nostalgic traces of this movement in the form of left-wing para-political organizations. Its impact on Quebec history, if indeed it has one, was related to anti-Semitism. In 1945, the Royal Commission inquiry into the Gouzenko affair asked why a relatively large number of Jews, about a dozen, were involved in the espionage intrigue. It sought an explanation in the trauma experienced by Canadian Jews who faced the double rejection of anti-Semitism and Nazism in Canada during the 1930s.

CHAPTER III

The Reaction of French Quebec, 1880-1945

A New Phenomenon: Anti-Semitism

Lawyer J. L. Cohen remarked in 1923 that he thought the majority in Quebec was tolerant toward Jews;[1] the minority was not. English-speaking society cannot be excluded from this minority, especially in the areas of industry, business and schools.[2]

His comment nonetheless raises an important point with regard to the Francophones. Ultramontanism created a deep and persistent division within French Quebec society, and the attitude toward Jews was one of the many forms it took. The dichotomy was also expressed in how French Quebecers perceived homogeneity and pluralism and conceptualized political autonomy within a federation having two distinct levels of government, as well as in how it treated immigrants and integrated them into the school system. The Groulx-Bourassa conflict is but one example.[3]

This dichotomy accounts for, though does not resolve, a historical contradiction in the eyes of the Jews. On one hand, French Quebecers had traditionally welcomed Jewish peddlers and relations between families were good, with Jewish and Catholic children playing together. Some French Canadians disclaimed the speeches of men such as Father Lacasse, Jules-Paul Tardivel, Monsignor Paquet, Arcand or Father Lionel Groulx and deplored the attitudes expressed in weekly religious bulletins from various dioceses. They could well understand Jewish apprehensions. On the other hand, French Quebec harboured a formidable generation of priests and politicians who formed a convincing and vocal intelligentsia. They preached the resumption of pre-conquest colonial ways, the severing of links with neighbours outside Quebec and the isolation of the Jews, if not a total ban on their entry.

Thus emerged an anti-Semitic current parallel to the first wave of Yiddish migration in Quebec, which would gather force until World War II. Oddly enough, the movement did not originate in Montreal where the Jewish community was concentrated, but in the countryside — the heart of rural Quebec, where the Jewish presence was felt less strongly. Montreal remained the principal meeting ground for the two communities, but a relatively small proportion of French Quebecers actually lived in Montreal at the end of the nineteenth century.[4] Most were recent arrivals who had poured in with the steady stream of rural folk attracted by the industrial boom. For the next several decades there were two communities in migration: one from the Quebec countryside and the other from Eastern Europe. In the streets of Montreal, they forged a path of mutual discovery and learned to live together.

French Quebecers accepted the idea of political co-existence with their English partners. In 1938, Aristide Beaugrand-Champagne wrote, in *Les Cahiers des Dix*, that although the English had settled in Canada more recently than the French and "are not as Canadian as we . . . they will become so in time."[5] Even Tardivel, an ardent ultra-nationalist, expressed to Henri Bourassa that English Canadians were not foreigners.[6]

The same was not true of the immigrants. Quebec was not a land of immigration in the way the western provinces were. We know that 684,582 people arrived in the province between 1901 and 1931 and that 822,582 people left it during the same period.[7] Few precise historical records concerning immigration were kept; in fact, immigrants were viewed as a burden, possibly a threat, rather than a valuable contribution. In Quebec, it was said that the main problem with immigrants or the "uprooted" was their ignorance of local traditions and customs which led to a supposed erosion of national unity. This was compounded by the fact that most entered the English-speaking community and swelled its ranks. The majority of French Quebecers thus identified them more or less with the English, and this tended to give them, at best, a recognized sort of status in the Quebec social landscape.

The Jewish community was unique in that of all the newly-arrived ethnic groups, it formed a distinct society (anti-Semites called it a "state within a state"), with a network of institutions such as social services and hospitals that made it autonomous in many ways. It also aspired to special legal status in the area of education. The French Catholic community had seen itself as homogeneous from the start, both ethnically and culturally. There was never any question of opening its schools and other institutions to the Jewish community, much less assimilating them.[8] Immigrants were guests, forever guests, with duties rather than rights. They had no claim to full equality with the people who considered themselves Quebec's original discoverers and builders.

That was certainly the position of radical anti-Semites at the *Goglu*:

> We officially recognize only one religion, Christianity, and two races, the Anglo-Saxon and the French. They alone have constitutional rights and legal privileges, and they alone shall have them in future. . . . Quebec is a Christian land, the homeland of French Canadians, and we shall fall rather than allow it to become the Promised Land of the Jews, a hotbed of Jewish anti-Christianity.[9]

Their attitude was echoed by intellectuals such as the Dominican Father Ceslas M. Forest: "They are immigrants just as Asians and Africans are. The civil equality they are granted by one law can be restricted by another."[10] This thesis was foremost an expression of anti-Semitism, but it should also be set in a larger context: the instinctive xenophobia of a people accustomed to seeing itself as both the builder of a Catholic and French nation and as an oppressed minority whose own survival is threatened.

The Jew in the Literature of French Quebec

French Quebecers generally had a rather vague and incomplete perception of Jewish immigrants from Eastern Europe. The only real point of contact between the two was business. There was the peddler, poetically evoked in a film by Jan Kadar and Ted Allen, *Lies My Father Told Me*. But mostly, there were the small shopkeepers and tradesmen of the city.

Perhaps the best judges of popular reaction to Jewish immigrants were the writers of French Quebec, especially those of the 1930s, for their memories reach back to the turn of the century. An Egyptian Jew, Victor Teboul, published a study entitled *Mythe et images du Juif au Québec*[11] in 1977, while he was completing his doctorate in French-Canadian literature at l'Université de Montréal. It describes the images of Jews that peopled the "collective imagination" of French Quebecers during the 1930s, the same imagination that was responding to the anti-Semitic discourse of the period.

First comes the image of the wanderer, which is closely linked to that of the immigrant. It contrasts sharply with the cult of the land and the habitant, so widespread in Quebec's French community. The habitant is close to the land and lives on the land, unlike the coureur de bois, who is unanchored. In his novel *Trente arpents*, Ringuet (Dr. Georges Panneton) uses this set of concepts to describe both the Frenchman Albert and the German family Schiltz. Before achieving acceptance, they must undergo an initiation period of working the land. "The Schiltz," says Ringuet, "were as Canadian as anyone, for they toiled over the Laurentian soil and lived close to it. A country," he went on, "is land, not lineage."[12] Inversely, adds Teboul, "Albert Chabrol, the labourer hired reluctantly by Euchariste Moisan to fill the void left by his son, refuses to bond with the land and is never fully accepted by Moisan. It thus appears that to achieve total acceptance, the other must have a will to put down roots or a predisposition to become firmly rooted."[13]

This image of rootlessness inevitably becomes associated with another image drawn from the old medieval heritage, that of the Wandering Jew. Here is how François Hertel presents his character Charles Lepic in *Mondes chimériques* (1944): " 'It's true that I am a wandering Jew,' he lamented. 'I have no right to become attached to anyone or anything. I must go, that is the categorical imperative which has come down from Golgotha. He told us to go. And so we go. I believed I could settle as a member of the nomad tribe.' "[14]

Another image to remember is that of the revolutionary. The journalist Olivar Asselin wrote in *The Canadian Century* that socialist ideas were so widespread among the Jews that they were the ones who organized the parades on May 1 to celebrate May Day.[15] Unfortunately, the Jewish left in Quebec was sixty years ahead of its time and throughout the 1930s, Francophone right wing supporters accused Jews within the province of being agents of communist revolution.

The mythical image of the Jew, common at the turn of the century, developed a harder edge as the anti-Semitic crisis intensified. This is evident in the literature that emerged after the war.

A 1960s writer, Yves Thériault, describes the Jewish immigrant of his youth quite well. In his novel *Aaron*, the two Jewish characters, Moishe and Aaron, are also condemned to persecution and flight. They live in what was then Montreal's Jewish quarter, defined by Mount Royal and Sherbrooke, St. Lawrence and Saint-Denis streets. The aging Moishe belongs to a family of tailors and lives by his work (as is the case in Jasmin for Ethel's family[16]): "The ties became closer that way, Jew between Jew, father and son working side by side."[17] He dreads the outside world and protects himself: ". . . against outside attack, against any unwholesome influence, against Gentile promiscuity. Moishe loathed this sewing above all else, it was the bane of Jewish existence! Worst of all were the people who did it to make their fortune, with no concern for preserving their spiritual or ethnic heritage."[18]

Thériault dwells on this refusal of the outside world; on the pain of culture shock: "Sounds rose from the dead-end street through the window, terrifying to Moishe, savage and demented: the cries, curses and laughter, the music from radios. . . . In Levine's place on the corner, the juke box blared out the century's new language."[19]

The old man, trapped, understands the generation gap in Jewish families: "Resolutely, Moishe turned his back to the screen. And so the evening went. The old man, back turned, read his newspaper, while Aaron, fascinated, never took his eyes off the screen."[20]

In another register, the literature of French Quebec represents Jews as avid scholars. Thériault's Aaron easily wins top honours in his class,[21] while Jean Laplante's Auguste Kramer is "superbly gifted. . . . He surpassed all his classmates by an unsettling margin."[22]

This portrait would not be complete without a look at the affinities between the Jews and the "English," understood in the sense of Power, as portrayed in a novel by Jacques Godbout.[23]

Jews seem to have been received by Montreal's English community much as they were received elsewhere in North America. Perhaps this observation by Ben Kayfetz about Toronto's Jewish community also applies in large measure to Montreal, at least English Montreal: "The Anglophile characteristics (if the term may be used) of the early Jewish settlers in Toronto were of great importance in the acceptance of Jews both as individuals and as a group after their arrival in Toronto."[24]

Immigrants in the 1880s and their successors in subsequent decades found that within English Quebec, especially in Montreal, there were leaders and spokespersons prepared to take up their cause. Add to this the immigrants' general perception that Quebec was an extension of Canada and the rest of North America, and it is no surprise that they integrated spontaneously into Quebec's English milieu. For them, French Quebec seemed to be a satellite society within the great British empire.

For the *shtetl* Jews in particular, French Quebec recalled the ethnic minorities of Eastern Europe under the empires that governed them. In addition, the French milieu was foreign to them; its language was unfamiliar and it was devoid of Jewish or even Eastern European influence which might have made them feel at home. In fact, there were virtually no Francophone Jews in Quebec before the arrival of the Sephardim from North Africa much later, during the second half of the twentieth century. It is fair to say that French Quebec left them no choice. Its people were Catholic, French-speaking and quite happy that there were just a few foreigners among them, especially within educational and social structures, where they were left to exercise their rights and prerogatives in peace.

Roots of Quebec Anti-Semitism

To arrive at a clearer understanding of the situation faced by Jews who arrived in Quebec between 1870 and 1930, it is necessary to retrace the roots of the hostility they encountered there.[25]

When the first wave of *shtetl* immigrants reached the banks of the St. Lawrence in 1877, Quebec Jews were just completing a century of good relations with the population, the French Quebecers. Theirs was possibly the best experience in the entire history of the diaspora.

Together, the two communities had struggled for their rights. Nowhere else in the world did Jews have greater freedom and more opportunity for personal and collective growth. While Canada's doors were closed to Africans and Asians, they remained wide open to Jewish immigration. From 1871 to 1931, Quebec's Jewish community grew from 518 to 60,087 members.

But the newcomers did not know that another wave, this one ideological, had swept into the Catholic segment of the intelligentsia a few short years before. In 1866, *La Gazette des campagnes*, a small rural newspaper managed by members of the clergy, published the first anti-Semitic text known in Quebec. It was followed in 1872 by a series of articles in the same vein signed by a member of the clergy from Quebec City named Alphonse Villeneuve. These were two warning signs of the immense darkness to come, when the ultramontane press propagated the myths that fed Quebec anti-Semitism for eighty years.

How can this sudden outburst be explained? The first anti-Semites surfaced in 1862 and had probably never come face to face with a Jew. Until 1871, there were just 518 Jews in all of Quebec, most of them in Montreal. They had been educated in Britain and were identified with the English for all practical purposes. As late as 1896, during a trip to France, journalist Tardivel responded to Father Lemann's[26] questions about Quebec Jews by saying that he did not know any, but that they were beginning to enter the country.[27]

Medieval Heritage

Analysis of the anti-Semitic discourse during this period reveals themes that kept recurring regularly: the Jew as a wanderer, incapable of national identification or patriotism, lacking all affinity with the land, neither peasant nor colonist but a deliberately unscrupulous merchant, exploitive and greedy for money.

These themes had their origins in the image of Jews that had come down from the Middle Ages. At that time, Jews were prohibited from owning property. This accounts for the myth of the Wandering Jews who was unable to settle on the land, and for the concentration of Jews in city ghettos, where they became involved in trades and business. Moreover, since Christians were forbidden to lend money at interest,[28] the Jews took on this essential economic function, leaving Christians free to brand them as moneylenders and bankers.

Another important influence was the history of conflict that surrounded the Judeo-Christian split from the earliest days up to the time of the Church Fathers.[29] This current of hostility left a deep impression on the judicial tradition of the Church and even filtered into the liturgy.[30] Quebec anti-Semites, consisting mostly of members of the clergy, were more or less consciously steeped in this tradition.

Heritage of the French Regime

This Christian atavism was compounded by broadly-based sociological factors going back to the early days of the French regime. The first was the ruling forbidding Jews and Protestants to take up residence in the colony. French Quebecers came to think of themselves as a monolithic people who had the right to banish all things foreign from their universe. During the nineteenth century, they fought the Freemasons, British successors of the seventeenth-century Calvinists, as well as the Jews.

Another no less important factor was the self-image developed by traditional French-Quebec society. Essentially, it perceived itself as a peasant culture with historical links to the nobility and later the aristocracy. Quebec was divided into seigneuries, and even today, especially in the Quebec City region, the memory of that era survives in names such as Place Royale, Côte du Palais and Château Richer.[31] Peasant culture looked down on the coureurs de bois, those itinerant adventurers of the fur trade who cared nothing for hearth and home. Its sympathies lay with the seigneur. Members of the gentry had been integral in founding New France: Paul de Chomedey de Maisonneuve, the founder of Montreal; Madame de Combalet, Richelieu's niece and founder of the Hôtel-Dieu in Quebec City; Madame de La Peltrie, founder of the Ursuline Order of Quebec; and of course Quebec's first bishop, François de Montmorency Laval. This French nobility had inherited a medieval tradition of loyalty to soil, king, country and Church. Its members were wholeheartedly conservative and idealistic too, with their mild disinterest, if not outright disdain, in matters of commerce and the pursuit of wealth.[32] These features resurface at various times in the mentality of French Quebec. At the dawn of the twentieth century they were expressed as a rejection of the industrial era; during the 1930s they emerged as a back-to-the-land movement.

Why, one might ask, was anti-Semitism expressed with more virulence and unanimity by French Quebecers than by other members of the North Atlantic family? One likely explanation lies in colonialism, which was much more oppressive for the Francophones. They belonged to a mini-society trapped in the Quebec ghetto and subject to three forms of domination by English Canada: economic, sociocultural and political. Denis Monière interprets their xenophobic reflex not as cultural atavism, since anti-Semitism did not exist before 1860, but as a "perverse influence of colonialism";

> Anti-Semitism developed in French Canada as a reaction to the power and class structures which dominated French Canadians. They felt threatened with annihilation and sought to affirm themselves, not by attacking the real causes of the situation but by turning on groups weaker than themselves. . . . The Jews threatened the economic base of the urban middle class, for they used the same means of social promotion as French Canadians: small business and the liberal professions. From this perspective, anti-Semitism was a weapon used by the middle class in its economic struggle. . . . Jews thus became the scapegoat, responsible for all our problems. . . . We held them responsible for World Wars I and II, the Russian Revolution, modernism, materialism, liberalism, communism and the emigration of French Canadians.[33]

The European Debate

The anti-Semitic tempest unleashed on Quebec can be traced to two distinct discourses circulating in Europe: ultramontanism, which set the Church against the secular state, and a fledgling racism which propounded the superiority of the white race.

Ultramontanism

The crucial issue for the ultramontanes was to determine who—Church or state—would control the imagination of the masses, whose allegiances had been divided since the time of Constantine.

The French Revolution had proclaimed the equality of all citizens, thus stripping the Catholic Church of its medieval powers. After eighty years of waiting, Rome declared war on the ideas that had inspired the revolution. In

France, this confrontation led to State control of the school system and the exile of several congregations (1900-14).[34] This brought to Quebec a number of priests, monks and nuns who only served to reinforce the defensive and suspicious tendencies shown by one branch of Quebec Catholicism.

During that period, ultramontanism was conducting a fierce battle against liberalism in France. On one side, there were strict Catholics such as Monsignor Gaume, who advocated a Christian reform of education and journalist Louis Veuillot of *L'Univers*. They crossed swords with Monsignor Félix Dupanloup and the Count of Montalembert, who wanted to "christen" the 1789 revolution and supported the Lamennais formula: "A free church in a free state."

What was the link between ultramontanism and anti-Semitism at that time? A clue can be found by reading a few paragraphs from the documents that served as ammunition for the anti-Semites. A case in point is the encyclical of Pius IX entitled *Quanta Cura*, issued on December 8, 1864. In it, the Pope condemned liberalism and rationalism and affirmed the "rights and liberty of a church faced with claims and encroachments by the secular state." Annexed to the document was a syllabus outlining the principal errors of our times, which contained eighty inadmissible propositions, including the following two:

> 7.7 In our time, it is no longer expedient to consider Catholicism the sole state religion, to the exclusion of all others.

> 7.8 It must also be accepted that certain countries, Catholic in name, have decided in their laws that foreigners who settle there should be entitled to practise their particular religions openly.[35]

In other words, from the Catholic point of view, other religions did not have the same rights as Catholicism and the Church did not agree with legislation granting them equal status.

These declarations by the Holy See were binding on the Catholic conscience. They were addressed to each individual, wherever the Church was in a position to intervene in issues involving the population as a whole, including Jews. They provided ammunition for both ultramontanes and anti-Semites.

By denying equal rights to members of other religions, the instructions of Pius IX and Vatican I had a broad impact that was even felt during the constitutional debates on the plan for a Canadian Confederation. The ultramontane bishops from Quebec launched an offensive against the separation of Church and state and the liberalism of the Fathers of Confederation. Intervention by Rome was required to prevent the attack from degenerating into open conflict between the church and the government.[36]

In less than forty years, ultramontanism would alter the liberal nature of Quebec's nationalist struggle and quickly transform it into a reactionary, anti-Semitic movement. Papineau would be replaced by figures such as Monsignor Laflèche and Tradivel.

The Racist Movement

The other discourse that began to circulate in Europe during the same period was more complex and its link with ultramontanism remains obscure. This discourse claimed to be scientific. It was initiated by Count Joseph Arthur de Gobineau (1816-82), who published his *Essai sur l'inégalité des races humaines* between 1853 and 1855. His thesis was taken up by a British Pan-Germanist, Houston Stuart Chamberlain, in an 1899 work entitled *Foundations of the XIXth Century*. Chamberlain was the son-in-law of German composer Richard Wagner.

Their thesis no longer defined man in the religious sense as an individual with eternal destinies, but as a biological being that had to be exterminated if it failed to find grace in the eyes of Power. It is difficult to imagine how an immoral and atheistic form of racism which had no room for religion, a kind of Hitlerism before the name, could possibly have received even the tacit support of church members.

In 1894 the Dreyfus affair exploded in France,[37] a scandal mounted largely by Christians. The accusation of treason against this Alsatian Jew unleashed a flood of hostility against all Jews that far surpassed the issue of his guilt. Society's most "distinguished" French Catholics sided with people who put the "honour" of the homeland and its army above justice and truth, thus unleashing a wider-ranging anti-Semitic campaign of unbelievable virulence.

The Dreyfus affair entered Quebec history through the Catholic and nationalist press. It haunted the popular imagination for almost fifty years. Voices as authoritative as *La Vérité* and *L'Action sociale catholique* persisted in stirring up public opinion against the officer, who was eventually exonerated by the Supreme Court of Appeals. But innocent or guilty, most French citizens had had enough of him — and of all Jews — and their reaction spread overseas to Quebec.

Precursors in Quebec

In an unexpected historical twist, the first known expression of anti-Semitism in Quebec goes back to 1866, two years after the Syllabus of Pius IX was published. Perhaps even more baffling is the fact that the text was signed by a member of the clergy, the Vicar-General Mailloux, and appeared in a small-town periodical called *La Gazette des campagnes*, published at the Collège Sainte-Anne-de-la-Pocatière in the Lower St. Lawrence. Mailloux denounced progress, luxury and fashionable clothing as Jewish inventions, a theme repeated for decades to come by Quebec anti-Semites. Who was this priest and how did he arrive at the idea of associating Jews with modernism, luxury and fashion? One thing is certain: his assault on the liberalism of non-Catholics in general and Jews in particular was but the first of a long series. Father Alexis Pelletier, a priest from the Séminaire de Québec who was at odds with his bishop, went to teach at the Collège Sainte-Anne-de-le-Pocatière in 1866 and published several similar articles.[38]

Not until fifteen years later were the classical anti-Semitic myths penned by a well-known and moderate Quebecer. Alfred D. Decelles was an author and librarian in Ottawa and a historian of the 1837 uprising. On December 1, 1881 he published a fairly moderate article on "The Jewish Question" in *L'Opinion publique*. In it, he analyzed the phenomenon of Jewish survival, touching on a number of familiar anti-Semitic themes: exploitation of the poor, international plots against Christians and wealth acquired by high-interest loans. He concluded his repertoire of myths with this final reflection:

> History has taught us that the Jewish people committed a great crime and that they accepted responsibility for it, both for themselves and their descendants. Do they not carry on, generation after generation, like the living and constantly reborn witness of the words they once spoke of themselves: "His blood be on us, and on our children"?[39]

Up to that time these isolated and distant voices had not received the support of church authorities. Eventually, however, it was a bishop who indirectly gave anti-Semitism the green light: Monsignor Louis-François Laflèche, in 1884. On the occasion of *Humanum Genus*, the encyclical of Leon XIII, the bishops of Montreal, Rimouski and Trois-Rivières published a commentary or pastoral letter for their diocesans, as was the custom. The bishop of Trois-Rivières alone added a short note to his text, referring readers to a work by Saint-André entitled *Franc-maçons et Juifs*. Saint-André was the pen name of Canon Chabauty,[40] whom Léon Poliakov dubbed the grandfather of French anti-Semitic priests. Such a prestigious precedent prompted increasing numbers of anti-Semites to make themselves heard even louder in Quebec.

Zacharie Lacasse

The first of the prolific anti-Semitic pamphleteers was the Oblate, Zacharie Lacasse (1845-1921), whose work contains the major myths that were exploited for decades by Quebec anti-Semites. Lacasse was born in Saint-Jacques de l'Achigan and had been a missionary with the native people of Labrador and the Inuit of Ungava before being called to the ministry in Lac Saint-Jean and the Beauce.

According to Magella Quinn,[41] his anti-Semitic campaign began in 1880 with an accusation against "the evil press," which consisted primarily of romance novels "published by Freemasons or edited by Jews."[42] His appears to have been the first attack of its kind in Quebec and it was particularly serious. Freemasonry had become a bugbear for Quebec Catholics and it stirred up powerful antagonism. By suggesting that there was complicity between Freemasons and Jews, two groups with no previous explicit links, Lacasse unleashed the whole emotional charge that had accumulated against the Freemasons and directed it towards the Jews.

Zacharie Lacasse waited until 1893 to publish *Une quatrième mine dans le camp ennemi*.[43] In the meantime, he joined Tardivel at the newspaper *La Vérité*. In his book, Lacasse called for an economic boycott of the Jews.

If all the business in Montreal and Quebec City falls into their hands, whose fault is it? . . . Are you going to give your money to sworn enemies of the Canadian Catholic cause because you pay two cents less for cloth worth but half its value because of the damage caused by moths in London warehouses? . . . We need an organization, for our money is going to our enemies. Jewish stores are always full of buyers being swindled right and left.[44]

His description of the Jewish peddler became a classic image among anti-Semites. Ironically it gives today's readers an idea of just how open relations were between these small merchants and Quebec's rural population:

They are fed and lodged by our people, who should know better. We must remember that these are not beggars, but merchants. They eat and sleep in the homes of our habitants; present a four-cent handkerchief in the morning as a gift, then turn right around and pass off worthless goods for a dollar. They do not want to eat lard and it is sometimes very embarrassing to have them in our homes. Others find people who will drive them around to two or three different places, then pay them with an old rag.[45]

Jules-Paul Tardivel

The leading Quebec anti-Semitic journalist and indisputable founder of *La Vérité* was Jules-Paul Tardivel, one of the fathers of Quebec nationalism as it is understood today.[46] He and Lacasse were among the first to establish what proved to be a devastating link between Freemasons and Jews. *La Vérité* of October 10, 1883 asked the following questions. "What do these words mean? Do they wish to introduce the capital of Freemasons and Jews into Canada?"

Tardivel was an unconditional enemy of Freemasonry. The administrators of l'Université Laval and the Archbishop of Quebec, Monsignor Elzéar A. Taschereau, came into conflict with him. This was just one of many skirmishes in the long battle between ultramontanes and liberals at the end of the century. It would have been irrelevant to Jewish history in Quebec, except that it fed a powerful myth that served as a war-horse for many anti-Semites: the Judeo-Masonic conspiracy.

Much later, during a trip to Europe in 1896, Tardivel met the Lemann brothers. They were Jewish converts to Catholicism who became priests and can be considered the true fathers of Quebec anti-Semitism.[47] In his *Notes de voyage*,[48] Tardivel recalls how Joseph Lemann confirmed all the anti-Semitic myths then circulating in the West. The traveller visited the Jewish ghetto in Rome and concurred with the wisdom of medieval canon law, which established a "Christian" way of dealing with its enemies: prevent them from causing trouble and give them the bare minimum for survival.

Tardivel had a sort of naivety that prevented him from maintaining a critical distance in relation to the information he was receiving from the Lemanns.

This shows up clearly in the following hare-brained episode that occurred in Paris in 1897. Tardivel went to see a converted Freemason reputed to have extrasensory perception, which he proposed to use in order to reveal the innermost secrets of the Order. The evening came and the great man appeared on stage before a hall crowded with curious onlookers. He shouted to the public that it was all a huge practical joke, then disappeared into the wings.

After he met Lemann, Tardivel resumed his anti-Semitic crusade in *La Vérité* with renewed zeal. His son succeeded him and continued his work for twenty more years. Tardivel was a pioneer of anti-Semitic journalism, which enjoyed a long career in Quebec.

One Wing of the Catholic Press

La Vérité was not an isolated phenomenon in Quebec journalism at the time. One wing of the Catholic press gave anti-Semitism a privileged platform and cultural credibility. Two diocesan periodicals stood out for their virulent anti-Semitism from the time they were founded. The first, *La Semaine religieuse de Québec*, was launched by members of the clergy in 1888 and became the property of the archbishop in 1901. For half a century, it took an active anti-Jewish stance that owed much to the work of pamphleteer Edouard Drumont (1844-1917). He had written an article entitled *La France juive, essai d'histoire contemporaine* (1886) which introduced a new form of anti-Semitism into France.[49] Drumont's influence in Quebec was so strong at the time that a number of writers quoted him liberally and a whole generation of periodicals called themselves *La Libre parole*. This was the name of the daily newspaper founded by Drumont in 1892, which had taken such an active part in the Dreyfus affair. The last incarnation of those *Libre parole* in Quebec was edited by Plamondon, a notary who appears later in our account.[50]

L'Action sociale catholique which, in 1915, would become *L'Action catholique* was yet another daily publication from Quebec City that held wide-ranging and deeply-rooted anti-Semitic views.

L'Action sociale catholique belonged to "the good press," publications that sprang up here and there during the period following the papal encyclicals: *Sapientiae christianae* of Leon XIII (January 10, 1890) and *E Supremi apostolatus cathedra* of Pius X (October 4, 1903). In a pastoral letter dated March 31, 1907, Cardinal Bégin initiated *L'Action sociale catholique* in his archdiocese.[51] Resembling works published in France and Austria, Quebec's *L'Action sociale catholique* began attacking Jews in its first issue and maintained that stance for many decades. Some of its managers and editors proved to be notorious anti-Semites. One was J. A. Huot, a priest who wrote one of the most virulent pamphlets of a black series entitled *Le fléau maçonnique* (Quebec, 1906). Another was the priest J.-Thomas Nadeau, who in 1919 penned an article entitled *En Passant*, which stated that "bolshevism, freemasonry, socialism, revolution and Judaism are one and the same." The special correspondent for *L'Action* in Montreal, Léon Trépanier, wrote a daily column about Montreal for several years. He looked for much of his news in the courts, focussing on offenses committed by Jews.

All the major cloudbursts of the anti-Semitic tempest sweeping Quebec in the early 1900s were echoed and supported by *L'Action catholique*. It gave special attention to accusations of ritual murder levelled at Beilis[52] in Russia and to the publication of the *Protocoles des Sages de Sion* at Quebec City in 1920-21.[53] The following quote from a 1921 editorial by the priest Edouard V. Lavergne sums up the image that Quebec anti-Semites had articulated of the Jews: "We do not reproach the Jews for the blood that flows in their veins or the curve of their noses, but for the violent hatred that generally animates them, and the profound scorn they profess for all things Christian."[54]

Action social catholique went beyond publishing the Quebec City newspaper. It also produced and sold many tracts, almanacs, manuals and books whose anti-Semitic discourse was echoed in *L'Action catholique*, as well as *Le Droit* in Ottawa and *Le Devoir* in Montreal. A long list of diocese and parish newsletters took up this discourse from one end of the province to the other.

L'Association catholique de la jeunesse canadienne (ACJC)

Among the most important of these publications was *Le Semeur* published by the Association catholique de la jeunesse canadienne (ACJC). Founded in 1903 by the teaching clergy, the organization propounded ultra-defensive nationalism. Both its publications and meeting records provide an invaluable archive for studying the propaganda and actions aimed at Quebec Jews during that period.[55] The minutes of the congress held in June 1908, preface by Sir Thomas Chapais,[56] are particularly revealing. They constitute a veritable manual of Quebec anti-Semitism and include a long text, written by L. C. Farley of the Cercle St-Michel, which qualifies as a classic of Quebec anti-Jewish literature. Here is but one pearl among hundreds:

> An ambitious Germany uttered a war cry some twenty years ago that resounded across the Atlantic. Minister Stoecker locked horns with the Jew Straussman and the alarm was raised: the Jews are our enemy! Hunted from the Vistula to the Rhine, Israel entered France. But scarcely had it begun to rise up when Edouard Drumont cried out loud and clear from the pages of *France juive*, "War on Israel! Death to the Jews!" and Russia finally followed the trend, or rather rose to fight the current by launching a bloody campaign against the Talmud's disciples.
>
> Now we find ourselves face to face with a very curious phenomenon: the hunt for the Jews.
>
> Israel must resign itself to the fact that France, Germany and Russia no longer wish to bear its yoke and that America will soon react the same way.[57]

An analysis of the phenomenon follows. The cause? Jews cannot be assimilated, they constitute a multi-faceted danger for other nations, especially because of their far-reaching involvement in politics, business, the press and revolutions. The author's conclusion is rather unexpected, in some respects:

> We do not wish to declare war on the Jews. We are Catholics, and as Catholics we act in Christian tolerance. But we are also French Canadians, and as French Canadians we mean business when we say to our countrymen: buy nothing from Jews, for some day soon the money you place in their hands will be used to make the bombs that shatter the foundations of our nationhood.[58]

The Theologians

Given the medieval roots of turn-of-the-century anti-Semitism and its affinity with Catholic ultramontanism, it should come as no surprise that members of the clergy and even theology professors joined in the battle.

One was the priest J. Antonio Huot, who died in 1929. We have already seen that as editor of the *Semaine religieuse de Québec*, he promoted many of the insane ideas concerning Jews that were then circulating in Europe. In 1906, he published *Le fléau maçonnique*, which linked Jews and freemasons.[59] In 1914, he resurfaced with the publication of a speech given in Quebec City before a chapter of the ACJC, when the Plamondon case was before the Court of Appeal. It was entitled, "La question juive, quelques observations sur la question du meurtre rituel."[60] Such was his lack of critical understanding that he did not hold his peace even after the myth was refuted by Cardinal Ganganelli of Rome.[61]

Huot was one of the first to sound the alarm against Zionism, which he perceived as a threat to the holy sites in the Holy Land.[62] He also used the *Protocols of the Learned Elders of Zion* to sow terror in the Catholic ranks. It made no difference that celebrated Jesuit theologian Pierre Charles of Louvain published a systematic refutation of the *Protocols*; the Quebec pamphleteer knew nothing about it and continued his campaign imperturbably throughout the 1920s.

Huot was a narrow-minded member of the clergy and his minimal influence reflected his lack of credibility. It is more difficult, however, to explain how a theologian as respected as Monsignor Louis-Adolphe Paquet (1859-1942) could have voiced the same ideas. His stance was a kind of catastrophe in Quebec during the 1930s, given the influence this great nationalist wielded over his generation and over Lionel Groulx in particular. His major work, *Droit public de l'Église*,[63] was published between 1908 and 1915. It describes the Jews as stigmatized with shame and as the enemy of other peoples; as professional usurers for whom deception is a virtue and hatred of Christians a dogma. Here is just one passage:

> Certainly "we must not hate these remnants of faithless Jerusalem over whom Jesus Christ weeps" (L. Veuillot . . .), but neither must we, through ill-conceived charity, deliver our society and the treasure

of our religious and national traditions into their perfidious and rapacious hands. The Jew, for us, is an enemy (not each individual, but the nation in general as it exists today). It either persists in nurturing its secular hatred of Christ's followers with Talmudic nonsense, or it sustains the corrosive action of free thought and places its hopes no longer in the restoration of the kingdom of Israel, but in the advent of a God-mankind glutted with gold and pleasure [ref. to Claudio Janet on the American Jews]. In either case, when its influence penetrates and dominates any Catholic people or group, it threatens them as well.[64]

The Ernesto Nathan Scandal

In 1910, an incident in the Italian capital unleashed an unprecedented anti-Semitic reaction in Quebec. Relations between Vatican and Roman authorities had been strained for more than half a century, since the confrontation between Pius IX and Garibaldi. Against this background, Mayor Ernesto Nathan of Rome, an Anglo-Italian Jew and Freemason as well, took the liberty of insulting the Pope.

Catholics the world over were outraged. Protests against the mayor's action and expressions of support for Pius IX poured in from Christian cities throughout the Jewish diaspora.

Reaction in Quebec was bitter. The anti-Masonic backlash also affected the Jews, despite the fact that Jews in Canada and Britain had publicly denounced Ernesto Nathan.

The Plamondon Affair, Militant Anti-Semitism

This wave of Quebec anti-Semitism foreshadowed that of the 1930s, gathering force and spending itself over the Plamondon affair, a court case which brought Christian and Jewish adversaries face to face in court for the first time. Until then, they had been mutually invisible. From this point of view, the case marked an important step in demystifying a long history of anti-Semitic conflict in Quebec.

For several months, two cities in the world shared the headlines with strangely medieval trials involving horrifying stories of ritual murder as well as plots against Christianity and the entire world: Kiev, in Russia, with the Beilis affair, and Quebec City, in North America, with the Plamondon affair.

In Quebec City, the stakes were enormous. The protagonists were locked in a fight to the finish before top-ranking jurors who brought their deepest convictions to the service of justice. It was a Quebec trial from beginning to end, with no outside participation, even in technical matters.

Here are the facts: J. Edouard Plamondon was a notary with an active practice in Quebec City. He was also joint founder and editor of a Quebec magazine called *La Libre parole*,[65] a title borrowed proudly from the French anti-Semitic writer, Edouard Drumont. Plamondon had carefully prepared a speech on the Jews to be given at the Cercle Charest of the Quebec City ACJC.

The text is a veritable anthology of malicious accusations against Jews, written by professors, members of the clergy, writers and European historians. He gave the speech on March 30, 1910 in the Saint-Roch parish hall before a large audience of priests, politicians, journalists and young people. The newspapers, especially *L'Action sociale catholique*, reported this cultural and religious event. The text was published in the form of a pamphlet and sold to the general public.[66]

The event caused a great stir. French Quebecers followed the advice of the speaker and stopped buying from Jewish merchants. Young people went so far as to throw stones through the windows of Jewish homes. An old Jewish man was harrassed in the street.

The handful of Jews in the city felt powerless before this assault. They did not have the intellectual resources to respond to the notary or the journalists and priests who supported him.

But this time a group of Montreal Jews led by S. W. Jacobs,[67] a lawyer destined to leave his mark on the young nation, decided to fight back. A Quebec City merchant, Benjamin Ortenberg, sued the notary Plamondon for libel.

His was a bold and courageous decision. The diaspora's history of inter-religious confrontation with surrounding societies had taught Jews to be wary of placing their reputation in the hands of the Christian or Islamic justice systems. The information available to Catholics about Jews, whether official, academic or folkloric, would certainly not encourage them to take action; nor would the legal precedents set in the courts of Europe, Austria, Russia, Syria and more recently, in France, with the Dreyfus affair.

Even so, the Montreal lawyers did not consult their colleagues in the United States or elsewhere, nor did they seek outside legal advice.[68] It is easy to imagine the consequences of a Quebec court decision perhaps based on a simple technicality, granting an anti-Semite the right to propagate the worst accusations against Jews (theft, ritual murder, hatred and immorality taught by their religion and so on); or of a decision ruling that the accusations were justified. And would society be any further ahead even if the prosecution won its case? The defendant himself had said that not all Jews were thieves and that the Talmud was not an immoral book.

Jacobs' decision seems even bolder in light of the extraordinary efforts needed at the Beilis trial to assemble a complete set of the Bombergo Talmud, the first and only edition in print at the time, by borrowing volumes from several countries. Mendel Beilis, it is true, had been brought to court by Russian anti-Semites, while in Quebec the situation was reversed.

No one knows exactly why the Montreal group decided to proceed, but the reasons can be deduced by looking at the ideology of this small Jewish society. Its members were confortably off, thoroughly acculturated to Canada's Victorian reality, confident of democracy and the Canadian judicial system and firmly dedicated to basing their community life on this kind of social and political optimism. Even the tactics used in the questions before Judge Malouin reflected their philosophy.

The trial was extremely complicated and involved many factors that went far beyond Plamondon's accusations against the Jews. Plamondon insisted that his speech was intended to inform the public and that the facts he revealed were universally known and corroborated by writers who were recognized and respected in Europe and elsewhere.

The witnesses fell into two strikingly different groups. The prosecution called on a young rabbi, Herman Abramowitz of the Shaar Hashamayim Synagogue in Westmount, merchants from Quebec City, Montefiore Joseph of Quebec's original Joseph family, De Young, a minister from the Eastern Townships and F. G. Scott, an Anglican cleric. The defence called on theology professors, priests and journalists, all of whom proved to be ignorant of the Talmudic texts underlying their arguments. Each repeated the errors and outrageous statements of the previous witness without reference to sources and without a basic understanding of the original language, traditions and ancient disciplines, which would have been essential to penetrate the issues. They had no arguments other than the myths peddled by international anti-Semites. The priest Joseph-Guillaume-Arthur d'Amours, a graduate in theology and canon law from Rome (1898) and chief editor of *L'Action sociale catholique* declared that "as a priest and journalist, he had become interested in the Jewish question and read some of the works mentioned by the defence," but that he "was not a Hebrew scholar, had not studied the Talmud in any detail and could not read the Hebrew in the text."[69]

Father Jean-Thomas Nadeau based most of his testimony on the works of Drumont. Another priest from the Séminaire de Québec, Langlois, brought an 1831 translation of the Talmud into court and admitted that he had found nothing in it to support Plamondon's accusations against the Jews.[70]

What remained were the legal technicalities used by the notary's lawyers to win their case.[71] Thus, they claimed their client was innocent on the grounds that libel legislation did not apply in the Plamondon case because Plamondon's defamatory allegations had not been directed at any one individual.

Their apparent victory was really a defeat, even from the anti-Semites' point of view. The Quebec City daily *L'Action sociale catholique* was not at ease being aligned with the Russian anti-Semites in Kiev. Nonetheless, it echoed the stance of some in Rome who continued to maintain that the Jews did practise murderous religious rites.

On October 13, 1913 the Kiev court rendered its verdict and freed Mendel Beilis, leaving Quebec virtually alone in the world to defend medieval anti-Semitic propositions. On December 29, 1914 Ottawa's Court of Appeal finally upheld Jacobs' appeal. Plamondon was abandoned to his fate and disappeared tragically from the scene.

World War I was approaching. *L'Action sociale catholique* changed its name to *L'Action catholique*.[72] Anti-Semitism took on new forms. The Jews were associated with the Russian revolutionaries and Zionists threatened the holy sites in Jerusalem now that the Muslims, friends of the Christians, had been driven out by the British. But the tone had cooled slightly. The 1920s were calmer as Quebec prepared for the Jewish schools issue and the problem of Jewish refugees fleeing Hitler from Germany and Poland.

Conclusion

This fifty-year history of anti-Semitism in Canada (1860-1910) reveals a network of factors that gave birth to a completely new phenomenon in the relations between Jewish and French Quebecers.

At first, anti-Semitism was fuelled by irrational concepts and subjective perceptions, many of which were myths in the broadest sense. These myths were supported by an odd assortment of sources: the Old Testament, Gospels and legend of the Wandering Jew; ideas of satanism, divine vengeance, usury and the cursed race; themes from medieval theology, plots, the cabala and its mysteries; by the desecration of the host and the consuming of Christian blood; by characters from Shakespeare and Dickens and by the *Survenant* of Quebec legend.

In fact, few of the players involved in this drama had ever seen, much less understood, the people they had chosen as targets. It took the Plamondon affair to bring the protagonists face to face, exposing the weakness and absurdity of the arguments put forward by one side and the complete self-possession of the other, who at a certain point decided to stand up to the challenge and strike back.

Jewish Schools

At the turn of the century, Canadian Jews formed a rapidly growing community. It expanded from 16,401 members in 1901 to 74,564 in 1911 and 125,000 in 1921, when it formed a higher proportion of the population than at any time before of since. But the Jews were far from the sociocultural monolith conjured up by the term in the minds of many French Quebecers. It was no more all-encompassing than the corresponding term "the English," which was often understood to include all the ethnic groups from the British Isles (English, Scottish, Welsh, Irish), as well as all the other European groups who had joined the English-speaking community: the Dutch, Germans, Scandinavians and sometimes even the Jews themselves.

The Jewish community was so small that few people suspected how diversified it really was. The group of old Montreal families whose ancestors had more or less adopted middle-class British ideology was literally submerged by the growing wave of new Yiddish-speaking arrivals from the *shtetl* who knew little or no English. This situation gave rise to social, economic, cultural and also ideological tensions that were played out around a number of issues vital to the survival of the community.

The most crucial issue of all seemed to be education and it created deep divisions in Quebec's Jewish community.

If ever there were an issue that French Quebecers could understand, this was it. Education had been their first constitutional battleground and they fought persistently to have the right to Catholic schools enshrined in the British North America Act. Their fundamental motives had much in common with the Jewish community's drive for a place within the Quebec school system: the same concept of integrated education in which religion is one with culture (in the Western sense), the same powerful link between language and tradition, the same desire to have full control over the education of their children and, therefore, the ideological orientation of their school system, the same status as a minority (French Quebec forming a majority locally but a minority nationally) whose survival was threatened by the surrounding culture.

A Question of Survival

The continuous flow of refugees from the *shtetl* restated the education issue in new terms. Whereas the original Jewish community had sought to become fully integrated into the English-speaking community through English schools, for example, many of the newcomers resented to placing their children in a school system over which they had no control.

For many of the new arrivals, as for many French Quebecers at that time, education could not be divorced from cultural survival. This concept was reinforced by the fact that they formed a distinct social and cultural entity which was evolving in a ghetto context. For them, the basic role of education was to introduce children to the Bible, Hebrew, Yiddish and in general, to everything that served to build their religious and cultural identity and helped integrate them into the group. No one could avoid such an initiation. In this sense the Jews had always practiced universal and mandatory schooling. From their point of view, a secular or non-religious education was inconceivable, for it would impose a foreign ideology on their culture and substitute "civil" religion for their own religious tradition.

But these immigrants arrived into a world that was poles apart from their way of thinking; a world in which religion and culture were dissociated. They were confronted by an urban, industrial society, for which their traditional education had left them ill-prepared. Even when they succeeded in mastering the language to a certain extent, the surrounding culture remained a mystery. They needed schools adapted to the new context, schools that would introduce them to the science and technology of the era. Their children were often born into poverty bordering on destitution and without Western-style education they would remain disadvantaged when they reached the labour market.

This situation became the source of deep divisions within Quebec's Jewish community. Many of the new immigrants soon began to dream of a self-administered separate school system offering a programme combining two kinds of subjects: those the children needed to adapt to society and those related to their Judaism — not an easy synthesis. It presupposed not just a Jewish administration, but also participation by Jewish teachers and educators.

The original Jewish community definitely did not share these views. They had assumed a liberal mentality and opted for straightforward integration into the public school system, despite the risk of creating a more or less definitive split between their religion and their adopted culture. What they dreaded above all else was the isolation of the ghetto. Consequently, they denounced the idea of separate Jewish schools as a form of segregation that could sooner or later lead to marginalization. By and large, they held to the great American dream of a democracy in which education is uniform, free and universally available.

The early pressure they had applied to both London and Quebec City was aimed at achieving just that goal. They had welcomed the 1832 legislation precisely because it threw the doors of Quebec society wide open to them. They had sent their children to English Protestant private schools until the late 1800s, but faced with the rapid growth of their community — from 518 to 7,607 in Quebec between 1871 and 1901 — they soon came to a formal agreement with the English authorities to send their children to Protestant public schools.

The Jewish Student Charter

The agreement, reached in 1894 and renewed in 1903, was passed and made law that same year (Ed. VII, ch. 16). It owed its existence to the fact that each of the three parties — the Protestant School Board of Montreal, the Jewish community and the Quebec Government — went out of its way to accommodate the others. The law stated that: (1) all Jewish children were from then on considered Protestant in matters of education (necessary so that the government could sidestep the Constitution, which made no provisions for non-Catholics or non-Protestants); (2) school taxes went to the Protestant organization; in return for which (3) Jewish children enjoyed all the same rights and privileges as Protestants (as we shall see, this clause excluded parents, teachers and other members of the educational institution); (4) religious education of children was protected by a "conscience clause."

The architect of the agreement, Maxwell Goldstein, rightly hailed it as the great educational charter of the Quebec Jewish community. Although many difficulties arose as the law was applied, it stood behind Quebec Jews as they faced the challenge to survive, even after the anti-Semitic crisis of the 1930s and the end of World War II.

Today we might wonder why the Jewish community gravitated toward the Protestant rather than the Catholic system. One obvious answer lies in the nature of French Quebec itself, which at the time cared little whether immigrants adapted or not. This resulted in a significant absence of social structures to welcome them, especially in the area of education.[73]

Why did French Quebec not open its doors wider to immigrants? Did it lack self-confidence as a colonized society? Perhaps, especially in relation to the Europeans — even the Francophones — who seemed to regard French Quebecers with a sense of unmistakable superiority. But the logic of history points to a more fundamental reason: the monolithic self-image that began to develop in the earliest years of the French regime. From an ethnic, religious and cultural standpoint, Quebec's French Catholic society viewed itself as a distinct entity within North America.[74]

Even so, some immigrant groups did manage to break into the Francophone milieu; particularly the Irish in the nineteenth century and more recently, the Sephardic Jews. The Jews themselves must therefore be asked why they turned to the Protestant school system. One obvious reason is that they perceived the French school as a training ground for Catholics. They saw its mission as essentially religious and, therefore, hostile to the survival of the Jewish community. A second reason, this one socioeconomic, is that for most Jews and other newcomers to Quebec, becoming Canadian meant joining the English community — specifically, the English Protestants who led the country. In the *shtetl*, they had looked to St. Petersburg, Vienna or Berlin. Now their eyes were on London, Washington and Ottawa. Joining a French Catholic society and aligning themselves with the French minority would have meant divorcing themselves from the rest of North America, from the Jewish diaspora, from an immense social and economic network.

Growing Crisis

The Jewish community was split in its relations with the English Protestants: the issue of representation on the Protestant School Board conflicted with the plan to establish a separate school commission. The two positions were diametrically opposed, but they sprang from the same concern for protecting fundamental rights and ultimately, cultural survival. Both groups wanted guarantees of equal opportunities and benefits for their children.

The first sign of trouble appeared in 1909. A new idea held that the Jewish community should be assured a role in administering Protestant schools. This idea was inspired by a principle which is close to the heart of Western democracies: no taxation without representation. The principle did not legally apply to the Quebec schools because the system was organized along religious lines and therefore administered either by Protestants or Catholics. But supporters of integration shot back that there was nothing at all religious about the Protestant schools in practical terms — they were simply Canadian and English, the latter having precedence.

This demand was related to the absence of Jewish teachers in the Protestant school system. Their spokesperson, S. W. Jacobs, addressed the issue in these terms:

> We ask for a simple measure of justice; there is not a single Jewish teacher in the schools of Montreal, although there are many certificated. The Protestant Commissioners consider the Jews good enough to pay fees and graduate from the teaching schools, but when they ask for positions as teachers the Presbyterian, Methodist

and Anglican clergymen say "they will not have the Christian character of their schools contaminated by Jewish teachers." This is an outrage. We have not complained because we thought we were not paying enough for representation, but now we know differently.[75]

The Protestant School Board of Montreal, confessional in structure, served the Anglophone community, yet was also charged with the education of Francophone Protestants. It was one of the bulwarks of the English language in the province, especially in the field of education. Jewish children were admitted in the system if only to assimilate them linguistically and culturally. The board resigned from any conversional programmes for these pupils. However, the negotiations which had led to the 1903 legislation clearly stated that Jewish parents could not serve on the school boards, nor could they work in the administration of the schools. The Jewish spokespersons who had been engaged in the school issue remembered this well; but two decades later, having become more bourgeois and aggressive in the face of an anti-democratic deprivation of due privilege, they insisted on open Protestant doors for their children and seats for themselves on the Protestant boards.

To complicate matters further, the notion of a separate Jewish school system began to take hold in the community. The spokesperson for the Protestant School Board, Reverend Barclay, was unequivocal when he stated that "the only solution for the Jews is to use their own taxes to establish their own separate schools."[76] Bram de Sola, on the other hand, was horrified at the spectre of segregation raised by this approach:

Does the Protestant community wish further to divide our population . . . by school segregation? Do we wish to force the Jews to remain foreigners forever? If not, let us be done with all this prating about a separate panel for the Jews: a suggestion which seems prompted by that spirit which has in all ages herded the Jews in ghettos, and forced them to wear a degrading badge as a mark of distinction from their Christian persecutors.[77]

Once the principle was admitted, he went on, the Greeks would have their board, then all the other sects and the state would eventually subsidize schools for every language spoken by the population.[78]

The debate was an open one. Protestant opinion gradually shifted, however, and people who had originally supported Jewish integration into their schools now began to reject the idea. Jewish migration from the *shtetl* became a tidal wave and no one knew where or when it would recede. In 1913 alone, 20,000 Jewish immigrants arrived in Canada, swelling the ranks of the Montreal community to 80,000. The proportion of Jewish students in the Protestant schools reached new heights. In 1924, they accounted for thirty-six percent of the total student population.

People began to worry about a threat to the religious identity and thus the very character of the Protestant schools. However, during this period, religion virtually disappeared from the curricula of certain schools. There was also concern about the growing administrative problems created by this influx of large, low-income families whose taxes, according to some administrators, covered only half the cost of educating their children.

Finally, the high proportion of Jewish students raised yet another issue: their religious holidays had to be added to the existing calendar of Christian and civic holidays. Confusion resulted from their absences and Protestant students felt unfairly treated compared to their Jewish classmates.

As a result, the Protestant School Board prepared a draft bill in 1921 grouping all non-Catholic and non-Protestants together in a "neutral" organization. At the time, there were between 500 and 1,000 students including Chinese, Muslim Syrians and Orthodox Russians and Greeks without legal status who would have come under the proposed legislation, which was aimed primarily at the Jewish community. Its members' objections were voiced by MLA Peter Bercovitch, who expressed the fear that sooner or later the legislation would lead to segregation.

The Protestants came back the following year with assurances that neutral students would be free to choose between the Protestant and Catholic systems. The bill was never passed, but the legislature amended the 1903 law (13 Geo. V, Ch. 44), raising the neutral tax in order to pay the Protestant School Board for the deficit it incurred in educating Jewish students.

The Jewish community was far from united on this arrangement, which some said made their children beg for their education and grouped them into a foreign sect. The debate between supporters of integration and separate school advocates resumed with new vigour. Some people even maintained that Canada had two Jewries.

A Jewish education committee was formed on January 1, 1922 to promote "co-education with children of other faiths." Michael Hirsch described its approach: "The intermingling of Canadian children of all faiths is likely to be productive of a better citizenship."[79]

The crux of the matter for this group was to prevent segregation and ultimately, ghettoization. Rabbi Corcos went so far as to say: "We want our children to be Jews in their religion only, but Canadians in all secular thoughts and actions. We want them to grow up useful, industrious, earnest, faithful, active and loyal members of the community. We want them to grow up true Britishers."[80]

Their opponents were the Jewish nationalists, who dreaded American-style public or government-rule schools because they held the treat of assimilation. Accepting them would be catastrophic for the Jewish culture, which had been passed on from century to century by a form of education that permeated every aspect of life. On October 28, 1923 a conference held in Montreal brought together thirty-two Jewish groups. It spoke out clearly in favour of a Jewish separate school system.

A few months later in 1924, the Jewish Community Council (Va'ad Ho'ir) was formed. Let by Louis Fitch, who had worked with Jacobs on the Plamondon case, its goal was to support the plan for a separate school system.

The wind was beginning to shift in government quarters. Until then, Premier Taschereau and his liberal team had shown remarkable openness and prudence. Essentially, their task had been limited to mediating a conflict betwen two sub-groups of a community unable to present a united front. Quebec's attitude was consistent with a long parliamentary tradition going back to the law of 1832. Sir Étienne Taché had already cited the 1832 legislation in order to reassure the Jewish minority, recalling that Lower Canada was the first British colony to grant political freedom to Jews.[81]

But another party joined the battle in 1925, this time with the whole weight and relative unanimity of Quebec's overwhelming majority behind it: the French Catholics. The legality of the draft bill on Jewish separate schools had been scrutinized by the Court of the King's Bench and declared *ultra vires*. The London Privy Council confirmed the Quebec court decision in 1926. Francophones were drawn into the legal debate, leaving the impression that the Church hierarchy, though silent, was evenly divided on the issue. Its position weighed heavily in the balance, for the Catholic Committee on Public Education was dominated by the bishops.

Catholic Reaction

Initially, Catholic reaction was fairly positive. Jewish schools were certainly a welcome alternative to the dreaded neutral schools. Such was the opinion of Jules Durion editor of the Quebec City newspaper *L'Action catholique*. In an editorial published on February 4, 1926 he nonetheless concluded with a remark that betrayed the insecurity of French Quebecers faced with an influx of immigrants who were swelling the ranks of the English community: "So here is where our immigration policy has led us."[82]

This favourable response was echoed by Henri Bourassa who had attended the Eucharistic Conference of 1910 under the banner "La langue gardienne de la foi" (Language, guardian of the faith). The previous year, the well-known member from Labelle had defended the rights of Jews to education in their own faith, adding that logically, Catholics should give Jews in Quebec the same rights which they themselves were demanding elsewhere. The Constitution recognized the Jewish religion, he continued, so there was no doubt that Jews were entitled to their own religious schools under natural right, civil law and simple common sense:

> Within the Jewish and Protestant communities alike, there are two currents of opinion: the integrationists and the advocates of separate and religious schools. We should clearly support the second. The school should remain an extension of the family and the church or the synagogue. . . . The Jews are part of our society and we cannot wish them away any more than we can eliminate the problems that spring from their presence among us. They have no specific rights in the area of education, but they do have the same natural and political rights as any other category of British subject and Canadian citi-

zen. After forty years of fighting for minorities, whoever and wherever they are, I am not about to turn my back on them now.[83]

He pointed out that Quebec legislation had given Jews the right to practise
their religion as they wished, just as they were entitled to maintain a civil reg-
istry. It also seemed logical to him that the government would permit them to
operate their own schools:

> In our present situation, it is more important to grant non-Christians
> such a right than to admit the principle of non-religious schools,
> which would lead to godless schools. The Catholic centralists, as well
> as the Jewish and Protestant integrationists are tending toward just
> that: schools are state institutions, transforming children into state
> property.[84]

His stance, however, was quickly attacked by the Catholic right. This was to
be expected in a monolithic society whose cornerstone was the religious
school system and whose very foundations were being shaken.

The Jewish community was growing so quickly that the Christian character
of some Protestant schools was changing. There was consequently no question of repeating the Protestant experience by setting up neutral schools in
Quebec and risking the breakdown of religion, first at school and then in society at large.

But the 1930s presented a broader challenge in the eyes of the Catholic
right. There were fears that Quebec's rapid industrialization and brutal urbanization would have two dire consequences: the de-Christianization of a society
already threatened by secularization, well under way in Europe; and Ameri-
canization, which filtered into Quebec in a thousand ways, from international
unions, to cinema, to a general fascination with the American way of life.[85]
Then came the crash of 1929, putting an end to the roaring twenties and trig-
gering one of the worst economic crises in the province's history. Panic
ensued. Catholic intellectuals were aware of the explosive situation that
might result, especially at a time when communism was intensifying its action
among Quebec's working class. The church was afraid of losing control over
the situation and of having to face questions it could not answer except by
exhorting its people to prayer. Confusion reigned among Jews and Protestants. Divisions abounded and there were claims, fears, demands, constitutional issues, court decisions and problems with the government.

To affirm their right to treat Jewish students in whatever manner they
wished, discriminatory or otherwise, the Protestants had refused a young student named Pinsler the scholarship he had won in 1902. His case had been
brought before Judge Davidson, who supported the school board. But it was
small satisfaction to win a legal battle over a cause that appeared no less
immoral after the victory.

People seemed to forget that thirty years earlier, the Catholic School Board
had helped the Shearith Israel synagogue to administer its own school for a
long period without interference, using school taxes collected from Jewish

property owners. This arrangement had proven very satisfactory and only ended because of disagreement among the Jews themselves. By the 1930s, however, relations between Jews and Catholics had deteriorated and the climate was no longer favourable to renewing the agreement of the 1890s.

To settle the issue, a decision was made in 1925 to go to the Court of the King's Bench, then to the Supreme Court and finally to the London Privy Council in an effort to clarify the rights, positions and options involved. In a lengthy judgement, London recognized the provincial government's right to establish a Jewish school commission if one was required.

This option did not have clear support among any of the parties involved, except a small fraction of the Jewish community. There was no alternative, however, so the Protestants and the Jewish spokespersons finally agreed to accept it.

The plan to establish Jewish schools acted as a catalyst for the Catholic community. Jews became targets in a wave of anti-Semitism comparable to that which had swept Quebec at the turn of the century.

The David Act of 1930: The Match in the Powder Keg

Since the Jews and Protestants still did not agree, the government was looking for a compromise that would satisfy everyone. The sponsors of the bill neglected to consult the Catholic Committee on all points, perhaps hoping for a degree of complicity from the church. This was an error in strategy and the Catholic opposition pounced on it. They were afraid of being forced, after the fact, to accept legislation establishing a separate and independent Jewish school commission that would break the educational monopoly granted by the Constitution to Christians alone. Much was at stake for the Catholics: constitutional and acquired rights, theology, Vatican directives and, as certain more circumspect minds recalled, natural rights as well. Above all, the whole issue struck a very sensitive chord among French Quebecers: they, like the Jews, considered schools absolutely essential to cultural and religious survival. From this point of view, neutral schools appeared to be nothing but a Trojan horse.

One of the first to open fire was the coadjutor to the archbishop of Montreal, Monsignor Georges Gauthier, who was more directly involved in the matter than any of his episcopal colleagues. He had been administering the diocese since Monsignor Bruchési had fallen ill.

On March 19, 1930, a ceremony was held at St. Joseph's Oratory on Mount Royal to honour the Feast of St. Joseph. Monsignor Gauthier led the proceedings and, before a crowd of pilgrims who had come to Montreal from across the province, he read the position paper he had just presented to Premier Taschereau, similar in content to the ones presented by his colleagues in Rimouski, Trois-Rivières, the Gaspé, Saint-Hyacinthe and Nicolet. He recalled the Christian character of Quebec's school system and the fact that ''non-Christians'' were dependent on a set of privileges:

I am aware of the Jews' sad history. We as Christians know why they must carry their burden, and God may keep us from doing them the slightest injustice. But we should ask ourselves this: what Canadian province, what world nation with its own history, laws and constitution, dreams of giving a minority such privileges, and where else would a minority dream of claiming them? Hundreds of non-Christians arrive every year in the United States and other Canadian provinces. Do they believe that they, or we for that matter, are exempt from the constitution of the country they have chosen of their own free will? . . . Is it so outrageous to think that one day they will be demanding exactly the same privileges we are proposing to grant the Jews? . . . Many good, wise and penetrating minds gaze with dread upon one potential consequence of these extraordinary innovations: that we will be creating such confusion and complexity in Quebec that the state will simply declare its intention to take the neutral tax for itself, and in return, set up a single educational system in the province, with a minister and a department to run it. And since it will have to abolish all sources of conflict, it will decide to teach only secular subjects in its schools.[86]

In his letter to the Premier, the Bishop added this remark, which did not escape notice by the Jewish community: "Do you not agree, Honorable Minister, that after accommodating the Protestants to the utmost and heaping absolutely unjustified sympathy upon the Jews, it is high time to consider the Catholic majority in this province?"[87]

There is no need to detail all the weaknesses of the prelate's argument, including his refusal to grant Jews the same rights and privileges that French Quebecers had struggled to win long before, joined by the Jews themselves, from a colonial administration that knew nothing of their culture and religion. Monsignor Gauthier was too involved in what was fast becoming a power struggle between the government and the episcopate to recognize the impact of his campaign. He gave voice to his actions by hiring a young, aggressive journalist who had shown his mettle as a contributor to two newspapers belonging to the yellow press (inoffensive up to then) which had been founded the years before by Joseph Ménard: *Le Miroir* and *Le Goglu*. The journalist was Adrien Arcand, who soon emerged as the future leader of the Quebec Nazi movement. It is doubtful the bishop could have foreseen his protege's career, but his gesture indicate just how determined he was to block the bill. From then on, in fact, the content of *Le Goglu* changed. It became serious, addressing one issue to the exclusion of all others: the Jews, the Jewish school question, the Catholic interest in not giving in to the Jews.

At the same time, Cardinal Rouleau of Quebec City, Primate of the Canadian Catholic Church, was lobbying the government as a mediator in a tone that was free of anti-Semitic rhetoric. On one level, he was in complete agreement with the Premier, who believed that the best way of avoiding neutral schools was to give the three major religions their own schools:

> Do not forget that there are twelve thousand Jewish children entitled to education in Montreal today, almost as many as there are Protestants.
> Jewish children are only accepted into Protestant schools under certain conditions, which parents find unacceptable.
> My studies in philosophy have taught me, I believe, that one of the most respected principles of natural right is the parents' right to educate their child. We fight to have this principle accepted in our own province, and in neighboring provinces as well. How then can we claim that it does not apply to Jews, and that they must send their children to schools of which they cannot approve?[88]

But Cardinal Rouleau could not hide his fears about the bill as it was presented to the House. The days of the declaration by his colleague, Monsignor Gauthier, he discussed parent control of schools in the pages of *L'Action catholique*: "Parents must be carefully monitored by the Council for Public Education. . . . One day, in order to overcome some obstacle, it is quite possible that they will try to impose upon us the neutral schools so often condemned by our Sovereign Pontiffs."[89]

Faced with this attack by the bishops, the government realized that it had to compromise. Taschereau and David held an emergency meeting at the home of Cardinal Rouleau on March 21, 1930, two days after the declaration at the Oratory, with Bishops Gauthier of Montreal, Courchesne of Rimouski and Comtois of Trois-Rivières. They agreed on two points: (1) to limit the legal jurisdiction of the law to the City of Montreal; (2) to refuse Jews access to the Council for Public Education.

That same day, the Protestant School Board reached an agreement with the government on an amendment to the bill, under which Jewish schools could only be created when the Jewish and Protestant commissions were unable to make any other arrangements.

Chain Reaction

Ideally, these preliminary steps would have averted the storm that was brewing. They did nothing of the kind.

The government acted quickly. On April 1, 1930 Athanase David presented a draft bill on the issue. On April 2, the legislation was adopted (21, Geo. V, Ch. 63), with a few slight changes added to achieve a typical political compromise. It provided for the creation of a Jewish school board in Montreal, composed of seven members. But it also abrogated the Act of 1903, thus limiting many of the rights and, especially, the guarantees that assured the Jewish community of legal integration into the Protestant community in the area of education. This crucial turn of events left the Jewish community in a state of uncertainty over its future. Then on April 24, without adequate consultation with the church, the government created the Jewish School Board under the provisions of the new law.

Catholic discontent erupted from the dioceses to the newspaper editing rooms, where it took on strong anti-Semitic overtones.

For the bishops, this law put the Jews on the same footing as Catholics and Protestants in the area of education, and unacceptable situation in a Christian society. They thus began lobbying the government with relentless persistence.

In May 1930, Cardinal Rouleau asked the Catholic Committee of the Council for Public Education to request a report on the impact of the new law (20, Geo. V, Ch. 61). The superintendent of education, Cyrille Delage, conducted an official inquiry into the Protestant and Catholic School Boards. He reminded them that the law permitted Jewish commissioners to reach agreements with them and asked whether any had actually been reached.

In September, the Cardinal requested another inquiry. Judge Paul Martineau understood the implications of his manoeuvre and objected; accepting his request could have been interpreted as giving the committee the right of scrutiny over Jewish schools, something it had never had over Protestant schools. That would go against the fundamental principles of the religious school system.[90]

Publicly, the clash between church and state was fought by intermediaries, especially in the columns of various clerical newspapers. They began by silencing Henri Bourassa, the longstanding champion of minority rights. He was removed from the editorial board of *Le Devoir* and a campaign was launched to discredit his grandfather, Louis-Joseph Papineau, who had long ago supported the Jews.[91] A whole wing of the clerical press, including publishing houses such as *L'Action sociale catholique* and newspapers such as *Le Goglu* and *Le Miroir*, joined in the chorus against the David Act.

Le Goglu was seized with panic and published headlines such as "Canada Home to Canadians, not Jews" (April 4, 1930) and "Handing Quebec over to the Jews" (April 23, 1930). The May 30 editorial shot out: "Accepting the David Act as it was passed in the Quebec House is to accept that all the races on earth can come here and expect the same rights as French Canadians and English Canadians; it is to accept that when we will fight in the west for our Catholic schools, we will be fighting for Jewish religious schools."[92]

Adrien Arcand could not forgive Camilien Houde, mayor of Montreal and defender of minority rights, for saying that the Jewish minority was entitled to protection "by all our institutions." That went further than even the David Act: "Whether Mr. Houde likes it or not, we are going to strike out against Jewish voracity until the Israelites no longer have the audacity to sabotage our school legislation, for example, and open their shops on Sunday."[93]

Faced with this sort of public protest, the government believed it had no choice but to back down. It put pressure on the new Jewish School Board to give up the right granted under the new law to establish Jewish schools and urged it to sign an agreement with the Montreal Protestant School Board, which gave Jewish parents no representative status at all.

The agreement was signed on December 4 and lasted fifteen years. On January 20, 1931 a similar agreement was signed with the Outremont Protestant

School Board. This was a double compromise that satisfied no one, for it re-established the status quo, except there was now a Jewish School Board in place to oversee how the agreements were applied.

The Jewish community was more deeply divided than ever between Jewish school supporters and public school defenders. Then, the entire Commission resigned *en bloc*. They believed that the law placed Montreal Jews in a position that was intolerable, unjust and against the traditions of the province, "which recognizes the equality of minorities and majorities." Once the commissioners were gone, there was no possibility of renewing the agreements passed with the Montreal and Outremont school boards and no one in place to see that they were respected. The new structure remained paralyzed in this way for decades to come.[94]

For the Protestants, the Jewish school crisis ended in partial success. Of all parties, they emerged the least dissatisfied. Although the religious and educational problems created by the presence of Jews in their schools were left hanging in the 1931 agreements, they scored two major points: they blocked the Jewish effort to participate in school board administration and, more importantly, they lightened their financial burden by obtaining from the government a substantial portion of the tax deriving from sources neither Catholic nor Protestant. Under the law, this tax should have been shared proportionally between the Catholic and Protestant boards. The money received from Jews and "neutrals" represented as much as eighty percent of their entire revenue; therefore, the Jewish presence actually helped them improve the quality of their schools at the expense of the Catholics.

Epilogue

There has been no movement on the issue of independent public schools for Quebec's Jewish community since then. After the mass resignation of the Quebec-created commission in Montreal and the tempest whipped up by the anti-Semitic press, it seemed that no one wanted to reopen that particular Pandora's box. The agreements reached fifteen years before between the Jewish commission and the Protestant boards of Montreal and Outremont were automatically renewed in 1945 without modification.

The Jewish community adapted to the situation and those who wanted separate schools developed a network of private institutions within the reach of moderate-income families. It was based on the parish school system devised by American Catholics. These day schools, open from nine to four o'clock, represented a first in the world diaspora. They gradually replaced the afternoon schools that had been offering programmes in Jewish studies since 1847. The original Jewish National Radical Schools are now known as the Jewish People's Schools. Others, more religious in orientation, are called the Talmud Torah.[95] All are recognized by other schools and universities and have been receiving government subsidies since the 1970s. Subsidies to Jewish schools are equal to the subsidies granted to private colleges, or eighty percent of the cost of public education.

The longstanding problem of Jewish representation on Protestant school boards was partially resolved in 1965, when the boards invited a Jewish observer to sit in on their meetings. Jews have since served in various capacities for the Protestant school system.

The Jewish school crisis left deep wounds in Quebec society that affected all the groups involved.

Jewish liberals of the Victorian era suffered a serious setback in their hopes of identifying with English Canada: the Protestants had refused them full integration into the schools by hiding behind their explicit constitutional rights in the area of religion.

The people of the working class, many of whom had demanded separate schools, now had to regroup and study the complexity of Quebec politics; they had to defend their position in the press, before the Protestant school boards and in the courts. In short, they had to pit themselves against the establishment, which was powerful and often hostile. The vitality which they demonstrated would emerge in other areas as well: demographic, economic and social. They were soon to be in a position to move into new neighbourhoods on the west island of Montreal.

There remains the fact that, in its collective memory, the Jewish community still retains painful images from this chapter in its Quebec history: the fierce Protestant resistance to sharing any aspect of school administration, the humiliation of students and parents at having to reintegrate into the Protestant schools under joint pressure from the Catholic Church and the government, the government's refusal to apply the principle of educational equality recognized in its own 1930 legislation,[96] the insidious anti-Semitism of Quebec Church leaders who openly struggled against Jewish schools and the anti-Jewish campaign conducted in the media during those years.

No less painful was the memory of the conflict within the Jewish community itself between different ideological approaches to education. Some people had wanted Jewish schools, while others believed that their children should be integrated into the Protestant system; some struggled for Jewish participation on school boards,[97] others were indifferent and a third group blamed the Jewish commissioners appointed under the 1931 law for caving in to pressure from the church and government.

French Quebecers were also deeply divided over the issue. Had it not been for the anti-Semitic aspect of the debate, this battle over religious schools would have quietly taken its place in Canada's history of school struggles. Ontario, Manitoba, New Brunswick and later British Columbia experienced many similar situations. Ironically, in most of these cases it was the French Canadians who suffered.

The Quebec government can be said to have held a moderate position on the issue, in keeping with its proud constitutional tradition. Although it had to yield to overpowering pressure by church powers at the last moment, it never stooped to the aggressive anti-Semitism of the time.

Perhaps that is the most positive aspect of the historic confrontation between the two communities, for it demonstrated the soundness of Quebec's democratic institutions. There can be no question that the church was broadly successful in preventing the Quebec school system from modelling itself on other unitary public school systems in North America. It also blocked the acceptance of a third religion — Judaism — in the educational forum, which would have altered the complexion of the school system and, with it, the monolithic image of French Quebec society. But the church could not force either the government or the Jewish minority to accept the status quo. Although Montreal's Jewish School Commission was inactive, its very formation created a legal precedent with potential that has yet to be fully explored.

The big loser in this episode was the Catholic Church itself. Since French Quebecers continued to perceive it as the bulwark of their survival, it retained support from most leading intellectuals of the time (Henri Bourassa remains one of the best examples of this unconditional allegiance). But its struggle against Jewish schools eventually undermined its credibility for an entire generation of writers and politicians. Such insensitivity to the basic rights and needs of a small segment of the population was one reason why many of them distanced themselves from the church, which could not rise above its short-term interests. They fought to maintain or establish limits in the areas of culture, language and politics — some even became committed to the class struggle. Never again, however, were they to be interested in defending religious interests. Paradoxically, the principle of confessionalism that had served as the clergy's final weapon in this battle was itself destroyed when they refused to apply it to Jewish schools.

In the long term, the worst loss incurred by the Catholic Church was perhaps to be found in Quebec society itself. Many dynamic forces lay captive in the isolation of the Montreal ghetto, and by stubbornly refusing to grant the Jewish community equal status in education, the church delayed their liberation. This deprived later generations of a major religious, cultural, social and political contribution, not to mention the economic vitality that would have come of more open relations between the two communities. The infusion of the rich Jewish culture into French Quebec could only have enlightened society as a whole.

The battle over Jewish separate schools illustrates how, even as it approached maturity, French Quebec reacted according to the inherited reflexes of a besieged minority.

Anti-Semitism in the 1930s

The resistance of Quebec society to Jewish separate schools, whether open or veiled, must be considered a setback in Quebec history. It not only deprived a minority of the natural right to educate its children, but more importantly perhaps, it opened the way to a new wave of anti-Semitism that spread to leading thinkers both inside and outside the Church and even to the general public.

Canadian Context

A look at the broad social and economic context of the period is useful in understanding Quebec anti-Semitism of the 1930s.

Although the goal of the Canadian government's immigration policy at the turn of the century was to settle the Canadian West, half of the new arrivals stayed in Ontario and Quebec. Montreal remained the main port of entry and the major centre for integrating immigrants. The city's population tripled between 1901 and 1931, growing from 267,730 to 818,577 inhabitants. The number of people who were of neither French nor English origin increased nearly tenfold, from 16,233 (4.5%) to 135,262 (13.5%)[98] and fully half were Jews from Eastern Europe. In statistical terms alone, then, the potential for assimilation problems in Quebec and especially in Montreal was serious.

Jewish Immigration Blocked

In an article entitled "The Line Must Be Drawn Somewhere: Canada and Jewish Refugees, 1933-1939,"[99] Irving Abella and Harold Troper describe the effects of the economic depression on Jewish immigration. They recall that after World War I, Canada's immigration policy became increasingly restrictive, especially for Jews. Of the 800,000 Jews who fled the Third Reich from 1933 to 1939, Canada admitted only 4,000. This gave it the worst record of all countries that accepted Jews, placing it far behind the others at the bottom of the list such as Brazil (20,000), China (15,000) and Australia (10,000).

By all accounts, this effort to stem the tide of refugees went beyond the question of immigration. With the advent of various forms of totalitarianism in Europe; not only in the Axis countries and the USSR but also in Poland, Austria, Romania and elsewhere, basic humanity commanded the nations of the free world to provide asylum for more than just a symbolic number of refugees. Some decades later, Canada would open its doors to the Hungarians, Vietnamese, Cambodians and Chileans.

Why did the Jews face these particular restrictions? In a study entitled *None Is Too Many*,[100] Abella and Troper discovered that the man who then controlled admissions to Canada was Frederick Charles Blair, Director of Immigration Services for the Department of Mines and Resources. Blair remained inflexible despite pressure from the Jewish community, pressure which eventually resulted in the creation of the Canadian Committee for Jewish Refugees in 1938 (CCJR), headed first by S. W Jacobs MP, and then by the dynamic Samuel Bronfman. Blair even refused to consider the plight of the *Saint-Louis*, a ship having on board 907 German Jews who were desperately seeking asylum in the spring of 1939.[101] The title of the work by Abella and Troper is taken from Blair's own words: "None is too many."

These facts imply that to some degree, Canada shared in the responsibility
for one of history's greatest crimes. Blair did not act alone. Who pulled the
strings behind this obscure civil servant? The government in power was
headed by W. L. Mackenzie King, Canada's undisputed political leader at the
time. We know that he admired his counterpart, German chancellor Adolph
Hitler.[102] Apart from the fact that he was no friend of the Jewish people, his
diary illustrates his conviction that the entry of Jewish refugees had to be limited because it threatened national unity. He felt that his hand was being
forced, particularly by Quebec whose cabinet spokesperson was Ernest
Lapointe. Indeed, Quebec's anti-Semitic press expressed its opposition to
accepting the victims of Nazism with stark brutality. "Why accept Jewish refugees?" asked *Le Devoir*, "Jewish shops on the St. Lawrence do nothing to
increase our natural resources." *La Nation*,[103] *L'Action catholique*, *L'Action
nationale* and other published similar articles. Federal Members of Parliament such as Liberals Wilfrid Lacroix, C. H. Leclerc and H. E. Brunelle joined
the chorus, as well as the Saint-Jean Baptiste Society,[104] municipal councils,
credit unions and the Knights of Columbus.

Moreover, the victory of Maurice Duplessis in 1936 sowed insecurity among
federal Liberals and convinced them that they had to assume a cautious attitude toward French Quebecers. King was convinced that "if the Liberal party
is to remain a national party, it has no choice but to concur with the opinion
of Lapointe and his French-Canadian colleagues in the House."[105]

Nation-Wide Anti-Semitic Propaganda

During this period, many elements of the Canadian press persisted in pro-
claiming the merits of Hitler and Germany. In the background was an echo of
anti-Semitism, which took different forms from one province to another. In
the 1930s, for example, Toronto witnessed its Swastika Clubs as well as vio-
lence at the beaches and parks; signs bore messages such as "For Gentiles
Only" or "No Jews Need Apply" and hotels and clubs catered to "Restricted
Clientele." Manitoba and British Columbia experienced similar phenomena.
Winnipeg had its Whittaker and Toronto its Joseph Farr, a member of Adrien
Arcand's party. A cemetery was desecrated in Kitchener; in Toronto, the Goel
Tzedeck synagogue was vandalized.

English Protestantism had its British Israel movement, affiliated with the
British Israel Society of England which distributed the *Protocols of the
Learned Elders of Zion* in Canada. On August 29, 1934 M. J. Finkelstein of
Winnipeg intervened on behalf of Vancouver's Jewish community in response
to Reverend Springett, the secretary of the movement in Canada:

> . . . there is no question in the minds of most of us here that he is
> strongly anti-semitic. He delivered a lecture here in a packed church
> to an audience of over two thousand people, and reliable Jewish citi-
> zens who were there reported that it was crammed full of anti-semi-
> tism along the lines of the infamous Protocols of the Elders of Zion.[106]

Finkelstein went on to report that the *Protocols* was being sold at a local British Israel bookstore: "In justice, however, to the rank and file of the British Israel Society here, I may state that the majority of them here in Winnipeg are opposed to anti-Semitic propaganda and a good many of them are personally hostile to Mr. Springett's actions."[107]

In 1938 Winnipeg City Council once again protested against this hate propaganda and *The Tribune* provided some details:

> The quantity of propaganda material circulated here and throughout the Dominion—circulated more or less surreptitiously but most persistently—is amazing. Most of it, though not all by any means, is anti-Semitic. Most of it originates in Montreal, though Winnipeg is also responsible for a share of it. It is circulated in such quantities as to suggest that the propaganda has quite extensive financial backing. . . . In origin, much of the material is made up from anti-Jewish, anti-democratic literature issued by the Nazi party in Germany.[108]

At its first meeting at Toronto in 1934, the Canadian Jewish Congress noted the growing distribution of anti-Semitic propaganda by Hitler sympathizers, as well as the customary social repression that followed in its wake. "There is not a single Jewish school principal or vice-principal in any western Canadian city."[109] The Congress also noted that Jews had been refused admission to nursing schools. In Ontario, a number of qualified Jewish teachers could not find teaching positions in the schools.

In Quebec

What was the situation in Quebec? We have seen that at the turn of the century, English Montreal opened its institutions to Jews at a time when the Jewish community, inundated by a flood of *shtetl* refugees, was striving to rise out of its misery and isolation.

But the demographic shift soon created educational pressures. The changes were sometimes dramatic. In the inner-city schools the proportion of Jewish students rose above fifty percent. The situation was compounded by religious, economic and cultural pressures.

English Protestant reaction was swift. Before 1916, the Anglicans of Montreal had refused to grant Jews access to the board of directors of the Protestant School Board. In 1921, the same board drafted a bill that grouped the "neutrals" into a different school system whose tax revenues would absorb the deficit of schools located in immigrant neighbourhoods.

From then on, the Jews fought against these measures, which they saw as the first step toward the segregation they had fled in Europe. English Protestants refused to grant them unqualified acceptance into the education system as teachers and administrators, and increased the pressure to relegate Jewish students to a separate system. Did the Jews believe that this treatment was an expression of anti-Semitism? According to R. Caux, author of a thesis on Adrien Arcand, anti-Semitism during that period was not limited to French

Quebecers. On the contrary, it was more efficient, though better concealed, in the English community. "But it became more generalized among Francophones and took more sensational forms."[110]

French Quebecers

The climate of hostility among French Quebecers during the 1930s was comparable to the situation previously experienced at the turn of the century. At that time Tardivel, Monsignor Paquet, *La Croix, L'Action sociale* and *La Semaine religieuse de Québec* had been at the forefront of anti-Semitic sentiments. This later anti-Semitism would take different forms: opposition to Jewish schools, the Nazism of Adrien Arcand, the Ligue de l'achat chez nous and the ethnocentric nationalism of Lionel Groulx and *La Revue dominicaine.*

To understand this resurgence more fully, one must consider the social, economic and political context of an era when Quebec society was gripped in panic. The economic depression was at its peak and government authorities were overwhelmed. Unemployment continued to rise. Between 1929 and 1931, it increased from 7.7 percent to 19.3 percent among unionized workers in Quebec, reaching a peak of 26.4 percent in 1932, a figure that has never been equalled since.[111] Those were the dark days of "direct assistance."[112]

The economic crisis conjured up the spectre of social revolution. There was talk of social credit, technocracy and communism. Fascism had not yet revealed its subversiveness; anti-communist discourse masked its own totalitarian nature. Fears were aggravated by the spread of dictatorship throughout the world and the ideological influences of foreign powers at home, manifest in the ideological and political groups that spread the socialist and totalitarian gospel.

Because of its strong position in Quebec society, the Catholic Church felt doubly concerned: it was both guardian of the established order and bastion against the modernism it had been fighting since well before the 1864 *Syllabus.* The Church feared communism more than anything else because of its avowed atheism, but also because of its activities in the province. The Communist Party of Canada (CPC) had been founded a short time before (1921). In 1928, it had no more than sixty members, but it would become more active in the 1930s. An abundance of Communist literature was circulating in Canada; the CPC and Labour Progressive Party (LPP)[113] tried to penetrate the French working class, but with little success. In order to combat their offensive, the Duplessis government passed its "padlock law" in 1936 with the tacit support of the church. The law prohibited individuals from using their homes to promote communism.

These problems in themselves had nothing to do with anti-Semitism. In Quebec as in Canada, however, the political and religious authorities failed to resolve them and thus sought a scapegoat—in this case the Jews. Their strategy was particularly effective because anti-Semitism was latent among the very people who bore the brunt of the crisis.

As a result, church authorities lent credence to the alarmist sentiments that had been circulating in Quebec for a number of years, such as those of Father Huot. Since the turn of the century, Huot had been spreading European myths of a supposed collusion between Freemasons and Jews, and a Jewish plot to rule the world. Even his allegations of ritual murder against the Jews did not succeed in alerting church authorities to the questionable value of his ideas. It is therefore not surprising that so many who cared so little for historical accuracy were quick to link the Jews with revolution and communism. After all, hadn't Marx himself been a Jew?

In the highly explosive climate of the 1930s, anti-Semitic propaganda first reappeared in chancelleries and newspaper editing rooms but soon spread to the young nationalist and political movements which were springing up to challenge the old parties. When the Rome-Berlin axis proclaimed itself Western Europe's breakwater against the communist tidal wave about to sweep the free world, the political right was strongly tempted to accept the Nazi propaganda published in the North American press. And when Germany invaded France, right-wing French Catholics lent their moral support to the Vichy regime, "the true France."[114] Quebec was neither isolated nor without influence, either. Ottawa, after all, despite all apparent diplomatic logic, maintained an embassy at Vichy throughout the war.[115]

The Catholic Church was highly influential and omnipresent in Quebec society at the time, but it seldom assumed an official role in these matters. Instead, it acted through its chancelleries, giving the green light to studies and articles intended for Church publications. This was particularly true of two of its official mouthpieces, *L'Action catholique* and *La Semaine religieuse de Québec* which combined with *Le Devoir*, assembled many of French Quebec's leading intellectuals. It is not exaggeration to refer to the Church as giving these publications the green light; at that time, all Church members in good standing who wished to publish anything at all first had to obtain an imprimatur from the Church bureaucracy. Most, if not all the texts cited here received no warnings nor were they listed in the *Index*; on the contrary, they were granted at least implicit permission to publish from the local bishop or superior Church authorities. This approval did not constitute official canonical support from the authorities, but it reassured believers that the material contained nothing that ran counter to their faith or morals.

Practically speaking, the Catholic Church held a key position in situations such as Francophone resistance to Jewish schools. A number of bishops played an instrumental role in that crisis, though they cannot be held fully responsible for it.

The Nazi Movement of Adrien Arcand

The causes for the surge of anti-Semitism in Quebec and other parts of Canada during the 1930s ran deep and cannot be traced to Hitler's diseased ideology alone, as the Adrien Arcan phenomenon might suggest. Nonetheless, this pamphleteer represented the most notorious of all its manifestations in Quebec, and his case deserves separate treatment.

Arcand was thirty years old when Quebec adopted the David Law on April 4, 1930. For Montreal Jews, the law approved the development of a Jewish school system similar to the Catholic and Protestant boards. For the Catholic clergy, it represented a dangerous precedent. As Adrien Arcand later stated in an interview, it was at the expressed wish of Monsignor Gauthier that he quickly launched a campaign against the David Law and its authors in the pages of *Le Goglu*.[116] For Arcand, this campaign was the starting point of a long path that eventually led him to Nazism. Réal Caux sketches the stages of his evolution in this excerpt:

> On the occasion of this campaign, the young journalist received ample documentation on the international Jewish question from several foreign countries, especially England. He set out to study the mass of information and a deep-rooted conviction began to form within him. The rather superficial anti-Semitism he had developed during the Jewish schools debate was transformed into fierce hatred of all things Jewish. His hatred led to other research, and slowly, a doctrine began to emerge. For it was a doctrine, if not an ideology. It included a dose if irrationality that transformed it into faith and an explanation, perhaps not of the world, but of the conditions then reigning in the world.
>
> Arcand's thinking is easy to summarize. He claimed that the international crisis, as well as various national and provincial problems, hinged on one factor: the Jews. The Jewish plan for world domination, developed thousands of years before, was perpetuated throughout the course of human history. Revolution, communism, economic crises and gold trading were but a number of means which Jews utilized so as to achieve their ultimate goal, one day in the future. White domination was threatened by the Semite, and self-defence was a must.[117]

Monsignor Gauthier probably chose Arcand because he had become acquainted with the young chemist during his training at the Collège de Montréal. He was also probably influenced by Arcand's sympathy for his own teachers, the Sulpicians. After setting out on a career in journalism at *La Patrie*, *The Star* and *La Presse*, Arcand joined forces with Joseph Ménard in 1929 to form a pair of similar weekly newspapers filled with cartoons: *Le Miroir* and *Le Goglu*. At first, they were not particularly radical. They supported the Conservative party, which helped to finance them, and backed Camilien Houde during the Montreal mayoralty election of March 1930.

Adrien Arcand entered the fight against Jewish separate schools with an abrupt and total about-face. Houde became the target of attacks that lasted for months in *Le Goglu*. His crime? He proclaimed that minorities were entitled to protection by the institutions of a free country. In February 1930 Houde responded sharply to these attacks, condemning *Le Goglu* and *Le Miroir* for their anti-Semitism. The debate began to intensify. The combined fire of *Le Goglu* and *Le Miroir* was first aimed at Jewish schools in an article appearing on April 4, 1930: "Le Canada est la patrie des Canadiens et non des Juifs" (Canada Home to Canadians, Not Jews).[118] This was followed the next day by a cartoon showing Premier Taschereau and provincial secretary David kneeling down before Peter Bercovitch and Joseph Cohen, beside an article entitled "Québec livré aux Juifs" (Handing Quebec to the Jews). In May, *Le Goglu* published "Pourquoi le sémitisme est un péril" (Why Semitism is a Peril).[119] In subsequent months, Arcand's attacks against Jewish schools appeared weekly and seemed to be carefully orchestrated. The articles were well-informed, clearly stated and kept close to the tactics and positions of the debate. This period probably represents the high point in Arcand's career, before he completely gave way to his obsession about the diabolical Jew. Here are a few samples of his work.

He attacked Montreal's Jewish School Commission, saying that after it was created, the Public Education Council would no longer have jurisdiction over questions of school order and that the only remaining liaison with government would be the superintendent:

> The government alone can intervene, but only on the recommendation of the superintendent. And what if that individual makes no recommendation? We will see the Jews act as they please, do anything they wish without control or supervision. They will enjoy a degree of independence that we did not even see fit to grant Catholics and Protestants.
>
> Since Jews alone will be able to advise the superintendent of public education about Jewish schools, both he and the school system itself will naturally become steeped in Judaism. He will lose control over Christian and Jewish schools alike.[120]

In response to Camilien Houde's statement that the Jewish minority in Quebec was entitled to protection by the province's institutions, he wrote:

> We wish he would tell us now whether or not he would be ready to grant the Jews a law — wherever it would come from — that gave them the same rights as French Canadians! We ask him to tell us once and for all whether our national and Christian traditions should dominate in this province, or whether Jews have the right, as Jews, to share our national life.[121]

Henri Bourassa did not escape his attacks: "We cannot even count on people like Camilien Houde and Henri Bourassa. The race, and indeed the country, thought that they at least would defend the principle of an officially Christian nation. But they have sided with the Jews and support their claims."[122]

The fight against Jewish schools was just one episode in Arcand's career. At the same time, he and Ménard were taking on Montreal's new municipal regulation permitting Sunday shopping.[123] In their last weekly, *Le Chameau* (founded March 30, 1930), they took Camilien Houde to task:

The Honourable Mayor Houde and members of the executive had no cause to arrogate rights they did not control. They were even less justified in denying their race and their faith to satisfy these anti-Christians [the Jews]. By violating (lawfully) the Sunday closing law, the Jews have issued a challenge to the French-Canadian and Catholic people of Montreal. We accept! May it bring them and their traitor-protectors public scorn and a black mark on their characters.[124]

But Arcand was already moving into the political arena. After launching the Ordre patriotique des Goglus in 1930, he founded an organization inspired by Hitler's fascism, the Parti national social chrétien, as well as the Parti de l'unité nationale du Canada, whose Quebec leader was Gérard Lanctôt. His writing became more prolific and more virulent. Perhaps the best-known and most widely distributed pamphlet was *La clé du mystère*, which the author confirmed to have been translated into German and used by the Nazis.

There is too little space here to describe all the events of his story in detail. We know that Prime Minister R. B. Bennett provided *Le Goglu* and *Le Miroir* with moral and even financial support, then turned around and suppressed them in 1933. Arcand himself was imprisoned from 1940 until the end of the war.

Arcand was certainly the most virulent and vicious of the Francophone anti-Semites. His violent rhetoric was exceeded only by that of his colleague Ménard, whose texts sometimes reached extremes typical of Nazi anthologies:

In their pride, the Jews claim to be a class apart. They believe they are superior and destined to dominate. Any nation that takes the risk of accepting them into its fold is expected to bow down before them. They are satisfied only when they have succeeded in gaining mastery by their gold or by usurping powerful positions. They aspire to power for just one reason: to perpetuate their hatred and destruction of Christians. . . . Two great races form the true foundation of the Canadian nation; we only recognize the official status of Canadians descended from the British or the French. We have admitted other nationalities as well, but their immigrants must be content to accept our laws and submit to our constitution. Of all the foreigners we have allowed to immigrate, the Jews should be the last ones to teach us a lesson or tell us how to run our affairs. Besides, they are the only ones who have had the nerve to use this arrogant tone. We intend to remind them of their true position within Quebec, because they are extremely dangerous and utterly contemptible.[125]

Quebecers today are led to believe that the Arcand/Ménard phenomenon was marginal and relatively unimportant. In terms of sheer numbers, however, we should point out that *Le Goglu* printed a run of 55,000 copies in 1930, and that Arcand managed to rally 13,000 votes for his candidate Saluste Lavery in the 1934 campaign against Camilien Houde. But its importance cannot be measured primarily in terms of numbers. The support, or at least the tolerance that Adrien Arcand initially received from the establishment could do nothing but help cultivate and reinforce Quebec anti-Semitism. This was especially true among young people, who received his message from the clergy in their schools and parishes.

As late as 1956, Jacques Hébert was lamenting the fact that Adrien Arcand, clearly recognized as a public enemy of Canadian society and Western civilization, still had access to parish halls such as St-Alphone d'Youville for his fascist rallies. He also wondered as to whether *L'Action catholique, Notre Temps* and other respected publications had ever printed a word against him:

> The people who are careful not to do so probably, like him, harbour a secret hope deep in their hearts that one day they will see our semblance of a democratic regime subjugated by a real dictator (a Catholic like Franco, maybe . . .), a dictator whose supreme authority "comes from God." He could cleanse our sacrosanct province of all communists, Jews, trade unions and intelligent newspapers (we could be so happy together, just us Aryans, with our dear "Fuhrer" Adrien).[126]

Arcand's post-war activities interest us only to the extent that they help us measure the impact he had on his own generation. The climate changed in Quebec after 1945. Revelations of Nazi atrocities were published and corroborated beyond a shadow of a doubt at the Nuremberg trials, sealing the fate of the province's Nazi movement as such.

Nationalist Anti-Semitism

More harmful perhaps was the covert anti-Semitism that often raged in the press, youth movements and political organizations, for it was cloaked in the religion and traditional nationalism familiar to all French Quebecers. Unlike European anti-Semitism, this sort of specialized xenophobia was limited to verbal abuse. It expressed the insecurity of a minority who refused integration and perceived the survival strategy of another minority as a threat to its own cultural and even economic survival. This other minority was of course the Jewish community, which relied on the Anglophone milieu.

During this period, Quebec society was experiencing right-wing nationalistic fervour. Taschereau's old-style Liberal party was opposed by small organizations such as Paul Gouin's Action libérale nationale, as well as groups led by Paul Bouchard and Philippe Hamel. All were recruited in 1935 by Maurice Duplessis' Union Nationale. The militants in these parties read *L'Action canadienne-française, L'Action nationale, L'Action catholique, La Nation* and of course *Le Devoir*. The Jesuits, basing themselves to follow on the initiative of Benoît XV, encouraged a Catholic action movement among young people, similar to Charles Maurras' Action catholique de la jeunesse française. The movement was the ACJC (Action catholique de la jeunesse canadienne-française), a curious mixture of Christian and nationalistic fervour founded in 1903 by Lionel Groulx and Émile Chartier.

This radical nationalism bore clear signs of anti-Semitism. Among its best-known promoters were Omer Héroux and Georges Pelletier at *Le Devoir* and André Laurendeau at *L'Action nationale*. But the entire press of the day joined in the chorus, from *La Boussole*, published by the Order of Jacques Cartier, to *La Revue dominicaine*: at best, they said, the Jews were guests in Quebec and not entitled to the privileges enjoyed by the "two founding races" (Arcand); or they were immigrants on the same footing as the Asians and Africans (Forest).[127]

To understand the causes and many manifestations of this movement, we have to go back to the leading intellectual of that generation, Father Lionel Groulx. He himself never officially published anti-Semitic material. In fact, he explicitly denied any such sentiments according to *La Nation*: "As Lionel Groulx recently explained, we are neither anti-English nor anti-Semitic. We are against no one; we are for the French Canadians."[128]

Nonetheless, his influence spread far beyond his post at the Université de Montréal and his published works on the history of French Canada, which forged close links between politics and religion and recruited Catholic youth, especially in the classical colleges, at least until the advent of the JEC (Jeunesse étudiante catholique) in 1932.

From 1920 to 1929 Father Groulx was a director of Action française québécoise. In 1932, he presided over the founding of the Jeune-Canada and Action nationale movements. He appears to have been a prominent member of the Saint-Jean Baptiste Society and of the Order of Jacques Cartier. All these movements were very active in the anti-Semitic battles of the 1930s.

Groulx's educational background reveals anti-Semitic influences which must be acknowledged, and which are outlined clearly by historian Mason Wade. During his university studies in Fribourg and Paris, Lionel Groulx was influenced by disciples of the Count de Gobineau, whose *Essai sur l'inégalité des races humaines* sought to establish the superiority of the Nordic race. This work ranked him, along with H. S. Chamberlain, among the precursors of Hitler's national socialism. The young Groulx had also discovered Action française, an ultra-nationalist political movement of the extreme right founded in 1908 by Maurice Barrès (1862-1923) and led by notorious anti-Dreyfusards such as Charles Maurras (1868-1952).

Such was the influence of these two men on Father Groulx, that he was quite unconcerned when Pius XI condemned Action française in 1926. He simply changed the name of the associated Quebec movement to Action Canadienne-française without changing its founding principle of integral nationalism. According to historian Mason Wade:

> Among the bases of this integral nationalism are the cult of the homeland and of the French language, folk hero-worship, Catholicism as a national unifying force, Caesarism or monarchism, and corporatism. As developed by Maurras, this nationalism is a breeder of hatreds of alien influences: Protestant, Jewish, Masonic, liberal,

republican, communist—and even papal, after the condemnation by
Rome in 1926. It inculcates the myth of "Latin" cultural dominance,
and bitter opposition to the democratic system of government."[129]

   Given his rejection of the anti-Semitic label, it might appear that his nationalism had not retained the anti-Dreyfus racism of Maurras, much less that of
the Count de Gobineau. His training as a historian should have warned him
that the tales told about Jews at that time were ludicrous. Some of his writings
indicate otherwise, however, such as an article he published in *L'Action
nationale* under the pseudonym Jacques Brassier. It was written to support
his young disciples in the Jeune-Canada movement after the Gesù counter-
protest held in response to anti-Nazi demonstrations in Canada as Hitler was
taking power. It includes several common anti-Semitic themes of the day:

> Politicians and Jews: Convincing our leading politicians to take
> action in favour of persecuted Jews living 4,000 miles from Canada is
> one thing . . . persuading them to do something for the Catholic
> minorities and even minorities among their own kin, collapsing on
> the doorstep, is quite another. . . . It is a public service to denounce
> these caricatures of pity who distort Catholic and national ideals.

> Intolerable Class: The members of Jeune-Canada have denounced
> another more serious error. These young people cannot tolerate the
> idea that an ethnic minority should be elevated to the rank of a privi-
> leged class when nothing suggests it should receive any special treat-
> ment. And yet this is exactly what we are doing for the Jews in Can-
> ada, and in Quebec more than anywhere else. We have carved out
> perfectly safe electoral seats for them in Montreal; practically private
> clubs where Jews can use and abuse their right of suffrage at will,
> voting to the tune of a hundred and ten per cent without any worries
> and, we have been told, with no threat of subjugating themselves to
> the tiresome matter of oath-taking. . . . We have also drafted a special
> Sunday closing law in Quebec for the Jewish minority. We allow the
> Jews to make Catholic and French-Canadian employees work seven
> days a week on the pretext of compensating the minority for a Sab-
> bath that does not really pose any inconvenience to them. We permit
> the Jews to open their shops on Sunday and thereby create the most
> unfair competition for French-Canadian business. We have come
> within a hair's-breadth of bungling the entire economy of our school
> system, all for the Jewish minority. . . .

> Jewish Dictatorship: What will be the end result of these absolutely
> unjustified privileges? To promote the creation of a veritable Jewish
> business dictatorship in Quebec, especially in Montreal. And Jewish
> internationalism will serve to make the entire process easier and
> more dangerous.[130]

   These sentiments might be considered a temporary lapse, a sudden change
of heart, or the polemics of a man carried away in the heat of the moment,

were it not for a letter that Lionel Groulx wrote to Lamoureux long after Hitler's demise. The letter was only published much later; it is nonetheless difficult to explain how, after the revelations of the Nazi Holocaust, such an irrational view could persist until the eve of the Quiet Revolution. Here are a few excerpts from the letter, which reiterate the myths that abounded in the 1930s about the Jews, from their revolutionary tendencies to their passion for money. By refusing integration in any form, he explained, the Jews became indifferent toward the social and political establishments and joined in "all the revolutions." This is what he had to say about Jewish involvement in economic life:

> We have to reckon quite as much with their innate passion for money—an often monstrous passion that makes them totally unscrupulous. They are prepared to do anything for money. It is not unusual to find Jews behind all kinds of shady operations and involved in every aspect of the pornography business: books, cinemas, cabarets and so on. . . . There is no need for me to tell you about the problems created by the Jews in our economic life. Their passion, or rather their ambition to dominate in this area gives them an extraordinary appetite for monopoly. They are not content simply to compete. Their lack of judgment makes them brutal in success. One example is the recent establishment of the chain grocery stores that are in the process of ruining small French-Canadian business.[130]

These few excerpts are necessary to understand why Lionel Groulx, the great national revivalist, failed to shield the generation of the 1930s from the anti-Semitic madness that was sweeping the entire Western world.

L'achat chez nous

There is too little space in this chapter to give more than a general idea of the extent of the anti-Semitic wave that swept pre-war Quebec. It permeated the entire collective life of French Quebec to varying degrees, leaving its mark on the economy, trade unions, culture, social affairs, politics and, naturally, on education and religion. The press of the period, from large dailies such as *Le Devoir* and *L'Action catholique* to a plethora of nationalist reviews (*Vivre, Les Cahiers noirs, Indépendance, La Nation, Le Patriote, L'Oeil, Le Franc Parleur, L'Action nationale*) expressed mistrust, hostility and even hatred toward Jews to varying degrees.

There were even cases of social discrimination at some clubs—Plage Laval, Val-Morin, Sainte-Agathe—as well as in the streets of Montreal bordering on the schools. Problems also existed at the municipal level, resulting in regulations to govern the opening of Jewish shops on Sundays.

One point deserves more detailed study, however, for it affected the population as a whole rather than a relatively limited segment of society, and it touched a very immediate aspect of people's everyday lives: their wallets. In 1930, an organization called the Ligue de l'achat chez nous, a patriotic organization which advocated that French-Canadians only purchase goods from French-Canadian owned businesses, was founded out of a movement, or rather a crusade, going back to the previous generation. A look at the newspapers of the earlier era reveals that the anti-Semitic plague was already spreading. These excerpts from an article in Montreal's *La Croix* of May16, 1908 provides a case in point. It was entitled "La conquête juive du Canada français" (The Jewish Conquest of French Canada, p. 4). The author hid behind the pseudonym J.-B. Gardavou, a play on words meaning "beware!" (the italics are his):

> In Montreal, as the *Action Sociale* of April 21 notes, French Canadians are alarmed by financial *judaization*. Montreal is becoming a Jewish city.
>
> The Jews buy up real estate with capital they extract by usury from Christian pockets.
>
> They deliberately settle in French-Canadian neighbourhoods, and like spiders, spin their webs where flies abound.
>
> And now, faced with this Jewish invasion, what shall we do, brothers? What defensive action shall we take?
>
> . . . It is no longer time to *complain*, but to *organize*.
>
> For want of a better solution, and as a first step, let's organize and *boycott* the Jews.
>
> We should follow the excellent example set by the Irish Catholics in their *boycott* of the Orangemen who wanted to invade the Catholic counties of the Emerald Isle.
>
> *Boycotting* is absolutely legal and legitimate, and means having no relations with the *enemy*.
>
> We will do no business with them, commercial, industrial, agricultural, financial, social or political.
>
> . . . This was a tactic used by our forebears in Europe against the Jews. It was successful then; why should it not succeed again today, in Quebec? Let's try it!

The movement of the 1930s used the same language. Maurras' influence was evident in the close ties it drew between religion and ethnicity.

> We need money if we are to spread the influence of our faith and our French spirit. In order to put our money to the service of Catholicism and French culture, we have to save it by *buying from our own people*, and increase it by *buying from our own people*.[132]

The promoters of the movement were, in fact, the various nationalist organizations of the day: Action canadienne-française, *Le Devoir*, the Saint-Jean Baptiste Society and, of course, the ever-present Lionel Groulx.

Whether the founders of Achat chez nous intended it or not, the movement became a weapon in the hands of anti-Semites obsessed with the Jewish peril, and they did not hesitate to use it. One of its main promoters was none other than Adrien Arcand:

> We are urging people to boycott Jewish stores so that French Canadians can take over the commercial control of their own nation. . . . Mr. Houde no doubt fears that this action will hurt the Jews, but for our part, we prefer to see French Canadians prosper in their own land rather than Jews.[133]

Le Devoir took Achat chez nous under its wing right from the beginning. On January 19, 1934, an editorial by Omer Héroux made the anti-Semitic potential of the movement crystal clear. It was entitled "La maison est à l'envers" (Our House Upside Down):

> In some parts of the city, mostly French, small French-Canadian businesses are in the process of folding under the pressure of foreign entrepreneurs, especially Jews.
>
> What is at the root of this reversal?
>
> There are many causes, but one is obviously the fact that in their day-to-day lives, French Canadians fail to follow the example of their non-French neighbours—the Jews for example—who provide mutual economic support on a regular basis without, for the most part, giving it a second thought. Who would dream of blaming them?
>
> To tell French Canadians how useful this strategy is—we do not have to remind the others, for it is a part of their everyday life—in no way implies hostility toward those others. And it is nothing like the boycott against German goods promoted by the Jews, almost an act of war.
>
> It is simply a way of re-establishing the normal balance of natural forces, which has been distorted by outside factors.
>
> We find it interesting that neither English, Italian, Polish, German nor any other Canadians seem to take offence at the campaign to buy goods from businesses owned by fellow French Canadians.
>
> Apparently, just the Jews are shocked; they alone refer to it as persecution and racist warfare.

The editor continues his argument by imagining a city whose population is three-quarters Jewish, in which a French-Canadian group comprising 10 to 12 percent of the population takes over a disproportionate share of business:

> Would the Jews close their eyes and not notice—and perhaps even say—that the French Canadians were taking up decidedly too much space? . . . But our hypothesis is fantastic [*sic*]. We would not expect the Jews to let another group take on a role that was logically theirs. We ought to admire and imitate this aspect of their character. . . . That is the goal of this campaign, which has been carried on here for a long time without hatred or animosity.[134]

The theme of the Jew as a threat to French-Canadian business resurfaced constantly in nationalist publications such as *La Nation*. This weekly approved the suggestion that Quebec renounce St. John the Baptist as its patron saint because he was a Jew. Such overt anti-Semitic nationalism would be confronted by Claude Hurtubise in *La Relève*, an influential Montreal philosophical journal which alerted Catholic Quebec to the dangerous radicalism threatening the roots, morality and traditions of the province.

When a Quebec insurance company refused to promote *La Nation*, editor Paul Bouchard shot out at French-Canadian business leaders who were indifferent to patriotism, in an editorial entitled "Notre faillite commerciale" (Our Commercial Bankruptcy):

> As Father Groulx said recently, our businessmen have been the first victims of a basic error: the notion that patriotism is not as important as business. Customers believe it too, and go off to shop at stores run by foreigners. Whose fault is that?
>
> The results are predictable. A foreign company comes to Quebec and uses all the cut-throat strategies of Jewish business practice to create ruthless competition for our merchants. Not only that, the company directors belong to a people with a strong sense of solidarity. And what happens? One of our biggest merchants rushes out to extend them a public welcome in the newspapers, to the great amusement of everyone else in town. We've really seen it all![135]

Even premiers Godbout and Duplessis, as well as mayor Borne of Quebec City endorsed the principles of Achat chez nous.

As could be expected, the movement took on disturbing overtones. An incident that occurred in one Quebec town was reminiscent of events in Eastern Europe. The local priest spoke out in favour of a boycott, and the next day a large sheet-metal sign was nailed to the door of a Jewish store with this message: "Don't buy from the Jews, because they are a cursed race of rotten sheenies, of anti-christian thieves and, often, damned deicides. Be patriotic and encourage our own merchants."[136] Needless to say, despite intervention by Member of Parliament T. D. Bouchard, the merchant went bankrupt.

Allusions to Eastern Europe are no coincidence. Countries such as Poland, Hungary and Latvia achieved independence in 1919 and 1920 after long nationalist struggles, and they too had seen movements similar to Achat chez nous. This weapon was rapidly turned on the Jewish minorities and was not limited to verbal violence. In fact, it was the beginning of what would later become the Nazi Holocaust. This apocalypse could not have spread throughout the Eastern countries so efficiently without a great deal of local complicity sustained over a long period by militant grassroots anti-Semitism.

But the promoters of Achat chez nous certainly did not accept anti-Semitism entirely. In 1933 Lionel Groulx wrote in *L'Action nationale*:

> Not only is Anti-Semitism not a Christian response, it is negative and foolish. To resolve the Jewish problem, French Canadians have simply to recover their common sense. There is no need for special legislation or violence of any sort. We will not even give our people the

order: "Don't buy from Jews!" We will simply say to our French-Canadian customers: "Do what everyone else does; do what all ethnic groups do: buy from your own people!"[137]

A nationalist paper representing the Order of Jacques Cartier, *La Boussole*, denounced the anti-Semitism of the movement as not only incompatible with Christianity, but an error in strategy as well. In it, Annai Loison commented on the decision by one member of an anti-Semitic women's group to stop buying goods from Jews and to patronize Eaton's instead:

> This all-absorbing anti-Semitism caused her to lose sight of her immediate goal. People are focussing on the means rather than the end, to the point that they will spend their money anywhere other than at Jewish stories. This promotes hatred against a particular group and sets aside one of life's most important principles, charity: love of our fellow man, our culture and our faith.
>
> From a strictly practical point of view, what would French Canadians gain if anti-Semites followed the example of this sincere zealot and went to shop at Eaton's? . . . They would unintentionally contribute to an inherent flaw in human nature; they would be cutting off their noses to spite their face.[138]

Jeune-Canada

Jeune-Canada emerged from the ferment of political initiatives that marked the awakening of Quebec nationalism during that period, a sign of the times. It was the direct heir of the Maurras-style nationalism promoted by Lionel Groulx, and included the young intellectual elite, led by André Laurendeau. His own development reflected the course of the anti-Semitic crisis during the 1930s.

Jeune-Canada had scarcely been founded (1932), when it attracted nation-wide attention by a startling action that was loaded with anti-Semitic implications.

The year was 1933. Hitler had just taken power in Germany and was launching brutal attacks on the Jews, in keeping with the racist, pan-German views he had previously made public with the publication of *Mein Kampf* in 1924. Jews were driven out of the universities and law courts. In Canada, as elsewhere in the Western world, there was reaction across the religious spectrum and protests were held. In Toronto, Roman Catholic archbishop Neil McNeil spoke out in unison with the Ontario premier and leaders of the Anglican and United Churches. In Winnipeg, the Anglican and United Churches joined forces, while in Vancouver, members of the Presbyterian and United Churches sided with the Jews in a common denunciation. The Manitoba government and the city of Winnipeg expressed the same outrage.

The Montreal Jewish community hastily formed a people's committee of protest against anti-Semitism in Germany. A protest rally was held at Mount Royal stadium. Senator Raoul Dandurand, former Canadian delegate to the

League of Nations, Mayor Rinfret of Montreal, who presided over the gathering and Honoré Mercier Gouin, the prime minister's representative were in attendance. All denounced Nazi violations of the most basic human rights of Jews.

Then Jeune-Canada acted. The following day, the public was invited to a counter-protest at the Gesù hall, which belonged to the Collège Sainte-Marie de Montréal.[139] Five young speakers appeared at the podium: Pierre Dansereau, president of the meeting, along with Gilbert Manseau, Pierre Dagenais, René Monette and André Laurendeau. The organizers' avowed goal was to convince the audience that the politicians had not acted in the interest of French Quebecers when they joined the Jewish protests, that the province's Jewish community did not constitute a legally-recognized minority and that they could therefore not demand the privileges that had been hard won by the early French settlers. These premises led to two conclusions, as a reader of *Le Canada* pointed out: "Close our doors to immigration and promote our own people."[140] The speakers went on to publish the records of the meeting in *Cahiers des Jeune Canada No. 1*.

Dansereau appealed to a patriotism that refused Jews the upper hand in commerce and industry. For him, the "Jewish danger was an imminent peril":

> The problems we encountered in organizing the present meeting have given us an even clearer idea of how much power the Jews hold in Montreal. . . . If Jewish money were all that enslaved us our protest would be less vocal. But every day, Jewish internationalism (which some call communism) is making inroads, even among our own people.[141]

Manseau's starting point was the principle that Canada is fundamentally a Christian country. No minority, not even the Jewish minority, could have rights identical to those enjoyed by the "French." He feared that Jewish aggressiveness over the schools issue could lead to a Jew being nominated as superintendent of public education. That was dangerous because it would eventually give the Jews a certain degree of control: "[It] would enable them to legislate against us, sooner or later demanding neutral schools and mass admission to all public schools."[142]

Dagenais attacked Canada's immigration policy, especially with regard to the "unassimilable" Jews, whose power had increased in proportion to their numbers, and who were using the Baron de Hirsch Institute and their influence in government to have more immigrants admitted.

Monette painted a picture of the economic ills that afflicted French Canadians and placed part of the blame on the Jews who were stifling Quebec agriculture and taking over entire business sectors. He cited alarming statistics on "Jewish success" (without indicating his sources) and concluded that "Jews follow gold and gold follows them."[143] His response was to buy from French-Canadians, speak only French and rescind the law that permitted Jews to work on Sunday.

However, the major theme of the gathering, "Politicians and Jews," was discussed by Laurendeau, the intellect of the movement:

> In early April, the Jews called a meeting to protest Hitler's alleged persecution of their kin. I say "alleged" because absolutely nothing has been proven of these reported atrocities. All, or almost all the news agencies, remember, are in the hands of the Jews. . . . Jews can be peaceful citizens and often are, but they nonetheless cherish a visionary and dangerous dream which must be eradicated at all costs: messianism. Everyone knows that the Israelites long for the happy day when their race will dominate the world. They belong to no nation, but reside in every land. . . . Jewish power is international. It backs Germany against the allies one day and helps France fight Germany the next, all in its own interest.
>
> The massive show of strength in the face of Hitler's "oppression" (remember, nothing has been proven in that regard) and the wave of protest sweeping across the entire civilized world indicate the degree of unity that exists among their forces. . . . And these are the oppressed, whom our public figures have risen to defend. This is the international minority we have attracted to live among us, say our wisest observers. Politicians be praised![144]

This indictment echoed the major anti-Semitic themes of the time and was not just the work of media hacks looking for scandal. Its five young authors were among the brightest of the new generation. In 1942, their leader left a lasting mark on Quebec political history by joining Georges Pelletier, Maxime Raymond, J.-B. Prince, Gérard Filion and Jean Drapeau to form the Ligue pour la défense du Canada and by launching the Bloc populaire canadien with the support, once again, of Maxime Raymond, Jean Drapeau and men such as Philippe Hamel, René Chaloult, Paul Gouin and Michel Chartrand. All were fervid nationalists and many were mildly anti-Semitic.[145]

The 1933 counter-protest at the Gesù hall will remain a prominent event in the history of anti-Semitism, not just in Quebec but in Canada as well. The occurrence of such an outcry poses serious questions concerning the education received by a generation whose sincerity was never in doubt.

Commenting on the event of April 8 under the pseudonym Jacques Brassier, Lionel Groulx came to the defence of Jeune-Canada by denouncing the Quebec establishment, in particular, for being "a veritable Jewish business dictatorship, created with dangerous ease because of Jewish internationalism." He recalled an Austrian bishop's denunciation of "Jewish internationalism as one of the most dangerous agents of worldwide moral and social degeneration." And he added: "In conclusion, then, this certainly does not support any form of anti-Semitism, but it does justify our youth, who are clear-sighted and proud in their appeal for more dignity and prudence in our leaders, and perhaps less naivety as well."[146]

Jeune-Canada pursued its anti-Semitic campaign, all the while denying that it was anti-Semitic. For months, André Laurendeau debated the issue in the pages of *Le Devoir* with H. M. Caiserman, a founder and secretary general of the Canadian Jewish Congress. He continued to show intransigence and lack of sensitivity toward Jews:

> You came to live among us wearing blinkers. Your frightful lack of tact, aggressive boldness in strength and insinuating meekness in weakness will cost you dear when misfortune comes your way. You must sense the exasperation that is universally provoked by your domineering presence, and exploited to the full by ideologues and demagogues. We have attacked the rash of immigration that brought useless nobodies to Canada, foreigners (including yourselves) who do not even try to work the land and instigators of social revolution. These people do not fit into any race; they form a state within a state in the name of their religion, their interests and their traditions. . . . We know that you cannot stand even the most harmless jokes about yourselves. A history of misunderstanding and conflict has made you sensitive. We respect and understand the great suffering of your race and know what it has done to the state of your nerves and your lives.
>
> But if you are wounded so deeply by these blows, why provoke them? Why these insidious attacks against people who mean you no harm; why rouse their hostility? Why transform a legitimate defence into a belligerent offensive?
>
> No. Bear your sorrow. Jeune-Canada is not anti-Semitic. It does not wish to suppress the Jewish element. It only wishes to be what it must be in all loyalty and justice.[149]

It took the demise and death of Hitler and the Nuremberg revelations of concentration camp horrors to open the eyes of this generation. In a 1963 article published in the French edition of *Maclean's* magazine, the man who was editor first of *L'Action nationale* and then of *Le Devoir* repented of his distorted views. This is what the changed André Laurendeau wrote in 1963 about the year 1933:

> What did we do here in Quebec when the German Jews were marching into exile?
>
> I belonged to a nationalist group, a band of arrogant youth called Jeune-Canada. At that time, Jews the world over were protesting against their treatment in Germany. They held a meeting in Montreal that was attended by a number of politicians, including Senator Dandurand. We organized a counter-protest. I can remember every last detail of what prompted us to hold each political meeting except for one, which we called "Politicians and Jews." Even now, I still wonder who or what put that idea into our heads. But hold it we did, because a cloud of anti-Semitism had polluted the atmosphere. It was the Depression, everyone had taken a beating and the search was on for a scapegoat.

I was one of the speakers at that meeting. I said a lot about politicians, and just a little about Jews. But it was still too much. Our speeches were horrifying. One of us went so far as to say: "We can't kick the Jewish dog in Germany without hearing it yap in Canada."

"Forgive them Lord, they know not what they do." And we really didn't know. The speeches of young twenty-year-olds reflect ideas that are in the air. And the ideas in the air then weren't always very clear or very nice.

But that's exactly what is so appalling. Take my four friends, the speakers that night. They were nice fellows every one of them. As far as I know, none of them became crooks or vicious anti-Semites. They were sincere and impassioned.

Just when Hitler was getting ready to kill six million Jews, they were giving sincere speeches about "alleged persecution" or "rumoured persecution" in Germany, which they compared to the "very real" ill treatment experienced by French Canadians in Quebec. I can still hear and see myself bellowing along with the best of them at that meeting, while in another part of the world, a German Jew was snatching his family from death by accepting exile. . . .

How many things do we refuse to believe today, things that are nonetheless true? Six million victims have not uprooted anti-Semitism. Some days, the progress of the human race seems hideously slow.[148]

The Jewish Response

The all-round offensive by the reactionaries in Jeune-Canada was the last straw. It broke down the final vestiges of resistance by the Jewish community, in Montreal as in the rest of Canada, to a bold project that had been stalled until then at the planning stages: the launching of the Canadian Jewish Congress.

The action of the young Laurendeau and his friends was unprecedented in the "civilized" world. They had given resounding public support to Hitler's anti-Semitic repression, while at the same time refusing his victims the right to organize their collective self-defence.

The Montreal community felt particularly targeted and threatened. Its members instinctively looked to their Quebec past for an adequate answer to the menace embodied in the Gesù hall meeting. A group of democratic and Zionist thinkers responded with a plan to set up national Jewish "congresses" in the countries of the diaspora. These congresses would unify community members on a democratic basis around common actions and issues. The name and structure of the organizations were inspired by the 1897 World Zionist Congress held in Basel by Herzl, who dreamt of universal Jewish unity. His dream was praised by idealists the world over, but it faced wide opposition as well. In Montreal, supporters of the project worked ceaselessly; national activists such as S. Schneour, Leon Chazanowitch, Yehudah Kaufman,

Reuben Brainin, Leib Zuker, S. Belkin, M. Dickstein and H. M. Caiserman. The Yiddish press—the *Canader Adler, Folkszeitung, Maccabéer* and *Der Veg*—tirelessly proclaimed the crucial importance of Jewish unity, grassroots mobilization and universal equal rights. But as the democratic spirit moved forward, it was opposed by the powerful and the affluent, who refused to be put on an equal footing with the poor and the ignorant, with recent immigrants and recipients of social aid. The reaction was the same worldwide. A congress was finally launched in the United States, but it did not secure the allegiance of the entire American community.

Canada, in fact, was the only country where the leaders of the immigrant society succeeded in laying the foundation for a truly representative Jewish Congress. The organization can be proud of a record that includes an impressive range of achievements and struggles for causes close to the heart of the Jewish community. From the very beginning it supported the idea of a Jewish state in Israel, thus again identifying the Zionist aspiration as an essential of modern Judaism. The community formed the JIAS (Jewish Immigrant Aid Society) to defend Jewish minorities in Europe against fascism, particularly in Poland and Germany, and to help those trying to flee Hitler to come to this country.

During this time Jeune-Canada appeared on the Canadian scene. The same committee that had organized the first meeting protesting Hitler's investiture in 1933 immediately decided to take on the defence of Jewish interests. The Canadian Jewish Congress sprang back to life in two short months after a lapse of twenty-five years. In early 1934, at a large hotel in Toronto, the Canadian Jewish Congress assumed its present-day form. The initiative for the Congress came from the leaders of the Montreal community: Rabbi Harry J. Stern, Michael Garber and H. M. Caiserman, who were joined in 1938 by Samuel Bronfman, a top-ranking figure from the business community, whose participation proved to be decisive in the renewal of the organization. Other important participants included Rabbi M. N. Eisendrath and A. B. Bennett of Toronto and Ben Sheps of Winnipeg.

The Congress survived the pre-war period with a tragic lack of resources and with the Nazi steamroller and Holocaust looming on the horizon. After 1945, it was able to receive tens of thousands of refugees from Nazi concentration camps, as well as from Hungary, the Arab countries and the Soviet Union. It also renewed the fight against a new form of anti-Semitism in Canada and on the international scene. The issues were no longer forced conversions, inquisitions and pogroms; the new anti-Semitism involved no less than the threat of annihilation for millions of Jews in the Near East, a threat ratified by the United Nations in 1974 when it equated Zionism with racism.

Resistance to Anti-Semitism in French Quebec

In French Quebec, early reaction against the anti-Semitism of the 1930s did not come from the Catholic Church, for it was part of the problem. At the very most, the Church began to develop a guilty conscience, if only because it did not want to be branded as anti-Semitic.

French-Canadian reaction against anti-Semitism would originate from anti-clerical circles. In 1926 Henri Bourassa returned from his conversation with the Pope so transformed that he rose in the House to defend the inalienable rights of minorities, including the Jews. But he soon found himself barred from the newspaper he had founded, *Le Devoir*, and was literally destroyed by a press campaign orchestrated against him and his grandfather, Louis-Joseph Papineau, the liberal spirit who had supported the Jews in their earlier struggle for equality before the law. The counter-attack was launched by people such as Olivar Asselin in *Le Canada*, and then in his own newspaper *L'Ordre* (1934) and Jean-Charles Harvey[149] in *L'Autorité* and *Le Jour* (1934). Their targets were Hitler sympathizers belonging to all sorts of nationalist and anti-Semitic organizations. Editor Edmond Turcotte of *Le Canada* fought at their side, along with journalists such as Lucien Parizeau and Henri Girard. On May 21, 1934 Girard invited Quebecers to become more competitive with the Jews, whose positive qualities he extolled. He was a believer in liberal economics, and urged his fellow citizens to face the facts and to accept that the thousands of Jews in Quebec were as Canadian as any French Quebecer. He added: "If we had the power to suppress competition by the Jews and the English, we would be well not to do so out of patriotism. This competition provides our people with a wonderful stimulant."[150]

The Jesuits, who had played an important role in the nationalist movement of the 1920s and 1930s—especially through the ACJC—became the avant-garde of the Judeo-Christian ecumenical movement in Quebec. The first Judeo-Christian meeting took place in 1935 between Rabbi Henry J. Stern and the Jesuit Joseph Paré, who was then the prefect of the Collège Sainte-Marie. Paré invited Catholic lay people and prominent Jewish figures to take part in open discussions. That was how the young Jesuit academic Stéphane Valiquette began his research into Judaism—research that prepared him for decades of involvement in the Judeo-Christian ecumenical movement in Quebec. Also in 1935, André Laurendeau rejected the anti-Semitism of *Le Goglu* (*Notre nationalisme*, No. 5). In the political arena, Jean-François Pouliot, Federal MP for Témiscouata, spoke out in favour of religious freedom in Canada before the Canadian Society for the Study of the History of the Canadian Church.

This was the dawn of a new era in relations between Jewish and French Quebecers. The anti-Semites, however, had certainly not been silenced. That same year, 1935, a Dominican priest named Forest fought against Jewish separate schools.[151] The following year he distributed an anti-Semitic Social Credit parable in parish halls and colleges. It would later be published by Louis Even in 1938 under the title *Salvation Island*, and is still distributed today by the Pilgrims of Saint-Michel de Rougemont, better known as the "White Berets."[152]

But a new discourse was taking shape in Quebec. Young people were sympathetic to it, for their outlook was shaped by the kind of Catholic action described by Pius XI. He talked of lay responsibility in the church as well as Christianity's international character and the universality of its evangelical message. Religion was no longer enslaved by nationalism. The youth of that period prepared the ground for the next generation, whose members would be found, during the 1960s and 1970s, in all the key sphere and positions in Quebec's social and political life.

Anti-Semitism clearly began to lose momentum in 1937. In Rome, Pius XI published *Mit Brennender Sorge*, which condemned Nazism and fascism. In Montreal, meetings continued between Jews and Christians.

Another sign of the times appeared in 1939. The Franciscan Gustave Bellemare, leader of a social studies group in Ottawa, had been doing his utmost to promote "more sympathy toward the Jews." In 1939, he wrote to the secretary general of the Canadian Jewish Congress in Montreal to inform him about two publications attacking anti-Semitism. One was from Montreal: the *Message aux aumoniers de la JEC* (Jeunesse Étudiante Catholique), published in April 1938 by the Montreal JEC Central Committee. The other was from Belgium: *La Nouvelle revue théologique* of January 1938, published by Casterman. It contained an article by the Jesuit Pierre Charles on the *Protocols of the Learned Elders of Zion*, which demonstrated the fallacies of the book. "I am pleased to bring them to your attention," wrote the Franciscan, "for the greatest good, which is social peace, and for the ultimate happiness and well-being of your people."[153]

In hindsight, and in light of the changed climate that has prevailed in Quebec since 1945, the immense anti-Semitic shroud of the 1930s can be read as a fit of collective paranoia. In fact, once the Nazi horrors and the reality of genocide were made known, Quebec society relegated the pre-war myths and fables to oblivion, from the incredible tales of the Jews' collusion with Freemasonry and communism to the *Protocols of the Learned Elders of Zion* and the distortions of the Talmud.

But we must not forget the pathological character of anti-Semitism. It is crucial that we remain sensitive to the danger it poses to the very foundations of civilization. Even a religion such as Christianity, which proclaims the supremacy of universal love, does not always succeed in checking the instinct for self-preservation that can grip masses of people on the verge of panic. In 1921 Father Edouard V. Lavergne, brother of the great Armand Lavergne, wrote an article in *L'Action catholique* which is particularly significant. Entitled "Haine aux Juifs" (Hatred to the Jews), it advocated love even as it declared an instinctive hatred for "the enemy":

Hatred to the Jews

Such an outcry is not Christian but unholy. . . . Our goal in denouncing the Jewish conspiracy against Christian civilization is certainly not to put these words into the mouths of Jesus Christ's disciples; it is to

awaken our brothers in faith who are too confident and too complacent in their charity. . . . It is our duty to love the Jews, both good
and bad, as neighbours, with a supernatural love, to the point that
we wish them well and even serve them if they are in real need. No
Christian can evade this duty.

The Jews—not individuals, but the Jews as a race—are our born
enemies. Their goal is to wipe out Christianity, even if rivers of blood
are spilled to accomplish it. This has been amply proven, and no
more needs to be said on the subject. Those who have read our
"Protocols" know what we mean. . . . Not only are we not offending
charity by warning our people of the danger they face and by exhorting them to "Know how to protect yourselves against the Jews who
hate you"; in fact, we are obeying the holy laws. . . . We want the
Jews to live in freedom, but on the condition that they do not strive
to bend us under their yoke. We want them to have food and clothing, but on the condition that they do not unite to take away our
share of food and clothing.[154]

Much of the intelligentsia in French Quebec had been influenced by European anti-Semitism, especially that of Maurras. But they read other authors as
well, such as Vries de Heekelingen, a Swiss Calvinist converted to Catholicism,
and Monsignor Gfoellner, the Bishop of Linz, not to mention the Nazi propaganda that filtered into the Canadian and North American press. They therefore said little during this time of paranoia. Only a few of the great figures—
some of them anti-clerical—such as Bourassa, Harvey and Asselin managed to
remain objective.

It is nonetheless reassuring to recall that political activity at all levels—
federal, provincial and municipal—was generally based on a respect for
minority rights and on North American political and economic liberalism.
Men such as Jean-François Pouliot, Alexandre Taschereau, T. D. Bouchard and
Camilien Houde quickly spoke out and acted on the most controversial issues
involving the Jews, despite constant pressure from the church hierarchy and
the intellectuals, who were always ready to speak out in the press and intervene behind the scenes of government. The attitude of these political figures
was consistent with Quebec's tradition of constitutional struggles to safeguard
human rights. It enabled the young Jewish community to survive the anti-
Semitic crisis of the 1930s without experiencing the tragedies of the Old
World.

Perhaps the biggest casualty of this ethnic and cultural battle was Quebec's
French-Catholic community. The Church did not follow Pius XI in vigorously
denouncing the domination of religion by nationalism as taught by Maurras.
It remained silent before the escalation of verbal violence unleashed by the
Nazism of Arcand as well as the intense anti-Semitism of Jeune-Canada and
the anti-Jewish press. As a result, Quebec's Catholic Church cut itself off from
the few remaining local intellectuals who were lucid, and from the major cur-
rents of renewal coming from outside the country.

On the whole, French Quebecers in the first half of the twentieth century failed where their forebears after 1760 had succeeded: integrating the Jewish community into the mainstream of Quebec society and creating harmonious relations among the Jews, the *Canadiens* and the English. Jewish young people were adopted by the Protestant school system and deeply influenced by their widespread assimilation into Quebec's English community. As a result, they were not in a position to join the Francophone majority in laying the foundations for contemporary Quebec.

Fortunately, the era of the Harts and Josephs would be renewed in the changed climate of the 1950s, influenced largely by the arrival of the Francophone Jews.

CHAPTER IV

The Quiet Revolution of Jewish Quebecers, 1945-76

World War II was not only a colossal armed conflict, another tragedy added to the infinite list of disasters that have befallen humanity; it also unleashed a global revolution whose consequences are still not fully understood. Hitler's death liberated a host of captive forces: a chain reaction among Third World nations seeking independence, movements for freedom and equality among Blacks and Native peoples, as well as a surge of interest in forms of counter culture, feminism and religious questioning. For the Jews, his demise sounded the death knell for pre-war anti-Semitism. It allowed the re-establishment of the State of Israel, an event that had major socio-economic, political and cultural repercussions and a powerful impact on the Jewish diaspora and humanity as a whole.

In Quebec as elsewhere, a new Jewish society replaced the Yiddish-based culture that had enjoyed a kind of golden era for half a century before it was suddenly wiped out. Here is how Joseph Baumholz and Saul Hayes, contemporaries of the period analyzed the transformation:

> The Jews learned to live together. People who had immigrated just a decade earlier now dealt with divisions in the community by founding the Canadian Jewish Congress. Growth kept pace with successive waves of immigration: first the Holocaust survivors, then the Hungarians in 1956, followed by the North Africans, Israelis and Russians. Increased population, economic success and the fight against anti-Semitism all served to enhance the reputation of Montreal Jewry. It became the envy of Jews the world over.
>
> Opposition changed to opportunity. The constraints on small merchants had vanished and their shops became chain stores. Tinkers who had dealt in scrap metal were now delivering construction

materials. Montreal's painters and musicians had access to all the public institutions on the continent, as did their fellow architects, builders and administrators.[1]

Saul Hayes, an important community spokesperson for forty years, summarized the developments of recent decades before the directors of the Canadian Jewish Congress:

> Our community is not the same as it was a generation ago. The majority of our present members were born in Canada. They pray to different household gods than did their parents and grandparents. A high proportion are under 35 years of age. The percentage of our young people attending college and graduating is higher, much higher than ever before.[2]

Cultural Revolution

A multitude of complex reasons accounted for this revolution in the Jewish world. They were neither specific to Quebec, nor were their consequences limited to Canada.

World War II was, in part, a war against racism. People experienced the horror of religious and racial discrimination; they learned that the most innocent acts could lead to unimaginable extremes when individuals were victimized. Free and liberated societies alike examined their consciences and discovered forms of slavery they had never before perceived.

The post-war generation has seen the abolition of oppression in many forms: the oppression of women, artists, children, the mentally and physically ill; of prisoners, Blacks, homosexuals and colonized peoples; of the Jews as well, and of nations such as Israel that had been deprived of their ancient homelands.

Quebec, and French Quebec in particular, joined Canada and the rest of the world in re-examining its history and past record in the area of freedom and slavery, not always an easy process. This gave rise to the economic, political and cultural-religious shift known as the Quiet Revolution. The ecumenical movement and new theological doctrines emerging from Vatican II literally convulsed the old religious order. Anti-Semitism is a case in point. French Quebec was virtually unanimous in rejecting a century of anti-Semitic indoctrination in social, political and religious terms to take its place among the most receptive societies the Jews have ever known. Anti-Semitic campaigns and activities suddenly ceased, except for these directed from outside by Israel's enemies. In almost a single stroke (the very stroke that destroyed Hitler and his regime), Quebec opened up so that Jews had free access to the economy and education.

This openness fostered a new generation of Jewish Quebecers whose biographies differed from those of their parents. They were young and born in Quebec though their parents were immigrants. They had shed the European identity of the previous generation to become much more like "Quebecers" in appearance and behaviour. More than fifteen thousand had fought beside English and French-Canadian soldiers. They were less "visible" and less vulnerable to discrimination; they were more apt to take their place as full-fledged citizens in all areas of society.

The visibility of old-world Jews has often marked the social scene of Quebec. For a long time after the great migrations of the 1880s, the Jews were the only visible minority in the eyes of the two "founding peoples." Quebec knew nothing of the sizeable Chinese and Japanese communities of British Columbia, the Eastern Europeans of the Canadian prairies nor the Blacks of the American south. The Jews were alone in their difference, a focal point for all of society's fear and aversion.

In time, other groups joined the Jews as "new Canadians," a term reflecting Canada's multiculturalism, and one that French Quebecers were slow to accept. The Jews gradually moved out of the spotlight. In Quebec, members of the Haitian community became victims of racism. Ontario was also under the grip of intolerance and racist attitudes as its newly-arrived East Asian community would soon attest. Ironically, in British Columbia it was the French Canadians who suffered.

In this new context, the experience of young Jews in the 1950s was closer to that of other Canadians. They had never known life in the European *shtetl* or anti-Semitism under the Tsar. Instead, their experience was based on European history between the wars and on the stories told by Jewish immigrants of their own generation, whose world view they shared. The Yiddish way of life was known to them only by hearsay.

A parallel evolution was already under way among the recent Jewish immigrants themselves. Major changes were occurring in Eastern Europe. The *shtetl* was disintegrating under the pressure of new social dynamics. Mandatory state-controlled education was conducted in the official language of each country and Yiddish was becoming marginalized.

The new arrivals therefore did not share the cultural sensibilities of their nineteenth-century predecessors. They found it easier to move from a traditional milieu into Quebec society. At home they spoke English, which was even beginning to attract interest from within French Quebec society. English became the working language of Jewish institutions, including organizations such as the Canadian Jewish Congress, which had been founded by members of the community who spoke Yiddish. This new generation took an active role in post-war Quebec. Each of its initiatives had its own justification and in many cases drew on a unique history that was new to the local Jewish establishment.

But whether Quebecers by birth or recent immigration, these young Jews were particularly affected by two major events that influenced the entire world at that time: the Holocaust and the establishment of the State of Israel. By casting doubt on the values and credibility of Judaism, the Holocaust created a wall between the Jews and those who did not believe they were the chosen people or found no compelling reason to accept them. People who now deny the Holocaust or try to diminish its importance bear the responsibility for the possible recurrence of such a catastrophe.

The restoration of a Jewish homeland, suppressed since early in the second century, enabled the Jews to experience a sentiment that went far beyond politics, religion, self-defense or survival through struggle and migration. Renewed faith in Israel became the beacon of Jewish religious idealism at the very time when its original traditions were being chipped away by the secularism that dominated contemporary societies.

Thus even for these young Jews, witnessing the Holocaust and fighting against Nazism had served to strengthen their resolve to refuse assimilation and remain within the Jewish community. This decision figured prominently in their choice of residence after demobilization.

Present-Day Jewish Schools

Since the 1930s, the issue of Jewish public schools had remained at a standstill. Jewish children continued to attend Protestant schools, yet their parents still had no say about what went on in the classroom.

The community sought an alternative in private schools. As early as 1911 it set out to establish a system of popular modern schools, the Jewish Peretz and People's Schools. They were more secular than religious in orientation, and ultimately served as a model for the whole North American diaspora. The system worked best in Quebec, however, because of the cooperation that existed between the provincial government and the Jewish community.

Men such as Shloimeh Wiseman, Moishe Dickstein, Jacob Zipper and Samson Dunsky led the movement in Jewish education. They modelled their institutions on the American parochial schools and used their own money to set up schools with a dual curriculum, combining the provincial programme and their own courses on Jewish culture, all within the time frame of the public school system. It was a bold solution that put a double load on students and parents alike. Teachers bore the heaviest burden, however, surviving on little or no pay at a time when poverty was widespread. Nonetheless, the schools quickly became successful and the formula spread from Montreal to the rest of Canada and into the United States.

From the beginning, the Montreal community sent a very high proportion of its children to these schools in comparison to other Jewish communities in North America. The quality of the programmes and teaching was soon recognized by the Protestant school authorities and students who transferred from the Jewish schools were given unqualified acceptance into Protestant classrooms.

In the United States, the Jewish school system remained very expensive. It was well beyond the means of lower-income families because of the double school tax: a compulsory one for public schools and a voluntary one for private schools.

It was not until thirty years after the war that Quebec recognized how the education system, though technically legal, was fundamentally unjust. The situation was finally resolved in a practical fashion. The Protestants had refused to give the Jews any hand in school board administration because they seemed a threat to the linguistic, religious and specifically Protestant character of the schools. However, in 1965 S. Godinsky was accepted as an associate member of the board. Several Jewish candidates then ran for school board positions in the Montreal suburbs and were elected. They sat on their respective boards and, lo and behold, the system did not crumble.

There were also financial problems to settle. Jewish taxpayers were already funding the public schools, often contributing a higher share than their Christian counterparts. They had to support the significant financial burden of their own schools as well. But the new climate prevailed; the Quebec government lent a sympathetic ear to the community, and toward the end of the 1960s, it authorized the Protestant system to help finance Jewish schools.

Later, provincial authorities assumed direct responsibility for funding the general education of children in the Jewish schools, just as it did for other Quebec private schools. Today's Jewish schools in Quebec enjoy an independent administrative status unique in the diaspora and surpassed only in Israel.

We must go back to the beginning to understand just how remarkable this development was. Montreal's original, pre-1880 community did not attach the same importance to Jewish education, as did the immigrants from Eastern Europe, nor transmit it with the same zeal. Traditional education, after all, had formed the very basis of religious life in Jewish history. This gave rise to the battles waged by the descendants of the two groups in the early part of the century. The West End establishment was anxious to prevent its children from being segregated and therefore preferred public school, while the Yiddish community fought for a legally-recognized, strictly Jewish education run by the community.

But the post-war revolution raised another question. How would the new generation, now the establishment, handle the education of their own children? In the end, they opted for a response that was quite close to the traditional position: prepare the children to live as Jews in Quebec by seeing to their Jewish education without neglecting their Quebec education. Jewish schools now offer public school programmes in English, French, science and the arts.

Despite their high cost, the schools are attended by a very high proportion of Jewish children. There are currently about twenty day schools, some English and some French. They are highly diversified at both the elementary and high school levels and offer a wide range of religious options. Some are Hasidic and others mitnagdic (dissident). Some are affiliated with synagogues while others are independent. Yiddish is taught in some; others offer religious instruction. There are also another twenty or so afternoon schools offering after-school Jewish education to children in the Protestant system.

In the words of Monette Amouyal and Edmond Elbaz, "the Jewish schools as a whole . . . unofficially play the role of 'Jewish school commissions.' "[3]

Practically speaking, they have been independent from the very start. They were the passion of their founders and gradually became the concern of the entire community. With the cooperation of these private schools, the Jewish Education Council of Greater Montreal was able to move beyond its limited role as a coordinator and representative. Many institutions now attest to the Jewish community's interest in education, including the Jewish Public Library, the Community Research Committee and the Educational Resource Centre, familiar to French Quebecers.

From Yiddish to English ... and French

While the Jewish schools were consolidating their success, language concerns continued to create tension.

The Jewish community felt the same strong attraction to English as did a substantial number of French Quebecers. As long as the vast majority of Jews were immigrants from Eastern Europe, however, Yiddish remained the language of the community.

As the number of Quebec-born Jews increased, the proportion of Yiddish speakers fell, slipping from 95 percent around 1880 to 25 percent in 1950. This drop coincided with the beginnings of the Quiet Revolution, which had sweeping and immediate consequences for the Jewish community. Everything changed: community leaders and spokespersons, ideas, interests, communication techniques, strategies, politicians, religion, literature, media, careers, the birth rate, the economy and the residential distribution.

English inexorably became the language of Jewish institutions—including the Canadian Jewish Congress. The *Canader Adler* disappeared as a daily paper; world-renowned Yiddish writers such as Segal, Rabinowitch, Zlotnick, Dunsky, Rawitch, Husid and Rachel Korn were aging and dying, and Yiddish literature in Quebec was dying with them. It lived on in the conversations of the older generation in the shopping centres on Van Horne Avenue, and sometimes in the traditional seminaries. It is true that the long-ignored cultural value of the language is now widely recognized, with the Université de Montréal, McGill and Concordia Universities offering courses in Yiddish language and literature. Yiddish literature is even considered one of the main branches of Canadian literature, along with English and French. And yet more courses are offered in Aramaic than in Yiddish at the Talmudic yeshivas, an unmistakable sign that the language of the *shtetl* has lost considerable ground in Montreal's contemporary Jewish community.

English has replaced Yiddish as the literary language of the Ashkenazic population since the 1940s. Artistic creativity has found new expression and a new public with the works of Abraham Klein, Leonard Cohen, Adele Wiseman, Irving Layton, Mordecai Richler and others.

A closer look at Jewish literature in English reveals that the first writers to express themselves in that language (all Montrealers) appeared to have inherited the literary maturity of the great Yiddish poets. They dealt with similar

Jewish subjects and shared the same ideals and social vision. Generally speaking, the writers who succeeded these English-language pioneers have shown less scope. They seem to lack the education and sophistication of their predecessors; it is as if they have to begin all over again.

It is worth noting that the first masters in the Yiddish tradition were self-taught, not graduates of the Western school system. Their successors have enjoyed the best in modern education and have gone on to become noted academics and professional communicators—one more sign of a promising renewal.

More recently, writers such as novelist Naïm Kattan have demonstrated that French has also become the language of Jewish literature in Quebec. Born in Iraq, Kattan was one of the first French-speaking Jews to immigrate to Quebec. His works opened a whole new chapter in Quebec literature. For the very first time, French Quebec readers unfamiliar with the Jewish languages (Yiddish, Hebrew, Aramaic) or English were given an intimate glimpse into the Jewish community that shared their destiny.

Economic Emancipation

The post-war period was one of liberation: the end of the war and the Nazi terror, the waning of conservatism, the acceptance of new ideas, the unmasking of anti-Semitism, the opening of jobs and education to all and the long-awaited recognition of human rights and freedoms. In the spirit of the times, young Jewish Quebecers and all other Quebecers could finally give free rein to their talents, skills and ambitions.

This enthusiasm and success were no coincidence. Until that time, the Jewish community had been confined by business to the socio-economic ghetto of the clothing industry and small shops. The end of the war would change all that for the Jews, breaking down the obstacles that barred their way to the professions, high finance and ultimately politics.

Jews of the post-Hitler generation can call themselves Quebecers by birth. They are, as a community, the most bilingual of all Quebecers and have become more familiar with Francophone traditions. Many took advantage of the new opportunities to explore non-traditional paths, seeking careers outside business and commerce and deliberately choosing to become graduate students rather than executives in the companies founded by their parents. They opted for the social services and liberal professions; forged careers as managers in large corporations and even as civil servants. University education led them to succeed far beyond their parents' wildest dreams and gave them new access to fields such as engineering, research, metallurgy, insurance, administration and transportation.

The community's traditional industries—the garment factories and small businesses—underwent a parallel transformation. The Jewish working class was replaced by successive waves of Italian, Greek and Portuguese immigrants. Shop owners became corporate managers; new names such as Steinberg and Pascal appeared on the Quebec business scene and were soon household words.

Statistics showed that the Jews' age-old passion for knowledge, once limited to religious study and community work, found a growing number of outlets in libraries, colleges and universities. Whether as students, professors or administrators, Jews took their place as accomplished researchers at every level and became judges, publishers, architects, corporate managers, communications experts, journalists, senators and political party presidents. Here are but a few: Bora Laskin of the Jewish Congress in Windsor and chief justice of the Supreme Court; David Lewis of the CCF; Judge Maxwell Cohen of the World Court of Justice; Herbert Marx, a constitutional expert, business leader and law professor at the Université de Montréal; Dr. Victor Goldbloom, who held several prominent provincial ministerial posts while in government; and Judge Alan B. Gold, a chief justice of the Quebec Supreme Court.

Needless to say, this injection of cultural pluralism had a stimulating effect on the economy, politics and culture of Quebec.

Trade Unionism

The economic emancipation of an entire generation cannot be explained simply by a fortuitous historical situation, nor by the traditional Jewish passion for education and knowledge. It also grew out of the enormous effort made by the *shtetl* immigrants to improve their lot. An anonymous mass of sweat shop workers, small shopkeepers and craftspeople fought to escape the poverty and misery so familiar to sociologists; the conditions that are found today in black American, Hispanic and other ghettos throughout North America.

Researchers who have studied the economy of contemporary Jewish society have noted how well the workers performed in the industries they created. General labourers often rose to more specialized positions, some to administrative or management posts, eventually becoming employers and owners. In short, they have reflected the gradual rise in income of the sons and daughters of the Montreal Jewish ghetto.

One can question whether this economic improvement was enriching or actually led to cultural impoverishment, especially since it was achieved at the cost of losing Yiddish and the quality of life of the old immigrant society.

In any case, the Quiet Revolution swept away most remaining vestiges of the old society and culture along with the union organizations that nurtured it. The Canadian children of former *shtetl* activists adopted new lifestyles, new ideals and values and new means of communication. The old ideological debates slipped out of fashion.

However, the post-war generation did not break from its past completely. Poverty among the elderly remains one of the most eloquent vestiges of the Old World; the prosperity of the younger generation has no more abolished it among Jews than among other communities. It is false to believe that the Jewish community is free from poverty or that fewer of its members are destitute. The community is aging rapidly and Jewish welfare agencies are constantly overwhelmed by the volume of people needing assistance. In a 1970 study on poverty in Montreal,[4] McGill University sociologist Jacques Torczyner concluded that 25 percent of the Jewish population was living below the poverty line. He showed that social problems were particularly serious for the people belonging to that group; most were elderly, ill and unable to contribute to the economy. Torczyner himself set up Project Genesis in 1974, a community self-help organization, to ease their burdens.

What is the current status of the Jewish community in Quebec society? It certainly shows all the signs of being more widely accepted than it was at the turn of the century, even in francophone circles. As a measure of the change, we need only recall the longstanding resistance of the old Canadian Wasp establishment to the young Jewish (and French-Canadian) dynasties rising to join its exclusive circle of top-level executives and bankers. The Bronfmans are a case in point. In his book *The Canadian Establishment*, Peter C. Newman recounts that Samuel Bronfman, a pioneer of the Jewish financial establishment, was never admitted to Montreal's Mount Royal Club. His son Charles was finally accepted as a member in 1970.[5]

As late as 1964, Ottawa's Rideau Club refused membership to two applicants because they were Jewish. Five prominent members of the Jewish community including Louis Rasminsky, then Governor of the Bank of Canada, had to intervene before the admission rules were changed.[6]

In Quebec, this new openness toward the Jewish community meant that its members were no longer perceived as foreign or new arrivals. As neighbours, business people and professionals, they had become part of the landscape. A number of the larger corporations founded or owned by Jews, such as Pascal's and Seagram's have practically become national institutions. It is difficult to imagine Quebec without them.

New Geography

The same revolution that opened unexpected paths for so many low wage-earners and immigrants in post-war Quebec also gave the Jewish community unprecedented mobility.

When they first arrived, the *shtetl* people had settled in the ghettos along St. Lawrence Boulevard. They did so out of fear or because they worked in the same factories, and generally speaking, required the same community services. But the neighbourhoods were not necessarily static as a result. The Yiddish-speaking community began to move north along St. Lawrence Boulevard. However, the Depression brought a halt to both construction and Jewish immigration, freezing local migration when the Jews were about to enter Outremont. It was a hiatus that lasted twenty years. When construction ground to a halt during the Depression and the war years, they had to make do with old houses that often verged on slums. Then came the Nazi defeat, putting an end to their confinement and to the open hostility of Quebecers. The 1950s gave Montreal back its mobility, that urban energy which is as old as cities themselves. It was of crucial importance to the Jewish community. The community could at last build itself new homes. Its members had access to different neighbourhoods with pretty streets; they were exposed to the majority languages and worked in jobs outside the traditional fields.

The Ashkenazic Jews, previously sandwiched between Park Avenue and Saint-Denis, crossed the barrier of Mount Royal Boulevard and began moving west toward Outremont. They also headed along Van Horne Avenue and Côte-Sainte-Catherine Road into Snowdon, Hampstead, Notre-Dame-de-Grâce, Montreal West and even the West Island. Others went north, following Laurentian Boulevard to Ville Saint-Laurent, as the community spread throughout greater Montreal.

This time, however, the "ghettos" formed spontaneously. They represented a new, post-Hitler Judaism and were home to the first middle and upper classes among the heirs of the great migration.

What price did the new generation pay for this sudden economic rise into the middle class, with all its new social trappings? Did it lose the dynamic heritage of the preceding generation and the highly colourful, heterogeneous character of the original ghetto? Or did it pay the price of dispersal into the larger Montreal community? The young people moved because they were earning more money, making new friends and distancing themselves from the institutions, families and influences of their original neighbourhood. Was this a first step in the assimilation and disappearance of the Jewish people in Quebec?

Surprisingly and reassuringly, it was not. Without being able to explain exactly how, the younger generation found its own way to avoid assimilation. In the purest of Jewish traditions, people continued to live together in neighbourhoods, close to their institutions. This was exactly how their own parents had managed to pass on their religious and cultural heritage under more difficult conditions in the past. The drive for continuity had inspired every aspect of family life and every effort to see that the children received an education. The children themselves spent their youth in the atmosphere of the Jewish neighbourhood, closely linked to the community by various internal and external factors which were interwoven to produce a sense of wholeness in space and time: geography, social morphology, intense family life, work sharing by fathers and sons and a uniform standard of living that kept families in one socio-economic group.

Thus the community was building everywhere, without discrimination or threats. What force could possibly hold this expanding constellation together? How and why would it maintain its former cultural cohesiveness when houses were so far apart with many green spaces between them?

Perhaps the answer lies outside the realm of urban sociology, rooted in the Jewish people's faith in its age-old promise to Abraham that his descendants would survive in ages to come. There are times when the definition of Judaism blurs; when the form and role of religion become uncertain and are questioned by the "chosen people" themselves. Then, the people reaffirm their identity and loyalty with concrete actions: an urban shift, a migration or the kind of exceptional population growth that occurred in Eastern Europe between 1850 and 1939. They reassert their will to be together and live together, united by a common anthropology and sociology.

The depth of this particular definition of Judaism does not come from theologians but from an instinctive consensus of the people. Witness the importance of custom (*minhag*) in the laws of the Talmud and Halakah. Even today, Jewish Quebecers have adopted a lifestyle in which neighbourhoods exert and enormous influence on behaviour, from politics to food to philanthropy.

As difficult as this may be to explain, one fact remains: the Hebrew people want to survive, and in order to do so, they must invent a whole new set of parameters to define themselves. The key to survival lies in the continuity of the community, for future generations as it did for their parents. The old neighbourhoods are part of Montreal's cultural history.

These neighbourhoods have seen decline and renewal. They have become the home of diverse ethnic and cultural communities. For Quebec Jews, the old stones remain the sacred places where the community first put down roots, just as certain cities in the southern United States are for black Americans. The back alleys of the old Yiddish areas, infused with nostalgia, have provided the settings for films such as *Lies My Father told Me* and *The Apprenticeship of Duddy Kravitz* and the inspiration for books such as the poetic autobiography of A. M. Klein. People return to the old Baron de Hirsch Institute, now in Chinatown.[7] They rediscover the old synagogues, witnesses to the tradition of Talmudic study and unforgettable devotion; the Jewish Public Library, home to the great Yiddish culture; the schools that shaped the minds of today's grandparents; the old people's home, forerunner of the present-day Maimonides Hospital; the small shops that first employed those who became the successful business people and affectionate parents of today's generation; as well as the restaurants where Romanian smoked meat was first served. They recognize the family homes of the Caisermans and Kleins, the rabbis Rosenberg, Cohen and Petrushko, the halls where Zionist meetings were held, the basement where the *Adler* was printed and the streets where the Richlers, Segals and Yelins lived, along with Ted Allen and his horse Ferdele.

The memories are cherished and tucked away on a different level of consciousness, far from the preoccupations of daily life, in the vaults of cultural archeology, like Yiddish courses in North American universities.

Contemporary Jews have ended their geographical and social migration and rejected the poverty of the past, as well as the ideological struggles, trade unionism and socialism that their parents sought to invest with meaning.

Church and Synagogue in Quebec

Despite millennia of common history and a unique set of affinities, Jews and Christians have experienced a tragic misunderstanding. Church and synagogue have long stood side by side in fierce isolation, though in Quebec, there are particular reasons that this has been so.

Under the French regime, the Catholic Church was the only religious institution. After 1760, it maintained its privileged positions with the Canadiens, who were cut off from their new masters by religion and language alike. The Jewish community associated itself with the English Protestants from the very beginning; as a result, it also developed in religious, social and cultural isolation from the French Catholics. The gap widened still further when the *shtetl* immigrants arrived, in flight from the far-reaching oppression of Eastern Europe and solidly entrenched in their Yiddish culture. The hopeless misunderstanding of anti-Semitism spelled the final rupture between these two communities, destined by history to a common future.

It is important to remember that the poisoned relations between Jewish and French Quebecers were not caused by the official policies of the Quebec government. Right from the start, Jews in the province enjoyed a legal status based on laws that were well in advance of legislation passed by any other Western government, and their status was never revoked. Progress in this area was generally opposed not by politicians, but by intellectuals whose leaders were church officials. In other words, Quebec anti-Semitism was above all a crusade of the clergy.

The social and economic pressures of the Yiddish migration could not help but affect the local people. Nevertheless, it is significant that the Catholic Church was primarily responsible for channelling the reaction of French Quebecers into a particularly virulent form of anti-Semitism.

Some have suggested that Quebec anti-Semitism was fuelled by ultramontanism, which claimed exclusive rights for the Catholic Church in countries with a Catholic tradition. In Quebec, this movement merged with the new, deep-rooted nationalism of the French-speaking people. Since their earliest days on the banks of the St. Lawrence, they had perceived themselves as a monolithic, French-speaking and Catholic society in a land where Protestants and Jews had no right to coexist peacefully with them.

In Quebec the great civil evolution of the mid-century which established certain relations between Jews and Catholics, was begun at the local level by several men of fresh initiative who were unknown to each other.

Saul Hayes had just been named director of the Canadian Jewish Congress in 1942, when he decided to appoint a press officer for the Jewish institution which had no national parallel. One of the first incidents in the annals of that office was the suggestion of a publicity consultant, Jean-Paul Guérin of *La Presse*, that it had been counter-productive for the community to blame all Quebecers for the anti-Semitic agitation and incidents which were then widely current in the province. Thus began a consistent national Jewish program of interaction with non-Jewish neighbours, a program which could only have been instituted in Canada, for only in Canada was there a democratic representative body mandated to this end.

The repercussions were immediate and numerous from many levels of Christian society. Notably, and clearly without premeditation, poet A. M. Klein issued his collection of Quebec poems, *The Rocking Chair*; hundreds of French Canadian readers responded with appreciation of the Jewish poet who showed such an understanding of the spirit of the province. Similarly Quebecers recognized kinship with the thousands of Canadian Jews who were wearing the national uniform, the unity which was binding them with other victims of Nazism and racism. Suddenly a tremendous body of Quebec moderation, decency and fair-mindedness appeared on the public arena of the province.

A Young Jesuit's Initiative

Paradoxically, the first ray of hope for the future of Judeo-Christian relations in Quebec, and perhaps the world, came during the darkest days of the 1930s from the Catholic Church itself. The person who sparked the dialogue was a young Jesuit theology student named Stéphane Valiquette. He was familiar with the Jews because he was born in their neighbourhood; he had played and scrapped with them. Father Valiquette had the good fortune to receive support—or rather cooperation—from Father Joseph Paré, a senior cleric at the Collège Sainte-Marie who had met the prominent rabbi Harry J. Stern from Temple Emanu-El in Westmount during a trans-Atlantic crossing. Driven by a desire to understand more about Judaism and armed with the necessary authorization, young Valiquette knocked on the door of Montreal's Canadian Jewish Congress on June 1, 1937. Founder-director Hananniah Caiserman was deeply moved. He shed tears before this Catholic, who was free of hostility and wholly committed to transcending the walls of prejudice by his listening.

It is impossible to understand the full impact of this unusual gesture without examining its historical context. In past centuries, the church had assumed a superior position in its relations with non-Catholics. Its intention, stated more or less explicitly, was to convert them to the "true faith." This attitude threatened the very survival of the Jews and inevitably provoked animosity.

But the young Jesuit's bold move revealed something else: the Catholic community's growing interest in the outside world. This interest was masked by the missionary tradition, which articulated its discourse and strategy in terms of conversion. However, a number of individuals who actively conversed with Catholics were able to grasp, though not without difficulty, the hidden truth—the deeper purpose of Catholicism. This was especially true of the Jews, whose history in Christian countries had alternated from ghetto to Inquisition and pogrom.

Rabbi Stern made his personal library available to the Jesuit student helping him complete his project: a thesis on liberal Judaism. Thus began a long pioneering ecumenical career that carried the young priest to the forefront of Judeo-Christian dialogue in Montreal, and in broader terms, brought Catholicism into contact with other religions.

From the time of his earliest research, Father Valiquette maintained contact with the Canadian Jewish Congress, which sent him many messages full of support for his initiatives and efforts to promote greater understanding between Jews and Christians.

In 1954 Father Valiquette opened the first permanent Quebec office of the Canadian Council of Christians and Jews. Later, and until recently, he was co-director of the Canadian Centre for Ecumenism in Montreal, where he continued working to bring Christians and Jews closer together.

New Aspirations

The natural progression of this story should come as no surprise. The world underwent a radical change after World War II, which could not help but influence the Jews' relations with the West, and with Christians in particular. No doubt because of the Holocaust, Westerners experienced a kind of catharsis. Suddenly, the Jewish people no longer appeared to be plotting aggressors who controlled world economics and politics, but rather the innocent victims of the most widespread and odious genocide in history. This led to a sense of guilt mixed with profound sympathy, an important factor in convincing Western nations to support the founding of a Jewish homeland in Israel. It also initiated a movement of encounters and in-depth studies in Europe — primarily in Switzerland, Germany and England — which produced substantial results.

The most impressive aspect of this story remains the initiative shown by the enlightened men of the 1930s — the Sterns and Parés, the Valiquettes and Caisermans. They were dedicated to a dialogue that transcended the age-old barriers of discord and to limiting the damage caused by the anti-Semitism of their time.[8] These initiatives were met with warmth and open-mindedness by the Jews; for the Catholics, they showed evidence of a new mentality that was already evident in the famous words of Pope Pius XI: "Anti-Semitism is unacceptable. Spiritually, we are Semites."[9] This new mentality signalled a change in the aspirations of French-Quebec society. Legal concerns gave way to something else that touched the very soul of Quebec culture: its religious structure. A positive answer was finally emerging in response to the question: Can and must Quebec make ample room for other communities who do not fully share its religious and cultural convictions?

Judeo-Christian Dialogue in Montreal

Ecumenical dialogue between Jews and Christians did not officially take place in Quebec until much later, during the 1950s; shortly after the Catholics, Protestants and Orthodox Christians began meeting in the spirit of the great ecumenist from Lyon, Father Couturier.[10] This development was linked to the personal growth, or more precisely the determination, of a remarkably intuitive and courageous woman, Sister Marie-Noëlle de Baillehache. She was born in France and entered a congregation called the Sisters of Our Lady of Zion, founded in the nineteenth century by two converted Jews who had become Catholic priests, the Ratisbonne brothers of Strasbourg. This congregation and its counterpart, the Fathers of Our Lady of Zion, seemed to have lost sight of their original vocation: converting the Jews. They were focussing instead on education in various countries around the world. With the support of several priests and nuns from the twin congregations, and inspired by the founding brothers' love for the Jewish people, the young nun took a completely new approach: ecumenical openness.[11]

Once the war was over, Sister Mari-Noëlle began studying Hebrew and continued exploring Judaism, first in Israel and then in Paris at the École nationale de langues orientales and the Institut catholique. By learning Hebrew and Yiddish, she won access to the great literary works and sensitivity of the Jewish people. Her tremendous intellectual honesty and humanity accomplished the rest: when the time was ripe, she was able to count on unwavering friendships in the Jewish community.

Sister Marie-Noëlle was sent to Quebec in 1959 to accompany a group of novices in training; later she would begin editing the newsletter issued by the Ratisbonne Centre. The Centre had been founded by her community in 1960 for the purpose of converting the Jews. The newsletter became known as *Dialogue* in January 1962. She began giving talks at meetings between Jews and Catholics and made contact with the director of the Jewish Public Library, the poet Mordecai Husid, Shloime Wiseman, the principal of the Jewish People's School, and the painter Jan Menses. She also wrote articles about Jewish schools (1963) and the Jewish state.

When the Faith and Order session of the World Council of Churches met at Montreal in July 1963, Sister Marie-Noëlle commented on how isolated Quebec nuns were from the ecumenical movement. That same year, she worked with the Sisters of the Assumption and the Anglican Sisters to lay the foundations for what eventually became the Rencontres oecuméniques des religieuses (ROR). The time had come for her to make a decisive move.

She convinced the highest authorities in her community to make the Quebec Ratisbonne Centre an organization with strictly ecumenical goals, which meant renouncing all activity in any way connected with its original purpose of conversion. To mark the change as clearly as possible, she renamed the centre using a Jewish name very familiar to Christians, that of the angel Michael (meaning "Who is like God?"). From then on, the Centre Mic-Ca-El became the focal point of Judeo-Christian dialogue in Montreal. The director's new purpose was to convert not Jews but Catholics, helping them to relinquish their prejudices and traditional attitudes toward Jews. She spoke, wrote, translated, gave interviews and expanded her network of contacts. The centre also established a multilingual library whose walls were hung with works by Chagall and posters of Israel, signs of a new Catholic attitude towards the Jewish faith.

Vatican II (1962-65) confirmed this new approach. Pope John XXIII wanted the council to study the problems of Judeo-Christian relations. One of his first official acts was to create the Secretariat for Christian Unity and entrust it to Cardinal Bea, a man open to ecumenical ideas. One of the organization's primary concerns was to study the Christian roots of anti-Semitism.

Quebec was now light-years beyond the time when bishops had closed their eyes to anti-Semitic campaigns. In Montreal, Sister Marie-Noëlle's activities were sanctioned by Cardinal Paul-Émile Léger, himself one of the ecumenical spokespersons on the council. They were also supported by the Canadian Centre for Ecumenism, directed by Father Irénée Beaubien, which counted Father Stéphane Valiquette among its members. In 1964 future Cardinal Roy presided over the Congrès des étudiants en théologie at the Grand Séminaire de Québec in Quebec City, where Sister Marie-Noëlle gave a talk on Judaism. While a chaplain at the Université de Montréal, young Father Paul Grégoire assembled his Pax Romana students for an intense consideration of the post-war Jewish scene. But the most significant of this priest's initiatives (since elected a cardinal) came in 1971, when as Archbishop of Montreal, he founded the Judeo-Catholic Dialogue, which played a leading role in reconciling church and synagogue. Its contributors included people such as Father Valiquette and Sister Marie-Noëlle, until she retired to France. One of the committee's moves was to issue a formal defence of Israeli prisoners who had fallen into Syrian hands during the Yom Kippur war of 1973.[12]

The move towards ecumenism progressed more slowly among the Jews. Representatives of non-orthodox Judaism were generally favourable to reconciliation with the Christians, but strictly orthodox Jews were ambivalent. Sister Marie-Noëlle analyzed these two perspectives in 1971:

> The orthodox wing . . . is divided between resolutely separatist traditionalists for whom dialogue is not even an issue, and representatives of the "modern" faith—the vast majority in North America—who are generally ready to support the action plan developed in 1966, which bears the stamp of their leader, Rabbi Joseph Soloveitchik. Its approach can be defined more or less as follows: *accept* dialogue with Christians on subjects of religious and moral interest to all humanity, such as war and peace, civil rights, more values and the threat of secularism; however, *refuse* to discuss anything at all on the subject of private religion, doctrine or rites, since Jews and Christians are believed to operate "within incommensurable frames of reference and evaluation."[13]

Modern orthodox Jews wanted to apply the principle of dichotomy to the Judeo-Christian dialogue, distinguishing between areas common to all people, and thus to both Christians and Jews, and areas specific to each. This was a more subtle task and, in fact, more dangerous than the complete openness required in the dialogue among Christians. Like the separatist attitude of traditional orthodox Christians, it arose from the orthodox Jews' fear of the vast North American melting pot, with its tendency to erode ethnic distinctions.

There is certainly still a long way to go in developing the trust which is so essential to ecumenism. In the words of Sister Marie-Noëlle: "It takes more than two decades to change a situation that has lasted 2,000 years."[14]

The process is a difficult one. In many ways it has barely begun, if only because the issues are so immensely complex, and perhaps also because the Catholic Church has traditionally discouraged its clergy from becoming personally and publicly involved in active politics. Up to now, the dialogue has dealt with "safe" issues such as conversion, genocide and even the role of the church during the Nazi horror. The controversial questions have not been broached, though they are more relevant now than ever before: the Jews' right to establish a state in their traditional Holy Land; the attitude that should be adopted towards the PLO (whose ideology vis-à-vis the Jewish state is, to say the least, not favourable) and the Israeli government's jurisdiction at the Holy Sites.

But despite slow progress, the pioneers of the 1930s and 1950s did begin the work of opening the wall between Jews and Christians. In this sense, every advance in Quebec's Judeo-Christian dialogue is of tremendous importance for the future – not only of the Jewish community, but of other communities as well. One should note that it is in Quebec that one of the world's first such bridge-building efforts did occur.

Religious Crisis

The old Yiddish world transplanted from the *shtetl* to Montreal was basically secular, or at least agnostic, and yet its roots lay deep in Jewish tradition, which is essentially religious. As a result, traditional culture was perpetuated in the discourse of radicals. Such was the paradox of Montreal Jewry.

The community included a substantial number of practising orthodox Jews (the word "orthodox" comes from the Greek and was introduced into Judaism during the Reform era). In reality, what people referred to as "orthodox tradition" was none other than the religious practice developed and perpetuated by the Ashkenazim in Eastern Europe. It is based on a life devoted to strict observance of tradition and to lifelong religious study according to the programs of the Talmudic seminaries. It derives its inspiration from traditions of education, thought, logic, music and conversation; an atmosphere imbued with the imaginary world of the Haggadah.[15]

In Montreal as in other Yiddish communities, this religion governed every moment, act and emotion of daily life. It followed the teachings and philosophy of the ancient texts and the examples of wise and holy figures. This was the life led by men such as Irving Layton's father, Mordecai Richler's grandfather and the Quebec founders of the Myerson family; J. I. Segal had attended an orthodox synagogue. This was the spirit that permeated the writings of radicals such as Dunsky, Wiseman and Zipper. It inspired the printing of the Babylon and Jerusalem Talmuds, Dunsky's Yiddish translation of the Midrash with its commentaries and the translation of books of the Bible by Rabbi Zlotnick and H. Hirsch. It was the tradition of first-generation rabbis such as Cohen, Rosenberg and Glazer which included the Talmud Torah School teachers such as Elimelech Levine and the instructors in the neighbourhood prayer chapels.

It was a life that confirmed the centuries-old saying: "Poverty sits well on Israel." Nothing was further from consumer society than this religion, whose affinities lay with the indigence of the *shtetl* and with the streets such as Saint-Dominique and Fairmount that made up the Montreal ghetto.

This religion virtually disappeared with the Quiet Revolution of Jewish Quebecers as did ideological conflict, secularism, radicalism, Yiddish, trade unionism and populism. The post-war era witnessed the emergence of a new lifestyle geared toward development and integration within the culture represented by the English Protestant middle class. It was a time when many people made a fresh and formal commitment to Judaism, just as for Christians, it was an era of full churches. But this external commitment was not necessarily accompanied by a deepening of ancient tradition for either group.

The new Montreal Jews became complacent in their urban, Western religion. They moved into comfortable neighbourhoods, leaving the *shulchelach*—little prayer rooms—behind and congregating around a smaller number of large, beautiful synagogues. These became community centres where the rabbi presided as he should and where people displayed all the proper signs of courtesy and mutual respect. In such a thoroughly polite and homogeneous environment, there was little room for the old folklore, theological arguments, Talmudic dialectic and clash of ideas. Bulldozers and graders smoothed over the differences in tone and personality, blurring colourful distinctions and diverse traditions. The religious spectrum became obscured and affiliations with the Cincinnati and New York "Vaticans," something completely foreign to Jewish tradition, did nothing to help.

But precisely because of their social, geographic and ideological accessibility, these synagogues efficiently fulfilled their role as meeting places open to everyone. Paying synagogue dues was new to Judaism, but now it became a sort of registration ritual in the local community. The dues almost always reflected the neighbourhood where the synagogue was located.

Attending services, particularly during holidays, became a way for many members to maintain contact and cohesion. The rabbi's sermons and advice were a part of community life and synagogue newsletters served as lines of communication.

It is difficult to describe or quantify the cultural religiousness of these communities, for it is impossible to compile statistics on personal commitment to prayer and dietary laws. Should synagogue attendance be interpreted as a purely social gesture, a socio-cultural act that consolidates and cements a community, or as the expression of a faith or belief? Do people keep their own kitchens kosher to comply with Jewish law, while eating seafood in restaurants, or are they attempting to maintain a traditional family atmosphere? More significantly, does not the adherence to kosher law simply reflect the traditional Jews horror at the sight of lobster, shrimp and bacon, or milk served on a table next to meat?

It is difficult to quantify religion just as it is difficult to pinpoint the religious motivation of Montreal's Jews and formulate a precise idea of how they maintain community contact. It is well known that a closely-observed chameleon changes its identity as it changes colour.

Anyone wishing to understand the spiritual life of Jewish uebecers comes up against one undeniable fact: the various traditions of Talmudic study and the many practices codified in the *Shulchan Aruch* (the Halakah, or legal part of the Talmud) are in the process of losing the unique place they held until recently for Jewish communities, and even for many contemporary rabbis. The essence of these religious traditions is no longer the distinctive mark of Jewish institutions nor, with some exceptions, the defining characteristic of Montreal Jews.

But just how has their relation to Judaism changed? Is it more universal, stronger and deeper than before? Is it more than a formal, external adherence to a credo? Does it take other forms, whether national, social, ethical, linguistic, cultural or familial? Do people express their faith through sharing in the fate of the Jewish nation, exploring Jewish literature or helping to keep a collective watch over the Jewish state – so very important to the community – and over a people rescued from the flames of history? Is there a heightening of national feeling; a deep sense of emotional and intellectual concentration so intense as to suggest ties to the community, family and history?

So many questions remain unanswered. And yet one fact remains: today's synagogue responds adequately to the new post-war Jewish society. It reflects the spirit and ideology that has produced this new generation of Montreal Jews and it will serve to ensure their collective survival.

The Disaffected

The Christian world has always known dissidence and reform movements. It has regularly faced disaffected members who reject traditional church structures and dream of going back to the beginning; to the primitive church. In post-war Quebec, this religious quest has taken various forms – pentecostal groups, scientologists, fundamentalists and charismatics. It has led people to seek inspiration in Asian religions and to practice meditation in the Hindu, Buddhist and Sufi traditions.

Jews have not escaped this contemporary phenomenon any more than the Christians. They too have a back-to-the-roots movements, whose goals are ultimately very close to traditional orthodoxy.[16] It is characterized by strict religious observance and an adverse reaction to the big, middle-class synagogues. These large institutions no longer met the needs of disaffected youth in search of guides (to aid them through their psychological, social, philosophical and religious questioning) as well as profound personal experiences.

These radicals seek truth everywhere—among prophets, unknown saints, dreamers, leaders, commentators and mystics—but especially in Israel, where there are many different schools and groups to welcome them. The phenomenon is difficult to define, for each person tells a different story. Together, they are often called penitents (*Baaleh Tshuvah* or *Chozreh Bitshuvah*).

The Hasidim

The single largest sect within this movement is the Hasidic renewal (from *Hasidim*, meaning "pious ones"). Hasidism is a difficult phenomenon to grasp in all its complexity. It is associated with a Judaic tradition known as the Cabala (meaning tradition), which is often translated incorrectly as "Jewish mysticism."

Believers trace the origins of the Cabala to the ancient authorities of the Jewish religion. This school of thought teaches an esoteric reading of the Bible, reserved for the privileged few who can understand it. The uninitiated, it is said, would only distort the meaning. Devout Hasidim and doubters alike have traditionally kept its secrets from being divulged and have utilized various means to thwart attempts at popularization. Therein lies the difficulty involved in understanding the sect and its history. All we know is that the tradition resurfaces from time to time and that a number of Jewish figures have taught the Cabalistic doctrines, adopting at the same time a particular religious behaviour.

Israel Baal Shem Tov (Master of the Good Name, 1698-1760) was one of these figures. He disseminated his Hasidic teachings to disciples who were then authorized to do the same, unleashing a great popular movement of mystic devotion in the provinces of southern Poland. This provoked lively opposition by the *mitnagdim*. The result was a deep schism within Eastern European orthodoxy that prevailed until the desolation of the Holocaust in the 1940s. In the interim, Hasidism spread throughout Europe. It accumulated a vast wealth of teachings, folklore, hagiography and music that have had a significant influence on Jewish culture, even in its secular form. In the *shtetl*, it created a separate Jewish community—a Hasidic world.

Neo-Hasidism

After the war, young Jews studying the works of the great religious masters met with the surviving *rebbe'im tzadikim* (saints) and charismatic leaders from the Polish communities, who had survived the extermination camps. A number of these *rebbe'im* (not to be confused with *rabbanism*, or rabbis) set up communities and yeshivas, or schools, in New York. But one, the Rebbe from Tash, chose Quebec.

The neo-Hasidim are known for their often aggressive preaching and conversion methods, including the use of modern media such as satellite television. They predict the imminent arrival of the Messiah and are able to create very strong ties within their groups. Followers of the Liubavitch, Satmar, Squir and Bobov *rebbe'im* have attracted many new neo-Hasidim to their communities.

Most Hasidim minimize contact with other Jews, even the devout. They have their own synagogues, schools and community centres. Their communities are strictly self-contained, except in the case of the Liubavitch Hasidim, who work outside the group to convert other Jews.

The Hasidim and their *rebbe'im* have little to do with the activities of the rest of the Jewish community. Their attitude to Israel is often ambiguous or even openly hostile. This problem offers more than one analogy to the highly complex international politics within Israel itself.

Unforeseen Directions

The search for religious and philosophical truth has led many young Jews far from the origins and paths of Judaism, sometimes as far as Asia. Like many other young Canadians and Americans, they have joined groups that practise meditation, an open window on other traditions and psychological experiences. At the same time, they have distanced themselves from the concerns of their own community. In that sense, their choices constitute a loss for the community and a threat to its survival.[17]

Culturally and spiritually, they have added their own contemporary chapter to the history of a community that continues to revere its Yiddish poets, secular theorists, pre-1917 revolutionaries and *chakranim* (perpetual speculators), as well as its folklore and the social life of the *shtetl*.

Arrival of the French-Speaking Jews

Of the 95,000 people who make up Montreal's Jewish community, about 20,000 are francophones. Most have immigrated to Quebec since the end of the war. Some are from Europe and others are from the Near East, but most came from North Africa.[18] All are linked to the world Jewish community by a great branch of the Jewish family that originated in Spain and Portugal, countries the Jews fled during the fifteenth century as they scattered throughout the ancient Ottoman Empire.

The francophone Sephardic community is of considerable interest to Quebec. It constitutes the province's largest influx of French culture since the conquest and affirms the undeniably "bicultural" nature of the Jewish community, which has too often been identified with the English. The Jews are unquestionably the most bicultural of the province's communities, including the original French Quebecers. It is interesting to note that no other groups of recent immigrants has been the subject of as many scientific studies.

Sephardic immigration began in the 1950s as North African countries gained political independence (Morocco and Tunisia in 1956, Algeria in 1962), and reached its peak from 1965 to 1967. Islamic-based Arab nationalism and tension between Israel and its neighbours forced the Jewish minorities in those countries to seek refuge elsewhere. Most peasants and craftspeople went to Israel, while the urban middle class of professionals, civil servants, specialized workers and students set out for France and North America. This accounts for the high level of French education among Quebec Sephardim.

More than one parallel can be drawn between the original Jewish community in Lower Canada[19] and the most recent one, despite the 200 years separating them. Both are linked to the Sephardic tradition, one through its connection to the Sephardic synagogue in London and the other through its roots in the Mediterranean branch of Sephardic Judaism. Cultural differences have undoubtedly evolved during the long period separating them, but the essential link remains intact. They share the same ritual language (Hebrew) and the same devotion to orthodox tradition.

In addition, both communities were prepared for joining Quebec society by a long period of acculturation. The earlier immigrants had lived in England, while the Sephardim came from Islamic countries that were strongly influenced by French culture. Their elite studied at French lycées in Morocco, Algeria and Tunisia and often earned degrees from French universities. This cultural factor contributed not only to their choice of Quebec as a place to settle, but also to their more rapid, almost spontaneous adoption by French Quebecers. Similarly the British background of the eighteenth-century Sephardic settlers had facilitated their integration into the English society of that period, as Ben Kayfetz has suggested in the case of Toronto.[20]

Still another analogy can be drawn, this time between the Mediterranean Sephardim and the early Ashkenazim who arrived prior to the great migration of the late nineteenth century. The immigrants from North Africa, like those from Eastern Europe, experienced difficulty in being accepted by the established Jewish community and by Quebec society as a whole. As we have seen, the German-Polish congregation was born out of opposition by the Sephardim of the mother community. Despite an unquestionably friendly welcome, the French-speaking Sephardim met with similar resistance from Montreal's Jewish community, which had moved away from its original Sephardic roots and embraced the Ashkenazic tradition.

Choosing a Culture

The first wave of Sephardic immigrants came to Quebec because they were attracted by the language. But on the well-intentioned advice of the venerable JIAS (Jewish Immigration Aid Society) no doubt, an organization that has been assisting Jewish immigrants since 1920, the French-speaking newcomers settled in neighbourhoods where the poorer members of the existing Jewish community lived (Park Avenue and St. Urbain Street, Outremont and especially Côte-des-Neiges). These areas were close to Jewish services and institutions that were operated, needless to say, by English-speaking Ashkenazim.

Like their predecessors of 1880, the new immigrants felt a strong need to stay together. In 1959 they founded a recreation centre-the Association juive nord-africaine or AJNA—and cherished the dream of a full-fledged Sephardic community centre.

The Quebec school system was ill-prepared for the sudden influx of a whole generation of French-speaking students who were neither Protestant nor Catholic. The Catholic system simply did not have structures in place for neutral students, while the Protestants had never adequately developed their French section, even for Protestant students. For its part, the existing Jewish community always associated and even identified with the English-speaking milieu and therefore had no French institutions to offer the North African immigrants. In all good faith, it actually believed that it was doing the North Africans a service by helping them integrate into the English system, just as it had for the Jews from Eastern Europe.

At its plenary session in Toronto in June 1962, the Canadian Jewish Congress was informed of the integration problems faced by the Sephardim. The Congress responded by advising the new arrivals to integrate into the Anglophone Jewish milieu, adding that they should no longer consider themselves the community's poor relations. To understand this attitude, it is useful to keep in mind that in addition to the Canadian Jews' longstanding affinity for the English-speaking community, the world's Ashkenazic Jews outnumber the Sephardim fourteen to one.

While the Congress's response may have seemed magnanimous in the eyes of Anglophone Jews, it was hardly satisfactory to the Sephardic community. This was their answer:

> As you know, our community's educational and cultural foundation is French. When our immigrants chose to live in Quebec, considered a French province, most hoped to provide their children with a French education. You can understand our disappointment when our children were forced to interrupt their French studies to be educated strictly in English.[21]

The Sephardim knew what was at stake in the drive to preserve their French cultural heritage and pass it on to their children. They also recognized the importance of the unique and irreplaceable role they could play in Quebec as members of the Jewish community: "These grievances are intensified by the francophones' desire to serve as a link between French Canadian society and the Anglophone Jewish community, of which it nonetheless wishes to remain an integral part."[22]

The Sephardic community steadfastly pursued its threefold objective: to remain a full member of the Quebec Jewish community, to preserve its adopted French culture and to act as a bridge between the province's Anglophone Jews and French-Canadian majority.

French Schools and Sephardic Synagogues

The Sephardim who wanted to transmit their cultural and religious heritage to their children had a limited choice: they could send the children to private schools or opt for assimilation into English by entering either the Protestant system or the Talmud Torah schools, which taught Jewish studies in the Ashkenazic tradition. The situation was made more critical by the fact that Montreal did not yet have a North African Sephardic synagogue. One observer even claimed that the community had to fight certain directors in its own association, the AJNA:

> We pressured the directors of the AJNA to pressure the Montreal Catholic School Commission and Department of Public Education, the forerunner of Quebec's Department of Education, so that our children could finally be admitted to French schools. The AJNA executive replied that they would do what they could, but that we shouldn't hope for too much, since we were in America and had to fit in with the economic majority/minority, which was English. In short, they (the community leaders) never acted, and it is their fault that a substantial number of adult Sephardim today are assimilated into the English community.[23]

Sephardic immigration to Quebec reached its peak between 1965 and 1967, as Canada relaxed its quotas for North African Jews. The same problems faced by the earlier immigrants now had to be handled on a much larger scale. The time had come for decisive action.

In 1965 a new committee was set up under the guidance of the Jewish Immigrant Aid Society and the Jewish Public Library, and called the Fédération séfarade des Juifs de langue française. It was replaced the following year by an association that eventually became the main organ of the Quebec francophone community: the *Association séfarade francophone* (ASF).

From then on, the Sephardic community began to set up a network of institutions to meet its growing numbers and needs. These included five synagogues, two community centres (one in Chomedey, the other in Montreal), a French Hillel House at the Université de Montréal, the Hevra Hakadisha[24] and a French section at the "Y" (Young Men's/Young Women's Hebrew Association), all added between 1966 and 1968.

The creation of the French section at the "Y" in 1967 was a good illustration of the kind of integration problems experienced by the young Sephardic community. Francophones had completely abandoned the "Y," and in a memo addressed to the organization, community leader Dr. Jean-Claude Lasry explained that this was because its personnel was English-speaking: "Since these organizers work exclusively in English, it is easier for our young people to go to French-Canadian centres. This could sooner or later result in a degree of community breakdown."[25]

His remarks were taken seriously and two francophones were hired a few months later. They were James Dahan, organizer of the francophone district of the "Y" and Léon Ouaknine, director and one of the founders of the Jewish Community Centre.

Lasry went further in his memo, calling for more aggressive francization of all Jewish agencies, particularly the JIAS and the Baron de Hirsch Institute. At the same time the ASF resumed its struggle with Canadian and Quebec Jewish institutions to obtain French schools.

The Jewish establishment began opening its eyes to the "French fact." A whole new image of a francophone Quebec emerged during the Quiet Revolution and the 1970s in particular. In Montreal, the Anglophone Jewish community quickly became aware of this and sought ways to adapt to the new situation.

At its fifteenth plenary session in May 1968, twelve years after the first North African Jews began arriving in Quebec, the Canadian Jewish Congress decided to support their fundamental option to choose French:

> The Canadian Jewish Congress, through representation from the eastern region, shall assist the ASF in creating a school that will enable children whose mother tongue is French to receive an education which respects the following criteria:
> 1) Education in the Jewish culture and its traditional values;
> 2) Education in the French language and preservation of cultural heritage.[26]

Quebec's Response

In just a few months, discussions between the Sephardic community, the government and the church produced something that 200 years of French-Jewish relations in Quebec had failed to obtain. Their achievement was an indication of the changing climate in the province, reflected in educational pluralism, immigration and the openness of the Catholic Church to Vatican II policies. It was also a sign of the progress made by French Quebecers in the area of ethno-cultural relations since the 1930s.

In August 1969 Jean-Claude Lasry chaired a joint committee representing the Association séfarade francophone and the Canadian Jewish Congress. It met with the Deputy Minister of Education, Yves Martin, to discuss implementation of the motion passed by the CJC in May 1968. The project was approved by the Catholic authorities, and the Montreal Catholic School Commission gave a wing of Saint-Antoine School to the Sephardic community the following month. The École Maimonides was born.

The École Maimonides was a turning point, and in light of the 1930s, a minor miracle in the history of Quebec intercultural relations. It was a practical consecration of the principle that Jewish Quebecers could now count on cooperation of the government as well as the French Catholic community, and that other new communities would be able to do the same.

The dream of the Sephardim was fulfilled in 1972. The École Maimonides, which they controlled, was recognized as an institution of "public interest" and the Minister of Education, François Cloutier, presided over the inauguration of its new premisses. This recognition gave the school new status as a private educational institution eligible for government subsidies. The initial subsidy stood at 50 percent but in 1978 rose to 80 percent, the same as for other private French and English schools.

Jewish Community Centre

Maimonides School, however, did not represent a final victory in the Sephardic community's battle to affirm its cultural identity. Jewish institutions in Montreal had long been steeped in a tradition of Anglophone assimilation, and they required more than a few short years to adapt to francophone needs. One such institution was Neighbourhood House Service (NHS),[27] an organization offering daycare, kindergarten and day camp services to immigrants. Its board was mostly Anglophone and "continued to pursue a policy of assimilation. The French-speaking element or character of the community was considered a kind of 'accident of history' that had to be 'incorporated' in the same way that Romanians, Russians, Hungarians and others had previously been assimilated."[28]

Francophone Jews literally began to dismantle the structures of the NHS in 1969. Léon Ouaknine became a full-time social coordinator in charge of a men's recreation department. The continuing education committee gradually became independent. By March 1970 it included thirteen Sephardic groups and associations, who united to form the Union des organismes séfarades de Montréal. Francophones joined the NHS board of directors the same year for the first time and opened a department for young adults. The movement culminated in 1971 with the complete reorganization of NHS: it was renamed the Jewish Community Centre (JCC) and chose a francophone president, Mr. Elalouf. The Centre's clientele changed rapidly, from mostly English in 1968 to mostly French (75%) in 1973.[29]

In 1971 the Jewish Community Council became a multidisciplinary organization committed to community development. One of the many problems faced by the Sephardim at that time was the anxiety of francophone children attending the English schools of the Protestant School Board of Greater Montreal.

The new board of directors quickly formed an action committee composed of members from the PSBGM, Canadian Jewish Congress, JIAS and the Association sépharade francophone. One of its initiatives was to hire social workers who could make the Sephardic community more aware of the sociological, psychological and familial problems experienced by children undergoing cultural immersion within the English schools. The Centre thus worked with schools and families alike, making schools more aware of the educational problems at issue and stimulating the parents' interest in French education.

Sephardic Integration

Despite the fact its members spoke the language of the majority, the Sephardic community faced the same difficulties as other immigrant groups when attempting to integrate into Quebec society. Generally speaking, its sociological profile was typical of any young community adapting to a new society. The following table was compiled by Fernand G. Filion for the year 1972:

No profession	27%
Owners, managers	5%
Liberal professions, technicians	8%
Small business	7%
Office workers	32%
Sales personnel	4%
Service employees	5%
Skilled labourers (specialized or not)	11%
Unskilled labourers	1%

It would seem that the Quebec Sephardim had reached a kind of social plateau. And yet the community had made spectacular breakthroughs in twenty years, of which the École Maimonides was just one. Today, members of the community are civil servants, social workers, doctors and nurses, journalists, film makers and even politicians. The Université de Montréal has helped welcome the francophone Jews by establishing a programme of Jewish studies under the guidance of Professor Jean Ouellette.

Filion also studied the marriage patterns of North African Jews in Quebec for the decade 1962-72. The proportion of Ashkenazic and Sephardic Jews who married within the faith was 93 percent;[31] among North African Jews, however, the number dropped to 50 percent (33% of women and 61% of men).[32] This indicates the importance of cultural affinities between francophones, but it also points to the lack of facilities for the Sephardim within the Jewish community itself.

Precursors of the New French-Jewish Reconciliation

It is possible, of course, that shared language and culture partly masked the "Jewishness" of the Sephardim in the eyes of French Quebecers. Were this true, it would indicate that French Quebec had still not relinquished the standard image of the Jew as a member of the English community, with all that image represents from the traditional perspective of the two solitudes.[33]

This is why the francophone Sephardim play such an important role in Quebec's Jewish-French relations. To the extent that they defend their French culture against assimilation by the Anglophone Jews, while at the same time maintaining a fundamental solidarity with them, the Sephardim help "repatriate" the Quebec Jewish community. In other words, they renew the tradition of an older Quebec which, for more than a hundred years, welcomed the first Jewish immigrants with unparalleled openness.

The 1976 Crisis

When the Parti Québécois came to power in November 1976 the Jewish community experienced a crisis whose effects have yet to be fully assessed. The crisis once again unmasked deep-rooted tendencies that have often gone unrecognized in Quebec society.

The election victory may have taken the English and the Jews by surprise, but not for lack of warning. The wall separating the "solitudes" is what prevented them from perceiving the depth and character of the nationalism sweeping French Quebec. Courses dealing with Quebec and its history were not part of the English school curriculum and Anglophones were not involved in the internal organization of Quebec's political parties.

The Anglophone community thus could not know of the aspirations and degree of dissatisfaction that existed in the province. The mood was not limited to particular groups; it had overtaken the entire population. The nationalist vote has always been a prime target of party strategy in Quebec, and by then it had become a barometer to measure the degree of public dissatisfaction that could be translated into separatism. This is yet another subtlety of Quebec's political tradition and a feature of French Quebec culture.

Without a fully integrated school system capable of presenting Quebec issues on both sides of the wall separating the two solitudes, Jewish immigrants and their descendants could only perceive Quebec as a kind of blessed land where even the unskilled, uneducated new immigrant could blossom in freedom. In their dreams, they envied the original French and English Quebecers for their mastery of one or both official languages, each universal; for being able to elect and overthrow two levels of government, provincial and federal; for their churches, powerful institutions with influence extending far beyond their walls. Quebecers were also envied for having and administering their own schools and universities; for having an army at its disposal and a civil service (all of the provincial and part of the federal); for creating political parties, establishing historic sites and patrolling their own borders. They could make mistakes, hold prejudices and even obstruct others in their own land, all within the limits of the law. Those who tried to advance the cause of their people, considering this a right, were not always able to mobilize the community effectively. Nor did they dare to call on new Quebecers in the name of fraternal patriotism. Just whose responsibility was it to make the first overtures? Who should have taken the initiative?

A widespread ignorance of French Quebec's own version of "Zionism" was just one of several particularly aggravating factors that accounted for the reaction of Quebec Jews, both Anglophone and francophone, to the 1976 election.

Like other Quebecers, the Jews are citizens of Canada as well as Quebec. They have adapted to the constitutional balance of the two founding nations. However, they are unusual in that historically, they have been admitted into the country by the Federal Government, usually a Liberal one. One of the many ways they expressed their attachment to the nation was by their considerable contribution to the war effort.

When the Jewish state was being created, Canada became a sponsor of the new nation through the intermediary of the Minister for External Affairs, Lester B. Pearson,[34] whose courageous stance helped convince the United Nations to approve the partition plan. There were many other political and social links between the Jews, the Federal Government and the Liberal party. The other Canadian parties could not maintain similar contacts and the left-wing parties could not weaken them.

There was therefore no valid reason for Quebec Jews to be discontented and wish to weaken or rupture ties with the Federal Government. For them, a "Yes" in the 1980 referendum was dangerous, to say the least.

But there was more to the situation. The Jews viewed the progress of the Quiet Revolution (begun under the previous government) with a certain anxiety. For a century, Quebec anti-Semites had all been nationalists, while the fascists had all been separatists and anti-Semites. These three groups appears to share a common identity. The ideologies they promoted, it seemed, had been quelled.

Nevertheless, memories of Arcand and Groulx, of church teachings, of editorials in *Le Devoir* and *L'Action catholique* were still fresh in the minds of Jewish Quebecers. None of the former leaders had been repudiated by the "Yes" movement. On the contrary, Duplessis and Groulx were about to be honoured publicly by the nationalists.

In other developments, the Parti Québécois had established contact with the PLO[35] and begun to distance itself from Israel,[36] while its leader expressed sympathy toward the Munich terrorists.[37]

Too often, the nationalist desire for change was expressed in a tone of demand tinged with revenge. The Jews had no guarantee that the movement would escape the pitfalls of hatred and excess.

The nationalist movement attracted an impressive range of highly diverse opinion and united people of widely differing convictions; extremists and moderates, believers and non-believers, unionists, fascists, racists, revenge-seekers, intellectuals, workers and artists all found themselves rubbing shoulders. The Parti Québécois had welcomed some of these groups, maintained contact with others and silenced still others, all with the greatest political discretion.

It is very important to be aware that the PQ coalition and the peripheral nationalist groups differed in their ideologies and objectives for Quebec society. Would it be monolithic by race, religion and colour? By equal rights? Language? Social justice? Who would be able to enjoy freedom in the new Quebec? What would an independent Quebec have to offer, and to whom? Some of the answers to these questions aroused and justified Jewish apprehensions while others were reassuring. But exactly who would finally answer them?

Everything rested on the man who had built the PQ coalition: René Lévesque. He possessed immense skill as a political planner and organizer of people, groups and strategies. But there was danger in his very talent. The outcome hinged on the intensity and duration of his political wizardry, the limits of his power and his own longevity. The future was being cast on fragile foundations and the situation invited catastrophe.

Another important point is that about a third of Jewish Quebecers were survivors of the European experience. They had seen political and social upheaval in Poland, Romania, Hungary, Lithuania, Germany and communist Russia. They had witnessed the development of nationalism, patriotism, political revenge, fascism and xenophobia. They understood the relation between economic boycotting and anti-Semitism, as well as its outcome in the death camp ovens.

Given their history, the Jews could not remain indifferent to the political changes of 1976, which were having a real impact on the public psyche. This reaction was noted – and even exaggerated – by outside observers attempting to write about Quebec. There is no doubt that a whole new body of literature has yet to be written on the reactions of Quebec francophones, Anglophones, Jews and business people to the events of 1976 and 1977.

We must also recall that this period was just one moment in an entire era lasting from 1960 to 1980, and that many of the after-effects of 1976-77 would likely have occurred even if specific events had not. Oil would have continued to gush in Alberta and Trudeau would still have wielded his power from coast to coast. Many businesses and business people would have moved. Toronto would have continued to grow and Montreal would have become more French in character, for better or worse.

In fact, it was the acceleration of several historical processes that shook Quebec Jews to such an extent. The Jewish community had espoused, for a number of years, an open attitude toward the French language Quebec culture. The Cercle juif de langue française was created within the Canadian Jewish Congress in 1948 by Rabbi Solomon Frank, S. D. Cohen and M. H. Myerson. Among its visiting lecturers were André Laurendeau, Gérard Filion, Father Émile Legault, Mme Thérèse Gasgrain and Jacques Madaule. The writings of Naïm Kattan were published; Le fait français committee was founded and French signs were displayed on public buildings such as the Jewish Public Library and the Canadian Jewish Congress. Following its 1976 election victory, the Lévesque government suddenly adopted Bill 101. The law was designed to restore the French face of Quebec and, above all, to promote a lifestyle more in keeping with the majority francophone culture. But it also contained clauses that many people believed discriminatory, including those dealing with signs, civil service language testing and, most importantly, restricted access to English schools for children whose parents were from outside the province.

Most members of Jewish community did not seem unduly concerned about the legislation. At least that was the feeling of spokesperson Alan Rose, executive vice-president of the Canadian Jewish Congress:

The Jewish community is adapting more and more to the changes in Quebec. We agree with the main objective of Bill 101, which is to protect the French language. Quebec is fundamentally moderate. . . . I do not say anti-Semitism couldn't happen again, but I don't think it is the issue. There is right now no overt anti-Semitism in Quebec."[38]

In fact, the rare outbursts of surprise and insecurity among Quebec Jews came from people who identified with the reactions of the Anglophone community. This was true of Montreal industrialist Charles Bronfman who, speaking to a Jewish audience on the eve of the 1976 election, threatened to pull his capital out of Quebec if the PQ won (he would later apologize for his remarks). This was essentially the case for two young Montrealers as well, S. Perel, a student at McMaster University in Hamilton, and H. Srebrenik, an instructor at Dawson College in Montreal. On January 22, 1982 they published an alarmist article in the Israeli newspaper the *Jerusalem Post*,[39] denouncing Bill 101 and concluding that all French Quebecers were anti-Semitic. The Canadian Jewish Congress and the B'Nai B'rith Human Rights League both publicly criticized the article as a complete distortion of the situation.[40]

Another important historical factor was the shift of economic activity westward. Many young Quebecers left to try their luck outside the province. This movement was beneficial to Toronto. It also helped Montreal affirm its French personality and character, thus enriching the entire nation.

From this point of view, the astonishing fact is not that Quebec lost some 15,000 members of the Jewish community during those two decades, but that it failed to lose many more.

Emotions played a decisive role in the process. This critical period kindled a desire on all sides to limit the damage to Quebec.

It is important to recognize that the PQ government, far from demonstrating hostility toward the Jews, openly rejected anti-Semitism. It backs its words with financial aid to Jewish schools, helping the community maintain the Jewish character of the education network, as it had previously done for hospitals and social services. Many of the gestures seemed politically motivated, however, and they did not alter the government's insensitivity on the sacrosanct subject of Israel. This may have been due in part to the lack of qualified interpreters in both camps. Once again, the wall separating the two cultures remained intact.

The Jews were quick to realize the gravity of the situation, and Charles Bronfman convinced the community to take a number of positive measures. Michael Yarosky, Director of the Community Research Committee, set up contacts at various social and political levels in Quebec. The community responded to its francophone members by setting up a series of institutions through which it could express its French character. The magazine *Jonathan* and other Jewish periodicals were as impressive as similar English publications, and the collection at the Institut québécois de la recherche sur la culture introduced major works on Jewish literature in Quebec.

Even more importantly, the 1976 crisis forced each member of every Jewish household to examine his or her personal attachment to the province. This is what kept emigration from rising even higher. Parents and children asked themselves how far they should trust Quebec society. They questioned their resolve to accept French in order to deepen their sensitivity to the quality of life in Quebec. They even pondered the moral weight of family tombstones in synagogue cemeteries and the price they attached to the history and traditions of the Montreal Jewish community. They reflected on their roots.

The "crisis of 1976" is now twenty-five years old. Referendum, constitution — what next? There are new prospects, new issues, new challenges, new openings, new restraints on commitment. This crisis, which provoked such anxiety, activity and upheaval, is certain to have far-reaching and lasting effects on Jews and other Canadians alike.

New Community Spirit

One word can be used to describe the hidden force driving post-war Jewish society in Quebec: activism. Jews wanted to act; everyone had a particular cause or organization to support. Rarely did people ask which one was most important to the continuity of the community. Underlying all this activism was an unspoken understanding that the social bonds created and maintained by the activities themselves constituted the common good of the community. The entire process was coordinated by the Canadian Jewish Congress and reflected in its structure.

The new democratic climate mobilized a vast number of volunteers. The thousands of donors and contributors included women, young people, administrators of schools, hospitals, synagogues and centres for seniors, less well-off militants, Zionists and participants in social clubs and summer camps. They also included campaign organizers for various causes such as the plight of Soviet or Ethiopian Jews, technical schools in Europe, families of Israeli soldiers and childrens' centres in the Holy Land.

Each agency and group had its own directors who were well established and respected in the community. Scandal was unknown in Jewish organizations.

This outpouring of initiative and achievement was grounded in common convictions, ideals and loyalties. The community movement often appeared chaotic and lacked established traditions and authority, yet during its long (more than 100 years) and active involvement within the community it had established its own — sometimes unwritten — set of practices, structures and rules.

Combined Jewish Appeal

The broad consensus that developed after World War II led to the launching of a fund-raising and planning organization called the Combined Jewish Appeal. It has become a truly common front founded on mutual trust and the absence of ideology. Indeed, the new post-war community resolutely closed the chapter on the ideological tension and conflict that had rocked the community in the past and sometimes torn it apart. Factions had no place in a new homogeneous society that agreed on one supreme value: action.

The Combined Jewish Appeal made it possible to streamline many tasks and functions including, to a certain extent, volunteer services. At present, the annual fund-raising drive alone raises millions of dollars and attracts thousands of volunteers. It is Canadian Jewry's most important institution.

In Montreal, CJA operations are centralized at the Allied Jewish Community Services on Côte-Sainte-Catherine Road. AJCS coordinates the administration of hospitals, social projects, libraries and programmes for young people and seniors. It also acts as liaison with various government agencies.

This superstructure is served by a team of professionals whose qualifications are steadily improving. Government has increased its involvement in volunteer organizations that were previously more independent, and the level of professional training has improved as a result.

Canadian Jewish Congress

Activities and issues of national scope are handled by the Canadian Jewish Congress, a coordinating body headquartered in Montreal. The very structure of the Congress represents an attempt to create harmony among the many opinions and activities of the Canadian diaspora. Its members include delegates from practically every Jewish organization, from Vancouver Island to Newfoundland, who meet every three years to approve an action plan and elect a new board of directors. Business is done through resolutions, discussion and open candidacy, in a spirit of total consensus. The CJC is dedicated to nothing less than the pressing needs of world Judaism; to issues that affect individuals, the Jewish people and humanity as a whole. These needs change constantly from country to country and involve everything from expulsions to immigration bans, economic boycotts and the erosion of civil rights.

The Canadian Jewish Congress was created by a group of young Jewish intellectuals early this century. Their goal was to establish an organization that could serve as a tool for the Canadian diaspora in responding to the incessant litany of problems and misfortunes experienced by Jews around the world. The project succeeded in Canada despite opposition which, in other countries, brought similar efforts to a standstill.

Today, the new community of Jewish Quebecers continues to meet challenges that the Congress has faced during the past seventy years, be it education, internal organization, civic activities or international aid to Jews. It also continues to promote religion, culture, archival research and government relations on various levels. And yet, despite—or perhaps because of—this impressive development of initiative and organization, one wonders whether the community will be able to cope with the latest threat to diasporas around the world: ideological demobilization. Contemporary, profit-oriented society tends to transform various fields of human activity into the cogs of a gigantic machine, from commercial sport, with its interchangeable stars shuttling from one city or even continent to another, to the media, which feeds us news emanating from a handful of press agencies in Paris, London and Moscow.

The issue is vital to Quebec Jews at this point in their history. Beyond the obstacles and threats that commonly obstruct their path, the major challenge facing the Jews in Quebec and around the world remains continuity, now more than ever before.

CHAPTER V

Where Is the Jewish Community Headed?

"In Canada today Jewish people live under conditions
of freedom which have not been exceeded anywhere in
the world."[1]

The Challenge of Continuity

Where do today's Jewish Quebecers stand? Where can they find a response to
the challenge of continuity they have always faced? Probably in the same
place Judaism has always looked, especially since the time of the Talmud: the
daily life of the community.

Long ago, when rabbis sought to formulate the essence of wisdom and
morality for the Jewish nation, they drew on popular experience. Disputes
were ultimately settled by custom (*minhag*) – according to one old saying,
"Custom breaks the law." Folklore has always played a predominant role in
Jewish culture.

The new Jewish society is perpetuated in the neighbourhoods of Snowdon,
Hampstead and Ville Saint-Laurent, at home as well as in cars, airplanes and
restaurants and meetings of groups and institutions. Its new middle-class
respectability does not tend toward controversy or ideological debate. Individuals take their place in the Jewish family by participating in its activities.
Private life, family life, friendships, associations and business are all woven
together in interpersonal relations, the very fabric of the community. It thrives
in this context, which in turn defines and consolidates Jewish society. Its fruits
are almost always harvested in community life rather than in solitude.

The Jews live in a society full of diversity, with its own structures, personalities and leaders. Its impromptu teachers lack professional training, but are
prepared to justify their activities and convince others to join them. Over the
centuries, the community has offered its members highly advanced study programs outside the schools. Knowledge has been shared in the *chevrot* (where

---

Notes for Chapter V are found on pages 176-77.

the Bible, Talmud, Midrashim and legal codes are studied) as well as in sermons, Zionist study groups, adult education courses, youth groups and summer camps. These programs complement the education provided by Jewish schools, study tours, trips to Israel and the retreats in the country, borrowed from Catholic tradition.

This immense effort to involve people as fully as possible in community activity raises other questions. What is, or should be, the focus of this activity, and what criteria can be used to establish priorities and an overall perspective? These questions, however, are not as compelling as they were in the past. Nowadays, the community establishes its priorities by reaching a consensus on current affairs: the economic and military crisis in Israel, the appearance of an anti-Semite in Alberta or a writer denying the existence of the Holocaust, legislation threatening the rights of Jews in Canada or Ethiopia, educational problems in the schools; all these issues have a place on the agenda. Each cause soon finds its champions and the community launches into action.

The Jewish community too, then, has experienced a Quiet Revolution. It has moved away from the ideological struggles of the period when Yiddish values were at the forefront to post-war activism; from social and political tension to unity in action. The architects of this revolution have been the men and women of action whose numbers now almost equal the Jewish population itself.

Quebec Today

However we interpret French Quebec's Quiet Revolution, one thing is clear: Quebec as a whole has reached a major turning point in its history. It is also clear that the Jewish community, which has bound its fate to that of Quebec, must face a pressing concern that surfaces here and there throughout the diaspora: the shape of the future. When all is said and done, the Jews' future in Quebec is closely tied to Quebec's future in Canada.

Where is Quebec headed now, with its heterogeneity, social and political structures, majority-minority relations and collective mentality? Above all, how will the current nationalism of French Quebecers come into play: their self-image as a people and a nation; their cultural attachment, history, folklore and political traditions; the network of associations and organizations that promote their collective interests? What will their role be in Canada, North America and the world?

Without analyzing this nationalism any further, we can safely state that it differs from the traditional Quebec nationalism of the pre-war years, which was centred on survival. The earlier movement was fuelled by the myth of ethnic purity, and cultivated carefully by certain intellectuals. They believed that as descendants of the original French colonists, the French-Canadian people should remain Catholic and French; faithful to their spiritual and cultural mission. Monsignor L. A. Paquet, a proponent of pre-war nationalism, put forth these convictions in a speech that has become a classic of its kind:

> Let us not descend from the pedestal where God has placed us, to follow the common path of generations who thirst for gold and pleasure. Let us leave to other less idealistic nations this feverish commercialism and gross naturalism which rivets them to material objects. . . . We shall fly the flag of ancient belief at full mast. . . . We shall display it before all America as the glorious emblem, the symbol, the living ideal of social perfection and true national greatness.[2]

Nationalism among today's French Quebecers is not just a secularized version of the old nationalism; it is receptive to the major schools of thought that influence contemporary nation-building. Significantly, the two political parties that survived the crisis of the 1970s are the Quebec Liberal party, heir of a political tradition open to social and economic innovation, and the Parti Québécois, promoter of a nationalism that is less ethnocentric than cultural and a socialism that claims ties to Europe's socialist movement.

According to people such as historian Michel Brunet, the nationalism of French Quebecers is a historical constant dating back to 1760. The crucial question now, however, is whether or not today's French Quebecers still perceive Quebec through the eyes of past nationalism as a monolithic society.

In this context, Gérard Pelletier's cry of "Unanimity is dead" marks the precise point of rupture between René Lévesque's "Old Quebec" and the Quebec we know today.

Shadows still linger over the scene. Memories of the FLQ and the War Measures Act persist. The FLQ raised the spectre of violence and dictatorship for the first time in Quebec history. Many Quebec nationalists, however, perceived the war measures that followed as violence imposed from without by the central power, in order to intimidate a colony dreaming of emancipation.

For the Jews, these changes have touched the most intimate aspects of collective life. They imply a radical adaptation process, with individuals and the community adjusting to a new social climate.

The Ambivalence of Nationalism in the 1970s

For the Jewish community, the main issue has little to do with how English interests will fare in the face of concerns over, for example, Bill 101. The important question before the Jews is whether or not they can still subscribe to the opinion of J. L. Cohen, quoted earlier: "The majority of Quebec professes or practises no desire to impose its character on others who reside within its boundaries."[3]

History has taught Jews in the diaspora to mistrust nationalism (including the nationalism that sprang up between the wars) precisely because of its tendency to breed enthnocentrism and cultural homogeneity.

From this point of view, no one would deny that a kind of ambivalence persists in the nationalism of movements such as the PQ, and that it takes various forms. Even in certain government texts such as Bill 101, the term "Québécois" includes all Quebec citizens regardless of language or origins in certain instances, while in others, it refers only to members of the long-established Francophone majority. These are the people who have been dubbed "real Québécois" by some nationalists. Another area of ambivalence, noted earlier, involves the Palestinian propaganda filtering into some Quebec circles. Asked about this by Warren Perley at the end of the stormy convention in December 1981, Gérard Godin, then Minister of Immigration and Cultural Affairs, answered that "It does not mean we endorse the PLO. Jews should not fear the PQ for talking to the PLO. We talk with everybody."[4]

Even so, Jewish concern about relations between the two political groups can only grow, as world Jewry loses face as a people victimized by the Holocaust, in the wake of events in the Middle East.

Exodus of Jewish Youth?

Under these conditions, pessimistic forecasts by various sociologists about the exodus of young people from Montreal's Jewish community in the late 1970s should come as no surprise. People vote with their feet, it is said, and so it is with the Jewish population leaving Montreal (numbers dropped from 114,000 in 1971 to 103,000 in 1981),[6] the facts seem to bear them out.

One thing is certain: the Jewish community was expecting the worst as the last census approached. According to a 1978 study by sociologist Morton Weinfeld of McGill University, Jewish parents predicted that 46 percent of their young adults would leave Montreal by 1983.[7] Whatever the next census reveals, the prospect of young people departing en masse is particularly traumatic for a community that has invested so much in educating them. But why leave Quebec? Once again, the situation is not clear and the motivations even less so. The ambivalent nationalist climate may explain why some Anglophone Jews left, along with members of other ethnic and cultural communities, including the two that have been there the longest. In a 1982 interview with *The Gazette*, Allen Rose observed: "there is a feeling among non-Francophone Quebecers that they're becoming second-class citizens."[8] There is certainly room for a study comparing the exodus of Quebec Francophones in general, with that of Francophone and Anglophone Jews. Francophones leaving for English Canada are no doubt obstructed by the language barrier. The same can apply to the Sephardic community, for its members have been less traumatized by recent European nationalism than the Ashkenazim. But if the nationalist climate in Quebec were as xenophobic and anti-Semitic as some of the English-language press suggested, it would affect Sephardic and Ashkenazi youth alike, which does not seem to be the case.

The problem becomes even harder to decipher in view of the economic situation in Canada and Quebec, particularly considering the earlier-mentioned flight of capital and manpower to western Canada, which has affected Toronto and Montreal alike.

From Ethnocentric to Cultural Nationalism

The new era in Quebec is characterized by more than just secularism. Despite reservations arising from apparent threats to national survival, it is expressed in the openness of French Quebecers to pluralism in all its forms — religious, ethnic and cultural. They have moved far beyond the traditional slogans "Catholic and French" or "Language guardian of the faith"; they now tolerate and promote pluralism, even in an area that was once inviolate: education. This new attitude first affected the universities, then the colleges[9] and has now filtered into the schools, as the current school reform demonstrates. Ideological pluralism has spread as well. Pockets of intolerance still exist, but since 1945, freedom of expression has been accepted in Quebec and censorship in all is forms has been banished as a thing of the past.

The most important type of pluralism to examine is ethnic pluralism. The old myth of ethnic purity still lingers on,[10] though works such as *La naissance d'une race* by Lionel Groulx no longer connect with the mentality of young French Quebecers.[11] For the first time in Quebec, the "revenge of the cradle" as been replaced by an immigration policy similar to the policies of most other Western nations. The need for this policy increases as the birth rate among French Quebecers plummets. In the past, practically the only way to become a French Quebecer was by birth. Today, there are facilities to help newcomers become integrated as Quebecers in the sociological sense, and despite racist episodes, there is also a more open attitude to ethnic and cultural pluralism.

For decades, the Jewish community, serious as it was, did not seek to study its own character and its own past. Most often it left this research to non-Jewish scholars, not always friendly. In part this was due to the discrimination against Jewish academicians. In the university faculties the few Jewish teachers were loath to devote themselves to Jewish themes: such concerns did not guarantee promotion. Hence Jewish studies remained in the hands of the gifted, dedicated men outside the preserve of the schools. Men such as Simon Belkin, H. M. Caiserman, Louis Rosenberg and B. G. Sack.

Suddenly, as late as the 1970s, Jewish academics could develop their own Jewish content courses. As the Congress archivist Judith Nefsky told the authors in 1985:

> Until recently the subject of Jewish history has usually been associated with the Holy Land and its environs, North Africa, Eastern and Western Europe. Canada as the newest nation of the New World, was invisible on the international map of Jewish history.
>
> The self-discovery that is now very much a part of the fabric of our Canadian community has penetrated the academic arena. The universities now incorporate study of the Jewish experience in Canada and Canadian Jewish themes emerge in many disciplines: literature, religion, law, sociology, demography, architecture, library science, political science as well as Canadian history.

The graduates of this generation are occupying executive positions in communal institutions. They, and many others are reading books written by Canadian Jews, seeing films written and produced by Canadian Jews about Canadian Jews, watching television programmes that deal with issues of concern to the community.

Cultural nationalism, however, does have its pitfalls. Culture can in turn become monolithic, exclusive and even imperialist. But French Quebecers by and large no longer seem to fear for their survival; they have largely overcome the insecurity that characterizes beseiged minorities.

Victor Goldbloom a former minister in the Bourassa cabinet and president of the Canadian Council of Christians and Jews, wrote in 1982: "Quebec Judaism is flourishing, well-established, and in comparison with so many other parts of the world, relatively calm. . . . As Jews, we in Quebec enjoy a very high degree of religious, social and cultural freedom."[12]

As a political figure accustomed to measuring the mood of the people, he asked frankly: "Is there anti-Semitism in Quebec? No, if we look at society as a whole. Yes, if we focus on occasional incidents. These incidents occur much less frequently than in the past, though, and do not represent any movement, general trend or strategy."[13]

One fact remains: the Jewish community, more than any other ethnic or cultural group in Quebec, is in a position to bridge the gap between English and French Quebecers, and create a bond to unite them.[14]

The Future Belongs to Quebecers

For anyone looking back at the Quebec of the 1980s, these words by Albert Memmi would seem self-evident. But in the context of 1980, when they were spoken, they ring out as a challenge. There is one slight change though, for at that time, Memmi was almost certainly referring to French Quebecers alone.[15] Now, however, the future belongs to *all the people* who live in Quebec, regardless of their ethnic and cultural roots and irrespective of their status or the role they play in society.

Why recall Memmi's words here? Because this writer, a Sephardic Jew from Tunisia, has been adopted as an oracle for a generation of French Quebecers. His *Portrait du colonisé*, published in the midst of the Algerian war, found an unexpected welcome among young Quebec nationalists. A pirate edition was printed and distributed free of charge at the doors of various educational institutions. It was re-issued in Quebec in 1972[16] and sold several thousand copies a year as late as 1980. In an interview with French literature professor Axel Mangey of McGill University[17] in 1980, Memmi opened up new perspectives on the 1960s. He suggested that French Quebec would benefit by associating itself with English Canada and the United States. Of nationalism, he said he had never considered it to be absolute. He saw no contradiction between self-affirmation by a relatively small group such as Quebecers, and the construction of large social mosaics such as the United States and Canada.

His were certainly not the only ideas being discussed in Quebec's nationalist circles. Nevertheless, they are accepted by the generation of French Quebecers who now hold power, and they confirm an attitude of openness toward other cultures.

Mangey asked Albert Memmi what he thought of that particular generation: "Returning here after ten years, I was struck . . . by the relative health of Quebec and its people. I found them less edgy, less humiliated and less rebellious as well. The collective social fabric seemed infinitely healthier. I was breathing the air of a democracy." When asked about the future, Memmi responded: "Quite honesty, I refuse to make predictions. The future belongs to Quebecers and hinges on their action. . . . I have a feeling there are great things to be accomplished here."[18]

These things cannot be done by French Quebecers alone, any more than by other Quebecers. To be considered a home by everyone, Quebec must become a place where all communities work together. Otherwise, it will experience the setbacks that have torn so many other nations apart. Intercultural sharing will only be possible when mutual ignorance has been dispelled, for ignorance breeds fear and scorn, and is the ultimate source of panic and conflict.

In order to escape from this vicious circle and create the climate of confidence essential to cooperation, there is a need for openness and outright affirmation. This must go beyond mere coexistence to create an environment in which others are accepted for their differences and all members of society can live together in social peace.

For the most part, French Quebec is turning its back on its earlier biological ethnocentrism. On the contrary, it seems to be developing a cultural nationalism that differs from both the American-style melting pot and the Canadian mosaic. An effort can now be made to achieve an open-ended nationalism in Quebec that will make it a place where many different ethnic groups are involved in dynamic interaction on every level, and where all Quebecers can find the practical means to flourish and still remain faithful to their roots.

The Jewish community contains the main elements for the success of this experiment, for it has been forging a similar path for thousands of years. Anyone who visits Israel can see evidence of this complex cultural mix. All the languages of Europe and North Africa are spoken there, as well as Yiddish and Ladino. The air vibrates with the folklore of the entire world diaspora.

Twenty years ago, few would have thought that so many Jewish schools would accept French and yet maintain their role as resource centres in their own tradition. Today, Quebecers can see Naïm Kattan at Quebec book fairs and Elie Feuewerker in Montreal biology labs, read Michel Solomon in *Le Devoir*, hear Paul Unterberg and Herbert Marx in the political arena, meet Jean-Claude Lasry in Quebec hospitals and encounter innumerable Jewish professors at the Université de Laval, the Université de Montréal and the Université du Québec à Montréal. Their presence is a sign that the Jewish community has left the Anglophone ghetto and that the language barrier is becoming blurred between Ashkenazim and the Sephardim as it is between Jewish and French Quebecers.

The growing pluralism of Quebec society is clearly limited to Western models and still excludes native people. Even so, it is characterized by a twofold cultural presence — predominantly French, but strongly English as well.

Because of its European and North African origins and the historical choices it has made, the Jewish community will always reflect this duality, while at the same time contributing the wealth of its own ancient culture. In Quebec as in Israel, its two branches — the Ashkenazim and the Sephardim — find themselves united in a common effort. Their goal in Quebec is to carve out an identity in the wake of the Quiet Revolution. They have gone beyond the painful immigration period, the *shtetl* and North Africa belong to the past as does the virulent anti-Semitism prior to the Second World War. The world inhabited now by the Jewish community is very different from the Old World. It is a more open society, in which Jews can share the richness of their traditions and human resources as freely and as long as their continuity is assured.

The Jews in Quebec

1290	Expulsion of the Jews from England.
1492	Expulsion of the Jews from Spain.
1496	Expulsion of the Jews from Portugal.

French Regime

1588	France: Royal granting of Canada to Noël de la Janaye; anti-Protestant clauses.
1627	France: Charter of the Compagnie des Cent-Associés, by edict of Cardinal Richelieu; open only to Catholics.
1655	France: Colbert (1619-83) prohibits non-Catholics from entering Canada.
1656	England: readmission of Jews after 350 years of banishment.
1685	France: Edict of Nantes revoked. Huguenots and Jews prohibited from settling in the colonies. The *Code Noir*: Jews expelled from the Islands.
1688	England: the Bill of Rights.
1697	England: William III of England grants Labrador to the Jew Joseph de la Penha.
1738 Esther Brandeau, being Jewish, prohibited from traveling in New France.	
1740	England: Jews no longer bound by Christian oath.
1744 The *Fort Louis*, ship belonging to Jewish shipowner Abraham Gradis, takes part in expedition to recapture Louisbourg.	
1748 David Gradis and Sons charged with supplying Canada and Ile Royale	

(Cape Breton).

1751	First Jewish immigration to Halifax.
1752	*Benjamin*, ship belonging to Gradis, arrives in Quebec City with provisions to ward off famine.
1758	Expedition to Quebec of 14 ships, 8 belonging to Gradis.

English Regime

1760	Arrival of Hart (Trois-Rivières), Jacobs (Saint-Denis) and Levy (Montreal).
1762	Eleazer Levy signs petition to obtain a legislative assembly in Canada— sent to London.

1766-83   United States: American Revolution.

1768	Quebec City: John Franks free to take Jewish oath. Trois-Rivières: Uriah Judah protonotary of the Superior Court.
1774	Quebec Act: religious freedom for Catholics. Influential Jews petition London for responsible government.

1776   United States: Declaration of Independence

1777	Montreal: founding of first Canadian synagogue: Shearith Israel.
1781	Montreal: first Jewish cemetery.
1784	New petition to London demanding a constitution and responsible government: 25 Jewish signatures.
1791	Constitutional Act creates Upper and Lower Canada.

1791 (cont.)   United States: Bill of Rights.
France: Civil and political rights for Jews.
France: Declaration of the Rights of Man and the Citizen.

1799   France: project for a Jewish state submitted to Bonaparte.

1801	Berthier and Montreal: Henry Joseph, leading shipowner, inaugurates Canada-England sea link.
1806	Jewish population: 100 (*Canadiens*: 250,000; English: 20,000). Quebec City: presentation of *The Jew and the Doctor*, a play by Thomas Dibden.
1807	Trois-Rivières: election of Ezekiel Hart to the Legislative Assembly.

1808   France: Napoleon declares Judaism an official religion.

1817   England: Jews given voting rights.

1818	David David, a founder of the bank of Montreal.	
1824	Aaron Ezekiel Hart and T. S. Jacobs, first Jewish lawyers.	
1830		France: first election of a Jew in Paris—Goudehoux (Seine).
1831	Jewish population (Lower Canada): 107.	
1832	Act (1st William IV, Chap. 57) granting the Jews equal rights.	
1837-38	Jews are divided between Constitutionalists (Loyalists) and Sons of Liberty (Papineau). Montreal: founding of the first Sephardic synagogue on Chéneville St.	
1841	Montreal: 30 Jewish families.	
1846	Montreal: charter to a German-Polish Ashkenazi synagogue (Shaar Hashomayim).	
1847	Montreal: Chair in Hebrew and Rabbinical literature given to Rabbi Abraham de Sola. Andrew Hays builds Hays Theatre.	
1848		Marx and Engels publish *The Communist Manifesto*.
1851	Montreal: Jewish population, 181. Quebec City: 40.	
1853-55		France: Count de Gobineau publishes *Essai sur l'inégalité des races humaines*.
1855		England: David Salomons, Lord Mayor of London.
1858	Cap-des-Rosiers, Gaspé: William Hyman, first Jewish mayor in Canada, held office until his death in 1882.	
1860	Montreal: dedication of the first Ashkenazi synagogue in Canada.	
1862	Sainte-Anne-de-la-Pocatière: first expression of anti-Semitism in Quebec by Father Alexis Pelletier in *La Gazette des campagnes*.	
1863	Montreal: founding of the Young Men's Hebrew Benevolent Society to aid German refugees.	
1864	First Jewish elementary school.	Vatican: Pius IX publishes encyclical *Quanta Cura*, with *Syllabus*.

Confederation

1867	Jewish population, Upper and Lower Canada, 1,300.	Germany: Emancipation of the Jews.
1868		United States, North Carolina: Jews

		admitted to public office.
1870	Quebec City: law authorizes Jews to pay school tax to either of the two religious school systems. First Jewish/Protestant school agreement.	England: religious schools, including Jewish schools, receive government financial aid.
1871	Quebec: Jewish population: 518. Father Alphonse Villeneuve published ultramontanist, anti-Semitic pamphlet entitled *Comédie Infernale au conjuration libérale aux enfers* (in 5 acts).	
1875	Montreal: Jewish population, 500.	
1877		*Shtetl*: start of huge Jewish migration from Poland, Germany, Austria, Hungary and Romania toward Canada and the United States.
1878		New Zealand: Sir Julius Vogel, a Jew, elected prime minister.
1880	Montreal: arrival of first wave of immigrants from the *shtetl*. First tour of Sarah Bernhardt.	
1881	Quebec: Jewish population, 989. Montreal: Jules-P. Tardivel founds *La Vérité*.	Russia: first pogroms in Yelisavetgrad and Kiev.
1882	Montreal: first reform congregation; construction of temple Emanu-El.	
1887	Montreal: Alexander Harkavy founds Yiddish-language newspaper, *Die Zeit*. Jewish journalist Jules Helbronner of *La Presse* founds weekly *Le prix courant*.	
1890	Montreal: naming of the YMHBS in appreciation of the Baron de Hirsch Institute.	
1894		France: the Dreyfus affair.
1895	Quebec City: *Le Courrier du Canada* and *La Croix du Canada* publish excerpts from *Juif talmudiste*.	
1896	Montreal: first Talmud Torah school founded.	
1897	Montreal: National Conference of American Rabbis. *Jewish Times* founded, first Jewish newspaper in Canada.	Switzerland: in Basel, Theodor Herzl presides over the first World Jewish Congress. Lithuania: Bund movement founded.
1898	Montreal: founding of Canada's first Zionist organization, Agudath Zion. President: Dr. David A. Hart.	
1899	Montreal: arrival of close to 3,000 Jewish immigrants, mostly from Romania.	Germany: H. S. Chamberlain, Wagner's son-in-law publishes *Fondements du XIXe siècle*.
1901	Canada: Jewish population, 16,401. Quebec: Jewish population, 7,607.	
1903	Montreal: Poale Zion founded.	

Quebec City: law settling the status of Jewish students in Protestant schools.

1904   France: Combes Act separates Church and State. Split between republican government and Holy See. Emigration of right-wing clergy to Quebec.

1905   Russia: preparation of *Protocols of the Learned Elders of Zion*.

1906   Ottawa: adoption of Sunday Observance Act proposed by Henri Bourassa.
Quebec City: law permits Jews observing the sabbath to conduct business on Sundays.
Father A. Huot publishes *Le fléau maçonnique*.
Montreal: publication of first Yiddish book in Canada, *L'éducation chez les Juifs*, by E. M. Levin.

1907   Montreal: Yiddish-language daily newspaper founded, the *Canader Adler* (Canadian Eagle).
Quebec City: founding of daily newspaper *L'Action sociale catholique*.

1908   Quebec City: Monsignor L. A. Paquet publishes *Droit public de l'Église (1908-1915)*.
Montreal: 30,000 Jews.
     France: Charles Maurras founds *Action française*.

1909   Sainte-Sophie, Quebec: Jews introduce the cultivation of Turkish tobacco.

1910   Quebec City: notary J. E. Plamondon promotes the boycotting of Jewish businesses. Plamondon/Ortenberg trial.
Montreal: Godefroy Langlois of the newspaper *Le Pays* defends an evicted Jewish tenant.
Henri Bourassa attacks Clarence I. de Sola, Belgian consul in Montreal, president of the World Zionist Federation. Jewish population: 40,000.

1911-13   Russia: Beilis affair in Kiev.

1913   Canada: arrival of 20,000 Jewish immigrants.
Montreal: 60,000 Jews.
Toronto: 30,000 Jews.
Winnipeg: 20,000 Jews.

1914   Montreal: Jewish Library founded with Quebec charter as library and people's university.
     Vatican: Maurras' *Action française* placed on the Index.

1916   Montreal: Anglican synod opposes

Jewish access to board of Protestant
School Commissioners.

1917   Montreal: Omer Héroux founds   England: Balfour Declaration on
       Action française. Federation of   Jewish national homeland.
       Jewish philanthropists of Montreal
       established.
       Ottawa: S. M. Jacobs elected to
       House of Commons.

1918   France: Maurras and Barrès found
                                            the Ligue d'Action française.

1919   Canada: founding of the Canadian
       Jewish Congress.

1920   Montreal: founding of Jewish Immi-   France: Monsignor Jouin publishes
       grant Aid Society. First collection of *Le péril judéo-maçonnique: les pro-*
       poems in Yiddish by J. I. Segal.   *tocoles des sages de sion.*

1921   Canada: 125,000 Jews.
       Ottawa: founding of the Order of
       Jacques Cartier.

1922   Canada: doors begin to close on
       immigration.
       Quebec City: Act (13, Geo. V, Chap.
       44) increases revenue of Protestant
       School Board through "neutral tax."

1923   Montreal: 32 Jewish organizations   Germany: Adolph Hitler publishes
       speak out in favour of Jewish sepa- *Mein Kampf.*
       rate schools.

1926   Quebec City: draft bill on Jewish   Vatican: condemnation of *Action*
       separate schools declared *ultra*   *française* in France. Henri Bourassa
       vires by London Privy Council.   meets Pius XI which leads him to
       Montreal: publication of *The Jew in* reject extreme nationalism.
       Canada, by A. D. Hart.

1927   Quebec City: *Action française* (Can-
       ada) disappears.

1928   Montreal: Lionel Groulx founds
       Action canadienne-française.

1929   Montreal: Adrien Arcand and Joseph   United States: crash of New York
       Ménard found *Le Miroir* and *Le*   Stock Exchange.
       Goglu.

1930   Quebec City: Unemployed Aid Act
       (21 Geo. V, Chap. 63) creates a sep-
       arate Jewish school commission in
       Montreal. *Achat chez nous* cam-
       paign begins. Founding of Ordre
       patriotique des Goglus. Founding
       of *Action nationale.*

1931   Quebec: 60,087 Jews, of whom 94%   Vatican: Pius XI publishes *Non abbi-*
       declare Yiddish their mother   *amo bisogno* against fascism.
       tongue.

1932   Cohen-Bercovitch draft bill (No.
       167) against group libel defeated.

1933   Canada: protests against Hitler.   Germany: Hitler appointed chancel-
       Montreal: Jeune-Canada counter-   lor. Jewish population about 1% of
       protest at Gesù hall.   total population.
       Quebec City: Paul Bouchard and

Philippe Hamel found *La Nation*.

1934   Canada: reorganization of Canadian Jewish Congress.

1935   Ottawa: Jean-François Pouliot, Commons member for Temiscouata, affirms religious freedom in Canada before Canadian Society for the Study of the History of the Canadian Church.
Montreal: André Laurendeau denounces anti-Semitism of *Le Goglu*. First ecumenical meeting between Rabbi J. Stern of Montreal and Jesuit Joseph Paré.
Toronto: defeat of Glass bill against group libel.

1936   Quebec: Maurice Duplessis elected premier.
Montreal: ecumenical meetings between the Jesuits Paré and Valiquette, laymen Gouin and Gérin-Lajoie and Rabbi H. J. Stern and H. M. Caiserman.

France: Léon Blum Prime Minister of the Front Populaire government.

1937

Vatican: Pius XI published *Mit Brennender Sorge* against Nazism and fascism.

1938   Toronto: S. Bronfman and S. Hays elected president and director of Canadian Jewish Congress.
Ottawa: Father P. G. Bellemare, o.f.m., de Pax et Bonum, attacks anti-Semitism in a message to the Aumôniers de la J.E.C.

Vatican: Pius XI to pilgrims: "It is not possible for Christians to adhere to anti-Semitism. Spiritually, we are Semites."
Germany: Kristallnacht. Violent acts commited against Jews, November 10. Hitler implements extermination plan.

1939   Ottawa: Canada refuses to open its doors to 907 Jewish refugees aboard the *Saint-Louis*.
Montreal: publication of *Canada's Jews* by L. Rosenberg.

1945   Montreal: B. G. Sack publishes *History of the Jews in Canada*.

1946   Canada: thousands of Jewish survivors admitted, victims of war in Europe, including Jewish figures well known world-wide.
Montreal: A. M. Klein publishes *Rocking Chair*.

U.N. divides Palestine creating two states — one Arab, the other Jewish.

1948

Israel: Ben Gurion proclaims the State of Israel.
U.N.: Universal Declaration of Human Rights.

1950   Montreal: founding of the Cercle juif de langue française. Death of H. M. Caiserman, general secretary of the Canadian Jewish Congress.

1954	Toronto: Nathan Phillips, a Jew, elected Mayor of Toronto.	
1956	Quebec: beginning of French Sephardic immigration.	Independence of Morocco and Tunisia.
1960	Ottawa: Canadian Declaration of Human Rights. Quebec: beginning of Quiet Revolution.	
1961	Canada: 254,368 Jews. Montreal: Leonard Cohen publishes *Spice Box of Earth*.	
1962	Montreal: Protestant School Board recommends Royal Commission on education and revival of Jewish school commission.	Vatican II: Council studies Jewish issues. Algerian independence.
1965	Massive influx of Sephardic Jews from North Africa.	
1968	Quebec: Private Education Act. Subsidies to private Jewish schools.	
1969		Israel: francophone population 400,000.
1971	Quebec: Jewish population 110,885 (1.83%).	
1975	Quebec: Dr. Victor Goldbloom named cabinet member in Bourassa government.	
1976	Montreal: publication of *Adieu Babylone* by Naïm Kattan. Quebec: Parti québécois government elected.	

Notes

Foreword

1 Robert Vachon and Jacques Langlais, eds., *Qui est Québécois?* (Montreal: Fides, 1979).
2 The oldest duly-constituted community. It is well known that there were Black slaves in Quebec from the time of the French regime (see Leo Bertley, "L'histoire du Québec vue par un Québécois noir," in ibid., p. 85-97). In addition to the fact that these Blacks were not immigrants, they did not yet form a community, properly speaking.

Preface to the Original French Version

1 "French Quebecers" in the sense of descendants of the first French settlers who came to this part of the world, now called Quebec, almost four centuries ago. The expression "French Quebecers" is intended to pinpoint a geographical area, as compared to the generic term "French-Canadian," while at the same time indicating the cultural background which distinguishes these people from other communities who share Quebec and are considered rightful "Quebecers" whatever their origin.

Moreover, the terms "Quebec," "Quebec society" and "Quebecers," French or otherwise, do not apply to peoples who do not recognize the geo-economic boundaries and political system imposed by "Quebec" society, such as the traditional native peoples. See Ka-ien-ta-ron-Kwen (Ernie Benedict), "Preface," in Vachon and Langlais, eds., *Qui est Québécois?*, pp. 9-13.
2 See, however, below, Part V, p. 251 and note 6.
3 Jan Kadar, director and Tel Allen, screenplay, *Lies My Father Told Me*, Montreal, Pentacle VIII, Production 1975.

Chapter I

1 Cornelius J. Jaenen, "Le Colbertisme," *Revue d'histoire de l'Amérique française*, 18 (1964), 252-66.
2 Denis Vaugeois and J. Lacoursière, *Canada-Québec: synthèse historique* (Montreal: Éditions du Renouveau pédagogique, 1978), p. 44.
3 See Foreword, n. 2. Blacks excelled as interpreters to the region's Amerindian people (Bertley, "L'histoire du Québec vue par un Québecois noir," n. 2).
4 Article 3 of the decree issued by Cardinal de Richelieu, dated May 7, 1627, specifies that associates of the company created by Louis XIII's Prime Minister for New France "could only admit French Catholics." The *Code Noir* of 1685 includes this article: "We charge all our officers with driving from our Islands any Jews who have settled there. They are ene-

161

mies of the Christian name, and we therefore order them to leave within three months, under penalty of confiscation of individuals, property and galleys" (Jean-Paul de Lagrave, "La présence juive au Québec," *Bulletin du Cercle juif,* and B. G. Sack, *History of the Jews in Canada* [Montreal: Harvest House, 1965], p. 1-2).

5 See J. P. Agus, *L'évolution de la pensée juive, des temps bibliques au début de l'ère moderne* (Paris: Payot, 1961), p. 398.

6 Vaugeois and Lacoursière, *Canada-Québec,* p. 194.

7 B. K. Sandwell, "The First Jew in Canada," *Saturday Night,* February 11, 1939.

8 A name meaning "of French origin" to the Ashkenazim. The corresponding name used by the Sephardim for Arabs and even indigenous Jews was Franco.

9 D. Rome, "On the Early Harts," Part 2, *Canadian Jewish Archives,* New Series, 16 (Montreal: Canadian Jewish Congress, 1980), p. 107.

10 The treaty guaranteed Catholics free practice of the Roman Catholic religion under the supremacy of the King of England.

11 Hilda Neatby, *Chelsea Journal,* 1, 1 (January 1975), 41-47. Even in Great Britain, the English, Irish and Scottish had to wait another half century to obtain these freedoms.

12 Raymond Douville reproduces much of the will in *Aaron Hart, récit historique* (Trois-Rivières: Édition du Bien Public, 1938), p. 146.

13 Ibid., p. 89.

14 Ibid., p. 186.

15 Anglo-sephardi in the sense that the true Sephardim came from the Iberian peninsula. It is important to remember that the Jews followed two main paths to reach Europe from their lands of origin, Babylon, Palestine and Egypt. One led them north-west, at about the year 1,000, to the borders of present-day France and Germany and from there to Poland. The other led them westward during approximately the same period into Spain. While the Sephardim adopted ladino, the Ashkenazim spoke a German dialect they called Yiddish-German and later Yiddish. The two branches later spread throughout the empires to which they belonged, often far from the capitals where repressive policies, such as those of the Inquisition, were devised and imposed on their people. Sephardi Jews could thus be found in Holland when that country was governed by Madrid. The Dutch Sephardim established a community in London during the 1660s. A century later it was submerged by a wave of Ashkenazi immigrants from the Slavic countries. The first Jewish community in Montreal and all of Canada remained faithful to this London Sephardic tradition in its Hispano-Portuguese synagogue.

16 Edited by Claude Perrault and published in Montreal by C. B. Payette (1969, xviii, 495 p.). The cemetery was located on Saint-Janvier Street, near today's Dominion Square.

17 The *Haskalah* ("The Light") was a secular and universalist movement whose goal was to free the Jews from their condition as perpetual wanderers through integration into European culture.

18 Benjamin G. Sack, "History of the Jews in Canada," in Arthur Daniel Hart, ed., *The Jew in Canada* (Toronto, 1926), p. 63.

19 One, David Salesby Frank, was destined to lead a lively political life. He was arrested for insolence toward the civil authorities and openly supported the Americans during the occupation of Montreal by Montgomery. He later became one of the minor heroes of the American Revolution. Because of his knowledge of French, he was twice sent by Congress on diplomatic missions, in 1781 and 1784, and was finally posted in Marseilles as American Vice-Consul.

20 Sack, "History of the Jews in Canada," p. 73.

21 D. Rome, "On the Early Harts," Part 4, *Canadian Jewish Archives,* New Series, 18 (Montreal: Canadian Jewish Congress, 1980), p. 363-67.

22 "He who chooses a region accepts its religion."

23 To the point that it passed unnoticed in the press of the day, which was preoccupied by a cholera epidemic sweeping the population.

24 D. Rome, "Samuel Bécancour Hart and 1832," *Canadian Jewish Archives*, 25 (Montreal: Canadian Jewish Congress, 1982), p.24.

25 Joseph Tassé, "Droits politiques des Juifs au Canada," *La Revue canadienne*, 7 (June 1870), 407-25.

26 Neatby, *Chelsea Journal*, 41-47.

27 Camille Jullian, *Histoire de Bordeaux* (1894), p. 542.

28 As his personal journal reveals, he maintained close relations with Montcalm, who clearly had confidence in Gradis. He writes to his mother in 1757: "Mr. de la Porte, director of the Naval Office, is so negligent that I must ask you to refrain from corresponding through him, and to go instead through Mr. Gradis, of Bordeaux."

29 Jean de Maupassant, *Un grand armateur de Bordeaux, Abraham Gradis* (Bordeaux: Féret et fils, 1917), p. 76.

30 "Archives Gradis. Recueil des lettres de 1757. Correspondance commerciale d'Abraham Gradis," *Rapport de l'Archiviste de la Province de Québec pour 1957-58 et 1958-59*, p. 11, 128.

31 Sack, "History of the Jews in Canada," p. 95-96.

32 From that time on, Montreal's Jewish community would have its "up-town Jewry," the aristocracy, and its "Yiddish gass," the new arrivals. In Toronto in 1934, people still spoke of the Jewish working class and the Jewish yahudim, the workers and the middle class, which was of pseudo-German origin.

33 Catholics who experienced the religious turmoil of the 1960s know how much commotion was raised in Quebec by introducing French into the liturgy and guitar into mass, which were then coined "masses à gogo," as well as by the clergy's decision to abandon its religious uniform. Even more disturbing was the reorientation of certain traditional doctrines, which convinced more than one Catholic that, "The church is going to the devil," which became the title of a book published during this period.

34 Early signs of the reform began to emerge long before the first reform synagogues were built. In 1857, for example, G. I. Ascher of Montreal, a fiercely orthodox Scottish Jew, wished to donate a scroll of the Torah and a Yod to the Toronto congregation. But he felt it necessary to demand that the recipients remain faithful to the orthodox tradition. The gift was only accepted after serious discussion on their part.

35 D. Rome, "Unpublished Notes," Book 10, p. 59. This debate conveys a sense of the reformers' pejorative attitude toward their brothers from the *shtetl* which can be related to their respective socio-economic levels. (See the New York weekly *American Israelite* of May 11, 1983.)

36 D. Rome, "Unpublished Notes," Book 10, p. 72. In fact, these nineteenth-century reformers thought that synagogues should look to the Christian model for their ceremony, architecture, appearance and behaviour, a trend which did not escape orthodox observers.

37 Ibid., p. 73. Here is the response of one Quebecer living at the time, after attending the funeral of a Jewish friend. It gives some indication of the problems involved in trying to read one culture from the vantage point of another. Even for a non-Jew, it also provides a glimpse into the trauma that can arise when two traditions clash, especially when they are light years apart and located in a universe as vast, diversified and yet consistent in its fundamental beliefs as that of the Jewish people. The text appeared in the *Leader* of May 26 and the *Mirror* of May 29, 1857. Its author suddenly found himself transported into a world that was strange and entirely different from the English-speaking world; a world steeped in the philosophy and folklore of the biblical and Babylonian Jewry of Eastern Europe. He notes the halting pace of the funeral procession and the way of singing, and is struck by the lack of decorum, the apparent disorder, the disregard for musical rules, the people's scanty

knowledge of Hebrew. The rites were carried out mechanically and with little solemnity. Our reporter was not particularly impressed, though he admitted that the moist eyes of the participants left no doubt as to their deep emotions. He understood the language of the ceremony though it was not his own, and his sensitivity to the artificial quality of language made the current of emotion seem even stronger. At first, he felt rather uneasy. He realized, when he saw the open casket, the children lifted up to look in and the relatives themselves throwing handfuls of earth in turn on the remains of their loved one, that he was witnessing something foreign to his culture but nonetheless very significant.

38 After the post-Solomonic split, the Jews were most apprehensive concerning further divisions and did everything they could to keep rebels within the community. Despite the experience of the Karaites, Judaism strove to assimilate Sephardim, cabalists, Hasidim, reformers, conservatives, Zionists, reconstructionists and others. From the outset, the Jewish reform itself was anything but homogeneous. It took various forms, some more intransigent than others. Rabbi David Corcos was as radical in his reformism as Meldola De Sola had been in his orthodoxy forty years earlier.

39 The word "philanthropy" is associated with the Victorian notion of assistance for the needy that prevailed at the time. It favoured the respectable poor; submissive and somewhat ashamed of having to beg, rather than the professional beggars who exploited the benevolence of others by their deliberate and untimely insistence on their own personal dignity. This middle-class notion persisted throughout the difficult period of massive immigration from Western Europe. It tended to select only the most respectable members of the crowds who flocked to departure points in Europe and American ports of entry. In Europe, Jewish agencies such as London's Mansion House tried to repatriate many eastern European immigrants to their homelands, while in America, there was such strong protest against the massive influx of problem cases to the New World that there were moves to simply close the door on them.

Chapter II

1 *Shtetl* (plural *Stetlach*) means village. It comes from the same root as *stadt, state* and *état*. The Jews from this part of Europe lived in villages for historical and sociological reasons.

2 A mystical religious movement very widespread among devout European Jews since the end of the eighteenth century founded by Reb Israel Ba'al Shem Tov (Master of the Good Name, 1700-60). Hasidism preaches the spread of cabalistic and mystical traditions. It found its counterpart in the *mitnagdim*, equally common among the faithful who observed the ancient law that prohibited the popularization of cabalistic teachings.

3 A nationalist movement that advocates the establishment of a State of Israel (Zion). Its founder, Dr. Théodore Herzl, convened the first international Zionist convention at Basel in 1897.

4 Rashi is formed from the Hebrew initials of Rabbi Salomon ben Isaac (1040-1105), of Troyes, France. His commentaries on the Bible and the Babylon Talmud are recognized as classics. The Troyes school was the leading authority among the religious schools in northern Europe and became the cultural centre of the Ashkenazi world.

5 From *gaon* (eminence), the title given to leaders of the Jewish schools in Babylon (589-1038). The *gaon* guided the interpretation and development of Talmudic law.

6 Dr. O. Juresco, in *Emigrantul*, No. 1 (May 21, 1900).

7 They worked up to eighty hours per week in filthy hovels. In Montreal, seamstresses working at home received between $2.00 and $3.00, the daily salary of a carpenter, for sixty hours of work per week.

8 These neighbourhoods formed for a number of reasons. The Orthodox, practising Jews sought proximity to the synagogue and kosher food shops, and everyone wanted to be near

schools where their children could maintain contact with tradition. In order to survive, they needed institutions, services, leadership and simply to see one another and talk about their wealth of experience, about the past, present and future. This phenomenon still occurs today in the form of spontaneous groupings of families from the same village or region.

9 The names of these institutions keep a Slavic toponymy alive in Quebec, perpetuating links to the regions of the *shtetl* that were home to its Jewish communities.

10 The *cheder* ("the room") is the traditional and very demanding school where young Jews learned the Talmud, the first books of the Bible or the prayers.

11 Vilno, once dubbed the Jerusalem of Lithuania, was incorporated into the U.S.S.R. after World War II. The whole city became the world's most important centre of Jewish culture, as expressed in the languages of Hebrew and Yiddish. YIVO was created in 1925.

12 These microfilms were prepared by the New York Public Library.

13 The Quebec government showed some interest in this Jewish cultural life. During Expo 67, the Minister of Cultural Affairs gave a dinner in honour of the poet Rawitch at the Quebec Pavillion. It also saluted the founding of the National Yiddish Committee by the Canadian Jewish Congress and Jewish Library. His department named the director of the Jewish Library to its Arts Council as a representative of the Jewish community. A funding program for Quebec literature, established by Cultural Affairs, subsidized the library as well as a number of Yiddish writers right from the beginning.

14 In 1967, the building became the Annexe Aegidius Fauteux of the Bibliothèque nationale du Québec.

15 Bavarian financier Maurice de Hirsch (Munich, 1831-Ersekujvar, Hungary [today Nové Zamky, Czechoslovakia], 1896) subsidized the *Alliance israélite universelle* and helped Jews expelled from Russia, especially to Argentina. His wife, Clara Bischoffsheim (Anvers, 1833-Paris, 1899) was also involved in the foundation and in supporting philanthropic works.

16 This distinction had been widely expressed by the early religious reformers in the following terms: "Be Jewish at home and a citizen outside."

17 Nathan Glazier is an American sociologist of religion.

18 See p. 127-29.

19 The Bund (literally "The Alliance") was founded in 1897 in Vilno. It brought Jewish workers from Luthuania, Poland and Russia together in the *shtetl*. It came into being the same year as Théodore Herzl's Zionist movement, but opposed the movement because it found the idea of a mass Jewish immigration into Palestine utopian. The Bund addressed itself to Jews who had to stay in Europe. It soon became a true socialist party in Russia, Romania and Poland. Lenin expelled it from the communist party because of its "separatism" and "nationalism."

20 D. Rome, "On the Jewish School Question in Montreal, 1903-1931," *Canadian Jewish Archives*, New Series, No. 3 (Montreal: Canadian Jewish Congress, 1975), p. 74. These words confirm the sentiments voiced by Sir N. F. Belleau during the debates on Confederation, concerning the "liberalism" of Lower Canada's French-speaking habitants (see p. 127, n. 79).

21 Ben Kayfetz, "The Evolution of the Jewish Community in Toronto," in Albert Rose, ed., *A People and Its Faith* (Toronto: University of Toronto Press, 1959), p. 27. Ben Kayfetz was an executive of the Canadian Jewish Congress from 1947 to 1985.

22 The original Jewish community contributed as well, partly by accumulating commercial capital out of proportion with its numbers (it included 30 families in Montreal in 1841). For more on this period, see P.-A. Linteau, R. Durocher and J.-C Robert, *Histoire du Québec contemporain, de la Confédération à la crise, 1867-1929* (Montreal: Boréal Express, 1979), p. 140. See also D. Rome, "Our Forerunners At Work," *Canadian Jewish Archives*, Nos. 9-10 (Montreal: Canadian Jewish Congress, 1978).

23 The Noble Order of the Knights of Labor was founded in the United States in 1869. It began as a kind of secret society and grew dramatically after 1880. The Order crossed the border in 1881 and came to Quebec the following year, where it remained a major union player until the end of the century.

24 *Jewish Daily Eagle (Adler)*, 1932, souvenir edition to commemorate the adoption of the 1832 charter of rights, p. 73 (Rome, "Our Forerunners At Work," p. 23).

25 Linteau et al., *Histoire du Québec contemporain*, p.147.

26 Jewish women rarely worked in factories.

27 The *Jewish Times* upbraided the thoughtless Jewish bosses at the annual meeting of the Baron de Hirsch Institute, urging the garment magnates to become philanthropists (February 8, 1898, p. 73).

28 Rome, "Our Forerunners At Work," p. 40.

29 Annex O of the Report of the *Royal Commission on the Relations Between Labour and Capital* (Ottawa 1889), p.72-75.

30 Linteau et al., *Histoire du Québec contemporain*, p.210.

31 Samuel Davis was an active member of Montreal's Jewish community. He presided over the Shearith Israel synagogue for seventeen years before joining the reform Emanu-El Temple in 1882, where he remained the president until his death.

32 Canada, Labour Department, *Annual Report on Strikes and Lockouts* (Ottawa, 1901-16). Quoted in Charles Lipton, *The Trade Union Movement of Canada, 1827-1959*. See also S. Belkin, *The Poale Zion Movement in Canada, 1904-20* (Montreal: Actions Committee of the Labour Zionist Movement in Canada, 1956), Yiddish, p. 85.

33 For more on this subject, see Marcel Fournier, *Communisme et anti-communisme au Québec, 1920-50* (Laval: Éd. coopératives Albert Saint-Martin, 1979).

34 The Labour Zionist was made up principally of Poale Zion (workers of Zion) and the *Ferbund*, or National Jewish Union. Since the beginning of the century, it had militated in favour of a Jewish labour society and state in Palestine. This workers movement was as active around the world as it was in Palestine. In Quebec, it was involved in launching the Canadian Jewish Congress, the Jewish Library, schools and camps for children as well as several literary and cultural projects.

35 Belkin, *The Poale Zion Movement*, p. 85. Poale Zion foresaw modern schools where Jewish children would learn Hebrew, Yiddish and history from a Zionist and Socialist perspective.

36 Ibid., p. 61-62.

37 The response of F. Blair, a senior civil servant in Canadian immigration, when asked how many Jews he expected to admit to the country. The answer reflected the anti-Semitism of the time, and served as the title for a book by Abella and Troper on the history of Jewish immigration to the country (see p. 85).

38 Another Canadian Jew by the name of Dave Barrett, also a social democrat, became the premier of British Columbia.

39 David Lewis, *The Good Fight, Political Memoirs 1909-58* (Toronto: Macmillan of Canada, 1982).

40 Since the Patriots episode in 1837, peace had been disturbed just once by a distant event, the Boer War (1899-1902). A few Jewish names can be found on the volunteer list, including a Franklin and a Lightstone.

41 Zionist Archives, Jerusalem. Document L6/34/II. Translated from French.

42 *Canadian Jewish Chronicle*, November 23, 1917.

43 For more on this topic, see Ivan Avakumovic, *The Communist Party in Canada. A History* (Toronto: McClelland and Stewart, 1975), in particular p. 51-53, 57 and 67.

44 He was reelected in 1945.

Chapter III

1 See p. 12.

2 The history of relations between the Yiddish community and English Quebec has yet to be written. As far as French Quebec is concerned, a number of studies provide a close look at how they dealt with the *shtetl* immigrants. One such study is by Victor Teboul, and we have drawn on it extensively in the following pages.

3 See David Rome, "The Jewish Biography of Henri Bourassa," *Canadian Jewish Archives*, New Series, Nos. 39 and 40 (Montreal: Canadian Jewish Congress, 1988).

4 In 1871, the island of Montreal was home to 352,673 inhabitants or 12.9 percent of Quebec's population. This percentage was still only 22.5 in 1901, with 371,086 inhabitants (Linteau et al., *Histoire du Québec contemporain*, p. 45).

5 D. Rome, "The Plamondon Case and S. W. Jacobs," *Canadian Jewish Archives*, New Series, Nos. 26-27 (Montreal: Canadian Jewish Congress, 1982), p. 174-83.

6 D. Rome, *Clouds in the Thirties. On Antisemitism in Canada, 1929-39, A Chapter on Canadian Jewish History*, Section 3 (Montreal, 1977).

7 Linteau et al., *Histoire du Québec contemporain*, p. 46.

8 In 1923, Cardinal Bégin of Quebec City still prohibited the Catholic school authorities from educating Jewish children with Catholic children. His was probably the only explicit refusal on the part of Catholics to open their school system to Jewish children (Jean Hamelin and Nicole Gagnon, *Histoire du catholicism québécois. Le XXe siècle*, tome 1, *1898-1940*, edited by Nive Voisine (Montreal: Boreal Express), p. 325.

9 Editorial entitled "Un Québec chrétien ou un Québec Juif?" signed Émile Goglu, *Le Goglu*, August 29, 1930, p. 2.

10 C.-M. Forest, "La question juive au Canada. Liberté religieuse et égalité. La question des écoles juives," *Revue dominicaine*, 41, 4 (November 1935), 274. Father Forest was a member of the Dominican team that published anti-Semitic articles in this prestigious review in 1935 and 1936. It also included the names of Fathers Mercier, J.-D. Brasseur, M. A. Lamarche, R. Garrigou-Lagrange, A. St-Pierre, R.-M. Martineau and B. Mailloux (*Clouds in the Thirties*, Section 3, p. 115-25).

11 Victor Teboul, *Mythe et images du Juif au Québec. Essai d'analyse critique*, collection "Liberté" (Montreal: Éditions de Lagrave, 1977).

12 Ringuet, *Trente Arpents* (Montreal: Fides, 1957), p. 59.

13 Victor Teboul, *Mythes et images du Juif au Québec*, p. 159-60.

14 Ibid., p. 41.

15 Olivar Asselin, "The Jews of Montreal," in *Canadian Century*, 1911 (French version "Olivar Asselin sur les juifs," *Jonathan*, March 1982, translated by André Daoust, p. 12-15).

16 Teboul, *Mythes et images du Juif*, p. 124.

17 Ibid., p. 129.

18 Ibid., p. 130.

19 Ibid., p. 133.

20 Ibid., p. 134.

21 Ibid., p. 65.

22 Ibid.

23 Ibid., p. 123.

24 Kayfetz, "The Evolution of the Jewish Community in Toronto," p. 19.

25 For more about this period, see D. Rome, "Anti-Semitism I, II and III," *Canadian Jewish Archives*, New Series, Nos. 26, 27 and 31 (Montreal: Canadian Jewish Congress, 1982-83).

26 Father Lemann was a converted Jew.

27 *Notes de Voyage* (Montreal:Eusèbe Sénécal, 1890), p. 246-47.

28 Loans with interest were considered a form of usury. They were strongly condemned by the Third Lateran Council (1179), the Second Lyon Council (1274) and the Vienne Council

(1311). See the *Dictionnaire de Théologie Catholique*, vol. 15, part 2 (Paris: Letouzey, 1950), Col. 2316-1390, under the word *"usure."*

29 Justin (100?-165?), for example, in his *Dialogue with Tryphon the Jew* and Eusèbe de Césarée (265-340).

30 Vatican II attempted to deal with this anti-Semitism by issuing ecumenical declarations. These led to a purging of liturgical texts (see in particular *Nostra aetate*, October 28, 1967, in *Concile oecuménique Vatican II. Constitutions, décrets, déclarations, messages* [Paris: Éditions du Centurion, 1967], p. 698.

31 As well as some names of businesses, such as the Château Frontenac, Gare du Palais and even now, the Fontainebleu, Château Fleur-de-Lys and Château Grande-Allée.

32 See, for example Michel de Saint-Pierre, *Le Aristocrates* (Paris: Éditions de la Table Ronde, 1954), or Jean d'Ormesson, *Au plaisir de Dieu* (Paris: Gallimard, 1974). In *Les Aristocrates*, Michel de Saint-Pierre writes to Mr. De Maubrun: ". . . money annoys me. I really believe I do not like money. And so I cannot bring myself to sympathize with people who have a lot of it" (p. 154).

33 Denis Monière, *Le développement des idéologies au Québec des origines à nos jours* (Montreal: Éditions Québec/Amérique, 1977), p. 281-82.

34 From 1915 to 1939, no fewer than sixteen congregations from France settled in Quebec. (B. Benault and B. Lévesque, *Éléments pour une sociologie des communautés religieuses au Québec* [Sherbrooke/Montreal: Université de Sherbrooke/Les Presses de l'Université de Montréal, 1975], p. 91.)

35 Pius IX, *Quanta Cura et Syllabus*. Documents gathered by Jean-Robert Armogathe, Holland, Jean-Jacques Pauvert, 1967.

36 See the history of visits to Canada by Dom Henri Smeulders and Msgr. George Conroy, cf. D. Rome, "Early Anti-Semitism: Threats to Equality," *Canadian Jewish Archives*, New Series, No. 31 (Montreal: Canadian Jewish Congress, 1983), p. 24 and 106.

37 Alfred Dreyfus, a Jew and French army captain, was accused of treason in 1894. He was found guilty and sentenced to lifelong deportation on the Île du Diable. When it emerged that someone had tampered with the evidence, a widespread movement was launched by anti-Semites, patriots, militarists, royalists and right-wing Catholics to oppose any review of the trial. According to them, the case involved a conflict between socialists, anti-clericals, republicans and Jews on one side, and France's army and honour on the other. The Dreyfus affair deeply divided the French people. It gave rise to a massive anti-Semitic campaign that left its mark on the history of Europe and the Jewish people. In the end, Dreyfus himself was cleared of all guilt by the court and reinstated in 1905.

38 At that time, a battle raged between the supporters of educational reform in the seminaries, based on ultramontanism, and the authorities of the seminary and archbishop of Quebec, who were accused of liberalism by the ultramontanes. Pelletier had attacked Msgr. Dupanloup and Mr. de Montalembert for their liberalism, which displeased the archbishop. (A Catholic [Father Alexis Pelletier] *La Source du mal de l'époque au Canada*, p. 33). See Rome, *Clouds in the Thirties*, p. 52-55.

39 Editorial, *L'opinion publique*, 12, 48 (December 1, 1881), 1.

40 Léon Poliakov, *Histoire de l'antisémitisme. L'Europe suicidaire, 1870-1933* (Paris: Calmann-Lévy, 1977), p. 52. In 1882, Chabuty re-edited his text under his own name and titled it *Les juifs nos maîtres*.

41 Magella Quinn, "Un prêtre bien de son temps, Zacharie Lacasse," in F. Dumont et al., eds., *Idéologies au Canada français*, vol. 1, *1850-1900* (Quebec: Laval University Press, 1971), p. 275-81.

42 Poliakov, *Histoire de l'antisémitisme*, p. 277-79.

43 Zacharie Lacasse, *Une quatrième mine dans le camp ennemi* (Montreal: Cadieux et Derome, 1893).

44 Poliakov, *Histoire de l'antisémitisme*, p. 62, 63 and 156.

45 Ibid., p. 153-54.

46 In the 1890s, he declared himself an advocate of French-Canadian nationalism: "The nation we now want to see founded with the blessing of Divine Providence is the French-Canadian nation." (Jean Hamelin, ed., *Histoire du Québec* [Montreal: Éditions France-Amérique, 1977], p. 430.)

47 In 1896, *La Semaine religieuse de Québec* published articles on the Rothschilds, who in its eyes were associated with the cult of the golden calf and the figure of the anti-Christ. (D. Rome, "Early Anti-semitism: The Voice of the Media," *Canadian Jewish Archives*, New Series No. 33 [Montreal: Canadian Jewish Congress, 1984], p. 87.)

48 Jules Tardivel, *Notes de voyages en France, Italie, Espagne, Irlande, Angleterre, Belgique et Hollande* (Montreal: Eusèbe Sénécal, 1890).

49 This book has been dubbed the "Defamation Directory." In it, Drumont accuses Jewish financial power of corrupting national traditions.

50 See p. 67. A similar phenomenon occurred in 1883 with another anti-Semitic newspaper whose title, *La Croix*, was borrowed by several papers with like tendencies on both sides of the Atlantic.

51 This initiative was launched by Leon XIII and Pius IX. In France, it gave rise to the Association catholique de la jeunesse française (ACJF) in 1886, and in Canada to the Association catholique de la jeunesse canadienne (ACJC). Not until the time of Pius IX did it take on specialized forms such as the JOC (1925), the JAC and the JEC (1929).

52 The Mendel Beilis affair had international repercussions. This Jew from the Kiev region was accused of the ritual murder of a child. See below, the Plamondon affair, p. 67.

53 This forgery appeared in London in 1919 under the title, *The Jewish Peril: Protocols of the Learned Elders of Zion*. The following year, it was translated into French and German. It was presented as the record of a secret meeting held parallel to the first Zionist congress in Basel in 1897, whose goal was to plan world domination by the Jews, relying on freemasonry and zionism. In reality, it was a French political pamphlet against Napoleon III and reproduced in large part by S. Nilus in his book *Le Grand dans le petit. L'Antéchrist considéré comme une proche éventualité politique*, which appeared in Russia in 1905.

54 Editorial, *L'Action catholique*, September 21, 1921, 3.

55 See Rome, "Anti-Semitism I. The Plamondon Case and S. W. Jacobs."

56 "Rapport du congrès de la jeunesse à Québec, 23-26 juin 1908," *Le Semeur* (Montreal, 1909).

57 L.-C. Farley, "La Question juive," in ibid.

58 Ibid., p. 132.

59 This pamphlet earned official recognition by Cardinal Bégin in the form of a pastoral letter.

60 Antonio Huot, "La question juive. Quelques observations sur la question du meurtre rituel," *Lectures sociales populaires No. 2* (Quebec: Éditions de l'Action Sociale Catholique, 1914). Speech presented under the auspices of the Garneau Circle of the ACJC at the Académie St-Joseph de Québec.

61 Report of Cardinal Ganganelli, Italian text and English translation in Cecil Roth, ed., *The Ritual Murder Libel and the Jew* (London, Woburn, n.d.).

62 See *La Semaine religieuse de Québec*, January 24, 1918 November 27, 1919 and volume 40, July 1928-29.

63 We are referring here to the second edition, entitled *Droit public de l'Église. Principes généraux* (Quebec: Imp. J.-A. K. Laflamme, 1916).

64 Monsignor Louis-Adolphe Paquet, *La Semaine religieuse de Québec*, p. 279.

65 It was founded in 1905 and appeared until 1911. (See André Leduc and Jean Hamelin, *Les journaux du Québec, de 1764 à 1964* (Quebec: Laval University Press, 1965).

66 The title of the leaflet was *Le Juif, conférence donnée au Cercle Charest de l'Association catholique de la jeunesse canadienne, le 30 mars 1910* (Quebec: L'Action sociale catholique, 1910).

67 Jacobs was an expert in Canadian law and director of the Baron de Hirsch Institute. In 1917, he became the first Jewish member of the House of Commons. He was a longtime friend of W. L. Mackenzie King. When the Canadian Jewish Congress underwent reorganization in 1934, he was elected president and continued in that position until his death in 1938.

68 Jacobs' team of Quebec consultants included one of Quebec's future premiers, Louis-Alexandre Taschereau.

69 *The Gazette*, May 22, 1913.

70 *Daily Telegraph*, May 23, 1913.

71 This is how Pierre Pierrard of the Institut catholique de Paris expressed it: "The mark of anti-Semitism is that it lives off its own excrement." (*Juifs et catholiques français, de Drumont à Jules Isaac, 1886-1945* [Paris: Fayard, 1970].)

72 In 1915, *L'Action catholique* took over from *L'Action sociale catholique*, founded in 1907.

73 As far as immigration was concerned, the Quebec government occasionally intervened in the selection of French-speaking immigrants at the source, especially in New England. Between 1928 and 1931, 9,920 Franco-Americans entered Quebec.

74 In their writings on turn-of-the-century Quebec nationalism (1897-1929), historians Linteau, Durocher and Robert observe that "the nation was defined as much by its Catholicism and rural origins as by its ethnic and linguistic characteristics" (Linteau et al., *Histoire du Québec contemporain*, p. 611).

75 *London Jewish Chronicle*, May 21, 1909, p. 11.

76 *The Jewish Times*, 1909.

77 "The Jewish School Question," *University Magazine*, 8, 4 (December 1909), 556-57.

78 *London Jewish Chronicle*, May 21, 1909.

79 D. Rome, "On the Jewish School Question in Montreal, 1903-1931," *Canadian Jewish Archives*, New Series, No. 3 (Montreal: Canadian Jewish Congress, 1975), p. 78.

80 *London Jewish Chronicle*, May 21, 1909, p. 79.

81 This echoes the words of Sir Narcisse F. Belleau, who in 1865 recalled the liberalism of Lower Canada's habitants, "liberalism which they demonstrated a very long time ago by decreeing the emancipation of the Jews long before any other nation in the world dreamt of such a thing." (*Parliamentary Debates on the Subject of the Confederation of the British North American Provinces* [Quebec: Queen's Printer, 1865] p. 183 and 286.)

82 "Les écoliers juifs," *L'Action catholique*, February 4, 1926, p. 3.

83 "Quelques problèmes de l'heure analysés par M. Henri Bourassa" (article signed L. D.), *Le Devoir*, January 17, 1925, p. 2.

84 Ibid. Henri Bourassa was probably right. Jewish presence in the Protestant schools led to secularization in that system, and as a result, reinforced the trend toward secularization in both school systems.

85 During the same period, Monsignor Georges Gauthier, archbishop and administrator of the archdiocese of Montreal, issued a warning to the Jews when he was addressing American film producers: "Moreover, I deny Americans and Jews the right to come and speculate on our morals this way! If they are not satisfied with the way we in Quebec censor their films, they can keep them!" (*La Patrie*, April 22, 1926, p. 1).

86 *La Semaine religieuse de Montréal*, March 20, 1930, p. 184-85.

87 Ibid., p. 181.

88 *L'Action catholique*, March 21, 1930, p. 3.

89 Ibid., March 19, 1930, p. 3.

90 Rome, "On the Jewish School Question in Montreal, 1903-1931," p. 127-28.

91 Robert Rumilly, "L'affaire des écoles juives, 1928-1931," *Revue d'histoire de l'Amérique française*, 10, 2 (September 1956), 222-44.

92 *Le Goglu*, May 30, 1930, p. 2.

93 Ibid., October 17, 1930, reproduced from, *Le Devoir* of October 8, 1930.

94 In 1964, the Protestant School Board of Greater Montreal made an unsuccessful recommendation to the Royal Commission on Education that this organization be revived.

95 This type of parish school had considerable influence on the Jewish education system both in Canada and the United States.

96 Ultimately betrayed by the very sponsor of the 1930 law, Athanase David revealed his hostility toward Jews in a letter to Mackenzie King dated November 25, 1938 (Rome, *Clouds in the Thirties*, p. 523-28). It is difficult to believe that this letter came from the same political figure who courageously came to the defence of Jews a few years earlier, and had been attacked by anti-Semites. Nonetheless, within a decade, David turned his back on his Jewish countrymen to the point of resorting to the verbal excesses of the people who had been his own enemies during the 1930s. He even attacked their desperate effort to save fellow Jews from the European fascists.

97 One member of this group was Michael Garber, the most highly-respected activist in the struggle for Jewish schools. He succeeded Samuel Bronfman as president of the Canadian Jewish Congress and became a central figure in the World Jewish Congress.

98 Linteau et al., *Histoire du Québec contemporain*, p. 416 and 422.

99 *Canadian Historical Review*, 60, 2 (1979), 178-209.

100 Irving Abella and Harold Troper, *None Is Too Many. Canada and the Jews of Europe* (Toronto: Lester and Orpen Dennys, 1982).

101 The *Saint-Louis* left Hamburg on May 15 and requested asylum in Argentina, Uruguay, Paraguay, the Bahamas, Cuba, the United States and on June 7, in Canada. Several Canadian figures pleaded its cause, but in vain. It was finally forced to turn back and unload its passengers in England, Belgium and Holland. Many were recaptured by the Nazis and died in the gas chambers.

102 It is possible that Mackenzie King, skillful manipulator of people that he was, used the anti-Semitic uproar in Quebec to pass off his own views, all the while maintaining that Lapointe had pressured him. He certainly had no hesitation in rejecting Quebec's position on other occasions, as in the 1943 referendum on the Canadian government's commitment not to impose overseas conscription. For more on the King-Blair administration, see Rome, *Clouds in the Thirties*.

103 In *La Nation* of September 1, 1938, for example.

104 The Society sent a petition bearing 128,000 signatures to the House with the member Lacroix. It opposed all immigration but especially Jewish immigration (*Débats*, 1939, 1, p.428).

105 H. Blair Neatby, *William Lyon Mackenzie King. III: The Prism of Unity* (Toronto, 1976).

106 M. J. Finkelstein to Leo Mahrer, August 29, 1934, Archives of the Canadian Jewish Congress, 2A 1934, Box 4.

107 Rome, *Clouds in the Thirties*, p. 64.

108 *The Winnipeg Tribune*, January 11, 1938.

109 Rome, *Clouds in the Thirties*, p. 26.

110 Réal Caux, "La parti national social chrétien. Adrien Arcand, ses idées, son oeuvre et son influence," M.A. thesis, Laval University, 1958.

111 Ontario was less affected: 4.3 percent in 1929 and 17.2 percent in 1931.

112 The federal and Quebec governments committed themselves to pay for the "food, clothing, fuel and rent" of unemployed workers (Vaugeois and Lacoursière, *Canada-Québec*, p. 507-08). However, fearing a new exodus to the United States similar to that of the nineteenth century, the Taschereau government adopted legislation concerning colonization. The church followed suit by supporting the back-to-the-land movement.

113 The LPP served as a front for the CPC.

114 In March 1941, Monsignor Chaumont, Vicar-General of the archdiocese of Montreal, gave imprimatur to a work entitled *La vraie France* (Montreal: Éditions Fides, 1941). It was written by Gilmard, the pen name of Father Gérard Petit, CSC, a Montreal priest. Among the great names appearing in the table of contents — Péguy, Claudel, Maritain and so on — is that of Philippe Pétain, who, in a sub-title on page 137, is proclaimed to be "the saviour of France." The true France, explains the introduction is "everything which is beautiful, noble and great in the Oldest Daughter of the Church." She perpetuates national tradition and is beyond "ousting the spiritual in favour of civil acts" and "materialist legislation." For right-wing Quebec, this true France was pre-1789 France.

115 Abella and Troper, *None Is Too Many*, p. 108.

116 Caux, "Le parti national social chrétien," p. 30, n. 45.

117 Ibid.

118 The editorial, signed Émile Goglu, concludes with a veritable declaration of war: "The outcry and the race war do not frighten us, and we shall answer the cry of the Jews with a formidable cry of national unity and Canadianism, until people all over this land agree that your status as Jews gives you no rights or privileges here; you must cease being Jews to become Canadians; you have your homeland and this nation is not the homeland of Jews but of Canadians. . . . If our laws, traditions, morals and tolerance do not satisfy you, there is but one thing for you to do: leave." (Editorial, *Le Goglu*, April 4, 1930, p. 2.)

119 Article reproduced from *Le Miroir* of May 11, 1930 and signed Adrien Arcand. It includes statements such as: "Wherever they go, the Jews carry this idea that Gentiles are not the children of God, that Israel will one day dominate the earth and claim all the other races as its servants." (*Le Goglu*, May 23, 1930, p. 3.)

120 Article signed by Adrien Arcand, *Le Goglu*, July 25, 1930, p. 6.

121 "M. Houde et nos journaux," *Le Goglu*, October 17, 1930, p. 3.

122 *Le Goglu*, June 6, 1930, p. 3.

123 Quebec anti-Semites and even nationalists fought this law, saying it was an unjustified privilege. In 1906, however, Bourassa had won Catholics a relaxing of former legislation based on the Protestant tradition, which was much more severe. Once the old law was relaxed, small shops could open on Sunday after mass in villages and neighbourhoods, contrary to the puritan custom of "Blue Sunday." As has often been the case in the history of anti-Semitism, hatred of Jews blinded its propagators to their own religion and national interests. The 1906 legislation was revoked during the anti-Semitic outburst of 1937.

124 From an editorial entitled "Un acte qui crie vengeance," signed "Oscar Chameau," in *Le Chameau*, October 3, 1930, p. 2.

125 Signed "Ti Luc Chameau," in *Le Chameau*, February 5, 1932, p. 2-4.

126 "Fascisme d'Adrien Arcand pas mort au Québec," *Vrai*, February 18, 1956, p. 12.

127 Forest, "La question juive au Canada," p. 226, 227. The author adds: "There is no question of that. But we do not see why we should turn our school finances upside down for the group of immigrants who have never wholeheartedly adopted another homeland."

128 Quoted by Albert Pelletier in "Xénophobie," *La Nation*, February 20, 1936, p. 1.

129 Mason Wade, *French-Canadian Outlook: A Brief Account of the Unknown North Americans* (New York: Viking, 1946), p.123-25.

130 Jacques Brassier (pseudonym for L. Groulx), "Pour qu'on vive," *L'Action nationale*, June 1933, p. 361-67.

131 Letter from Lionel Groulx to M. Lamoureux, dated November 19, 1954. Quoted by J. P. Gaboury, "Le nationlisme de Lionel Groulx. Aspects idéologiques," *Cahiers des sciences sociales*, No. 6 (Ottawa: Éditions de l'Université d'Ottawa, 1970), p. 35-36.

132 *La Conquête, Une publication de la Ligue de l'Achat Chez Nous*, No. 16 (Montreal, 1938).

133 *Le Goglu*, October 17, 1930. In a speech given to the Association catholique des voyageurs de commerce, Lionel Groulx himself acknowledged the brutality with which the anti-Sem-

ites were conducting their campaign. (*Orientations* [Montreal: Éditions du Zodiaque, 1935], p. 220-30.)

134 *Le Devoir*, January 19, 1934, p. 1.

135 *La Nation*, March 7, 1936, p. 1. Paul Bouchard, a radical nationalist, founded *La Nation* in 1936, at the same time as the "Faisceaux républicains," who were separatist in orientation.

136 *Jewish Daily Eagle*, July 1934.

137 Brassier, "Pour qu'on vive" (April 1933), p. 243.

138 Annai Loison of *La Boussole*, "L'antisémitisme et notre restauration économique," reproduced in the neighbourhood newspaper *Chez nous dans l'Est* (Montreal, September 1939), p. 8.

139 This college belonged to the Jesuits. Premier Taschereau protested to Monsignor Gauthier. He said in public that the people who took them in should not forget that they would be the first to disappear in case of revolution.

140 Philippe Ferland, "A propos des Jeune-Canada," in "Tribune libre," *Le Canada*, April 25, 1933, p. 3.

141 "Politiciens et Juifs, discours prononcés le 20 avril, 1933," at the Gesù hall by Pierre Dansereau, Gilbert Manseau, Pierre Dagenais, René Monette and André Laurendeau, *Les Cahiers des Jeune-Canada*, No. 1 (Montreal: Le Devoir, 1933), p. 12-13.

142 Ibid., p. 23.

143 Ibid., p. 46.

144 Ibid., p. 55-56 and 62-63. See also *Le Devoir*, April 21, 1933, p. 1.

145 We must note here that one segment of the Quebec intelligentsia did oppose this wave of aggressively ethnocentric nationalism. The day after the Gesù counter-protest, *Le Canada* published a warning by a reader, P. Ferland, in its open forum. He cautioned against parochialism and the propensity of Jeune-Canada members to gobble up Nazi propaganda. He noted a declaration by Cardinal Verdier and an account by the French writer René Pinon, both concerning the persecution of Jews in Germany. This is what Pinon wrote in the *Illustration de France*: "The most violent wave of anti-Semitism is now sweeping across the Reich, the likes of which we have not seen for many long years in a modern state." He referred to unprovoked assaults "of revolting barbarity, worthy of the Russian pogroms." In an editor's note, the newspaper responded to the letter in these terms: "What we do not want to see is the development of French-Canadian nationalism that derives its only inspiration from racial animosity." (*Le Canada*, April 25, 1933, p. 3.)

146 Brassier, "Pour qu'on vive," June 1933, p. 364-65.

147 "Les 'Jeune-Canada' et l'antisémitisme," *Le Devoir*, January 30, 1934, p. 2.

148 André Laurendeau, "Why Keep Reminding Us That He's A Jew," *Maclean's Magazine*, 1 (1963), 275.

149 We know that his novel, *Les demi-civilisés*, was considered immoral in 1934, which led to his resignation as editor-in-chief of the Quebec City newspaper *Le Soleil*. (Teboul, *Mythes et images du Juif au Québec*, p. 177.)

150 *Le Canada*, May 21, 1934, p. 3.

151 Forest, "La question juive au Canada."

152 It is a fable about five Canadians shipwrecked on a desert island. Each one has a skill: carpentry, farming, stock breeding, agronomy and prospecting. They set to work and soon become established. The only problem is that they have no money. Meanwhile, a refugee, Oliver Gluckterlingmann, arrives from Central Europe. He is a banker, and they ask him to help them set up a monetary system. The prospector brings him gold as a guarantee for the system. Oliver hastens to bury it in secret and distributes in its place one dollar bills on demand, except that he asks for interest on each one. After a while, money runs short among the borrowers and the banker is doing business in gold. He is exultant. He evokes Rothschild. He dreams of dominating the world. The parable ends on a sensational note. A

chest washes up on the beach containing Social Credit publications. The Canadians realize that they can get along very well without the banker. They discover evidence of the "fraud"; the barrel of gold really contains nothing but stones. They send the banker back to Canada on the next passing ship. (Summary of a reprint of the booklet dated June 1981 in *Michael Journal*, at Rougemont, Quebec, entitled "The Money Myth Explored.")

153 Letter dated June 20, 1939, Archives of the Canadian Jewish Congress, ZA 1939, June.

154 *L'Action catholique*, September 21, 1921, p. 3.

Chapter IV

1 National Archives of the Canadian Jewish Congress.

2 Ibid.

3 *Le Devoir*, Vol. 3, August 24, 1984, p. 7.

4 Jacques Torczyner, *Client and Community Needs: How They Can Be Better Met* (Montreal: Ville-Marie Social Service Centre, 1974).

5 Peter C. Newman, *The Canadian Establishment*, vol. 1 (Toronto: McClelland and Stewart, 1975). As Charles Bronfman confided to him: "It's pathetic, when you think of it, that my father was the first Jewish director of the Bank of Montreal. I mean, that's almost incredible. And then you had all those token French-Canadian directors. This is all definitely changing, and changing for the good" (p. 180).

6 The major clubs in western Canada took even longer to open up. The Manitoba Club in Winnipeg, for instance, did not accept its first Jewish member, Gerry Libling, until 1972.

7 In 1902, the Institute moved to 2040 Bleury Street, the present-day site of a subway station.

8 Another important hurdle was crossed when the priests agreed to participate in the Annual Institute of the Temple Emmanuel. Rabbi Stern presided over the event.

9 From remarks made during a private audience to pilgrims from Belgian Catholic Radio and published in *Documentation catholique*, 39 (December 5, 1938), Col. 1460.

10 The initiative for these meetings came from the Jesuit Irénée Beaubien and goes back to 1958. One significant step in this process was the creation of a Christian Pavilion at Expo '67 through the united efforts of eight Christian churches in Canada (see, among others, the interview with Father Irénée Beaubien, S.J., entitled "Le dialogue oecuménique ou le désir de mieux comprendre," which appeared in *Revue Notre-Dame/RND*, 1 [January 1982], 16-27, as well as "Irénée Beaubien, 30 ans au service de l'unité des chrétiens," *L'Église de Montréal* [January 1982], 7-9).

11 A number of colleagues came from Brazil to France to work with her in Quebec with this new perspective.

12 More recently, one of the most remarkable gestures of Catholic support for a cause which was often controversial but fundamental for the Jewish people, came from Montreal during the war with Lebanon. At a time when anti-Israeli propaganda was rife in some educational circles, Father Valiquette denounced this campaign of vilification by the enemies of Israel from atop a truck during a demonstration by members of the teachers' union.

13 Sister Marie-Noëlle de Baillehache, "Le dialogue judéo-chrétien vu du côté juif," *L'Église canadienne* (May 1971), 158.

14 Denise Robillard, "Soeur Marie-Noëlle, une pionnière du dialogue judéo-chrétien," *Le Devoir*, August 22, 1981, p. 4.

15 The Haggadah (literally, The Story) is different from the Halakah (The Way) in that it forms the non-legal part of the Talmud. The halakah supplements the scriptural law of Judaism, while the Haggadah passes on historical, biographical and folkloric traditions as well as proverbs, discussions, biblical commentaries and so on.

16 Francophone Jews from Africa and Asia faced a different issue. Their Sephardic culture is infused with religion, perhaps even more than for the majority of Ashkenazim, and their

faith is often very inward-looking. Unlike the Ashkenazim, they had not experienced Europe's radical lay movement and were not nationalistic. Unlike the young Europeans, they had not forged a synthesis of Western civilization, Zionism, Jewish culture and the religious values which lay at the very base of the European communities. Many young Sephardim had come to reject the Jewish ideologies of Africa and adopt a more French attitude which included the cosmopolitanism of the Sorbonne. As twentieth-century Jews, it was difficult for them to define their faith and allegiances in relation not only to religion, but to the community and the nation as well.

17 This type of spiritual adventure was described by Josh Freed in his book *Moonwebs: Journey Into the Mind of a Cult* (Virgo Press, 1980). The 1981 film *Ticket to Heaven* was based on this book, in which Freed tells the story of a successful attempt to lead a young Jew involved in a cult back to his Montreal family.

18 According to Fernand G. Filion, "La Communauté séfarade de Montréal: une analyse ethno-historique des structures communautaires," M.A. thesis, Laval University, 1978. In 1956, the community was divided as follows: 78 percent from Morocco, 8 percent from Spanish Morocco, 4.5 percent from Europe and Israel and 9.5 percent born in Quebec or other Mediterranean countries.

19 The term anglo-Sephardim is actually more precise; this community retained nothing of Sephardic culture other than its rite. The first Montreal Jews traced their roots to Europe (England and Germany), and so rite was their only cultural link to the original Sephardic tradition.

20 Kayfetz, "The Evolution of the Jewish Community in Toronto," p. 19.

21 Note from Pinhas Ibghy to Saul Hayes, vice-president of the Canadian Jewish Congress. Roger Cohen-Scali, Guy Bouzaglou, Yossi Levy, Léon Ouaknine, *Être nous-mêmes. Histoire des Juifs marocains depuis leur arrivée à Montréal* (Montreal: Jewish Community Centre, n.d.), p. 11.

22 Ibid.

23 Filion, "La communauté séfarade de Montréal."

24 A benevolent association created to subsidize certain religious needs within the community: prayers at funerals, visits to people in hospital, presence at births and when setting up a new home.

25 Cohen-Scali et al., *Être nous-mêmes*, p. 31.

26 Ibid., p. 33.

27 6645 Darlington Street, Montreal.

28 Cohen-Scali et al., *Être nous-mêmes*, p. 40.

29 Ibid., p. 46-47.

30 Filion, "La communauté séfarade de Montréal," p. 16.

31 In their study "Jewish Intermarriage in Montreal, 1962-72," *Jewish Social Studies*, 37, 3 (Summer 1975), 267, Jean-Claude Lasry and Evelyn Bloomfield-Schacter attributed the high rate of endogamy "in part to the few partners available on the side of the French-Canadian majority." It is true that the rate of endogamy among French Quebecers was 96 percent.

32 This rate is still relatively high in comparison to other ethnic groups such as the Egyptians, Iraqis and Lebanese, for whom the rate was just 19 percent.

33 In his memoires, future NDP leader David Lewis recalled this aspect of Montreal life when he was showing the city to tourists: "One of the questions we were invariably asked by American tourists, particularly by teachers, was how the English and the French got along. For some months I was stuck for an answer. I didn't know because I had almost never seen them together. This led me to compose an answer which I believed to be true and which I repeated word for word dozens of times: 'They get along very well together by keeping studiously apart. In hindsight I see how very true this aphorism was, and how very sad, for I uttered these words without appreciating the consequences of this condition for Canada."

(David Lewis, *The Good Fight, Political Memoirs 1909-1958* [Toronto: Macmillan of Canada, 1982], p. 26.)

34 The Honourable Louis Saint-Laurent was prime minister at the time.

35 On October 15, 1969, for example, one of the round table discussions organized at Laval University by the Comité palestinien de Laval and the Mouvement de libération populaire mondiale, was attended by René Lévesque, then president of the Partis québécois, as well as Michel Chartrand of the CSN (*Le Soleil*, October 17, 1969). He accepted the invitation because "in the near future, Quebec will be speaking out internationally" (Report of the meeting, National Archives of the Canadian Jewish Congress). Among other things, he maintained that it was a serious political and moral error to "make Palestinians and Arabs pay the cost of reparations to the Christian and German world." In practice, he seemed to favour the creation of a Palestine belonging equally to the Arabs and the Jews.

36 *La Presse* of May 10, 1978 published an article by Jean-Pierre Richard and Pierre Saint-Germain on page B-4, entitled "Froissé par un accroc au protocole, Lévesque refuse d'assister aux fêtes juives." It was the thirtieth anniversary of the founding of the state of Israel. According to officials in Quebec City, the premier received the invitation of the last moment without the required formalities and so he appointed Gérald Godin and Yves Michaud to attend the celebration. At a time when alarmist articles by Jewish observers in Canada and the United States abounded, his absence clearly worried the Jewish community.

37 In the *Journal de Montréal* of September 6, 1972, René Lévesque described the Munich incident as an act of despair by a nation that found itself forgotten, isolated and betrayed after the Six Day War. Its activists had no choice but to cast themselves into the most absurd extremism. In an article entitled "The Jewish Question in Quebec," Morton Weinfeld conceded that the reaction of René Lévesque was personal and not that of his party. Nonetheless, it came from a political leader who subsequently became premier of a province and aspired to leading an independent state in North America. It certainly provided grounds for dismay on the part of Jews in Canada and the United States (*Midstream*, October 1977, p. 28).

38 Warren Perley, "Exodus of Young Worries Montreal Jews," Part 5 of the series "Quebec's Troubled Minority," *The Gazette*, Montreal, March 26, 1982, p. A-1 and A-8.

39 Reproduced in translation in *Le Devoir* of February 17, 1982, p. 9.

40 *Le Devoir*, February 22, 1982. Reverend Claude de Mestral of the United Church, well known in ecumenical circles, commented on this article in a letter to *Le Devoir*. He pointed out that the two students remained remarkably silent on the question of contemporary French Quebec: "The Authors of the article in the *Jerusalem Post* probably don't know a thing about it . . . because they live 'in English.'" His reaction was similar to that of Asen Balikci, a member of the Jewish community and a professor of anthropology at the University of Montreal. Commenting on the same article, he wrote that "the massive anglicization of the Ashkenazim has meant that they now maintain very close ties to the English community." (Asen Balikci, "Les 'souffrances' des Juifs montréalais," *Le Devoir*, February 23, 1982, p. 7.)

Chapter V

1 Abraham Arnold, *Jewish Life in Canada* (Edmonton: Hurtig, 1976), p. 87. Speech delivered at the golden anniversary celebration of the Saint-Jean Baptiste Society, June 24, 1902.

2 Yvan Lamonde, *Louis-Adolphe Paquet*, Collections Classiques canadiens, 45 (Montreal: Fides, n.d.), p. 59-60.

3 Rome, "On the Jewish School Question in Montreal, 1903-1931," p. 74.

4 Perley, "Exodus of Young Worries Montreal Jews," p. A-8.

5 The small Hasidic community alone does not share this way of thinking, and for very particular reasons. Because of their essentially religious and apolitical stance, the Hasidim do not side with any group, Anglophones included. Their neutrality takes the place of openness and constitutes a guarantee of their growth in Quebec society.

6 Louis Noveck, *Meeting the Needs of the Jewish Elderly in Canada* (Jerusalem: Broakdale Institute, 1985), p. 14. Nonetheless, it is worth noting that Jewish immigration to Quebec from Europe and North Africa rose (from 451 in 1971 to 571 in 1981).

7 Perley, "Exodus."

8 Ibid.

9 Significantly, the CEGEP legislation gave private colleges the option of establishing an official religious affiliation; only two out of thirty did so.

10 An increasing number of studies are examining the contributions of various ethnic groups who helped to build French Quebec society. The most important seems to have come from Canada's Indian people, and the revival of native studies has begun to clarify Quebec's ethnic and cultural debt to that group.

11 This is true of everything that comes under the teaching of history.

12 Victor Goldbloom, "Le judaïsme québécois. Une communauté vigoureuse, bien enracinée et assez sereine," *Le Devoir*, April 8, 1982, p. 36 and 38.

13 Ibid., p. 38.

14 Without prejudice to those who do not identify with either group, such as the native people.

15 He cites the names of Gaston Miron, Gérald Godin, Paul Chamberland and Jean-Marc Piotte.

16 Montreal: Éditions de l'Étincelle, 1972. Preface by Jean-Paul Sartre.

17 Translation in *Relations*, No. 463 (October 1980), p. 272-75. Alex Mangey is the author of *Poésie et société au Québec* (Quebec: Les Presses de l'Université Laval, 1937-70).

18 *Relations*, p. 274-75.

Bibliography

Abella, I. and H. Troper. *None is Too Many: Canada and the Jews of Europe*. Toronto: Lester and Orpen Dennys, 1982.

Agus, J. P. *L'évolution de la pensée juive, des temps bibliques au début de l'ère moderne*. Paris: Payot, 1961.

Anctil, Pierre. *Juifs et réalités juives à Québec*. Québec: Institut québécois de recherche sur la culture, 1983.

_____. *Le Devoir, les Juifs et l'immigration, de Bourassa à Laurendeau*. Québec: Institut québécois de recherche sur la culture, 1988.

_____. *Le rendez-vous manqué*. Québec: Institut québécois de recherche sur la culture, 1988.

_____. "Laurendeau et le grand virage identitaire de la révolution tranquille." In Lucille Beaudry and Robert Comeau, *André Laurendeau, un intellectuel d'ici*. Québec: Les Presses de l'Université du Québec, 1990.

Arcand, Adrien. "A bas la haine!" *La Vérité* [Montréal], 1965.

_____. *Chrétien ou Juif, les Juifs forment-t-ils une minorité et doivent-t-ils être traités comme tels dans la Province de Québec?* Montréal: N.p., 1930.

_____. *Clé du mystère*. Montréal: N.p., 1937.

_____. "Discours-programme exposé des principes et du programme du parti national social chrétien." *Le Patriote* [Montréal], 1934.

_____. "Fascisme ou Socialisme." *Le Patriote* [Montréal], 1933.

_____. *Key to the Mystery: The Jewish Question as Explained by the Jews Themselves*. Montreal: N.p., 1937.

_____. *La république universelle*. Montréal: Service canadien de librairie, 1950.

_____. *La révolte des matérialismes*. Montréal: N.p., n.d.

_____. *Le Christianisme a-t-il fait faillite? Notre devoir devant les faits*. Montréal: Service canadien de librairie, 1954.

_____. *Le communisme installé chez-nous*. Montréal: N.p., n.d.

Arnold, Abraham. *Jewish Life in Canada*. Edmonton: Hurtig Publishers, 1976.

Asselin, Olivar. *Pensées françaises*. Montréal: Editions de l'A.C.-F., 1937.

Avakumovic, Ivan. *The Communist Party in Canada: A History*. Toronto: McClelland and Stewart, 1975.

Baldwin, Earl of Bewdly. *The Plight of the Refugees*. Ottawa: Canadian National Committee on Refugees and Victims of Political Persecution, 1939.

Belanger, A.J. *L'apolitisme des idéologies québécoises, le grand tournant de 1934-36*. Québec: Les Presses de l'Université Laval, 1974.

Belkin, S. *The Poale Zion Movement in Canada, 1904-20*. Montreal: Actions Committee of the Labour Zionist Movement in Canada, 1956. (In Yiddish.)

Benault, B. and B. Lévesque. *Eléments pour une sociologie des communautés religieuses au Québec*. Sherbrooke/Montréal: Université de Sherbrooke/Les Presses de l'Université de Montréal, 1975.

Benet, Stephen Vincent. "Jacob and the Indians." *Saturday Evening Post*, May 14, 1958.

Bergeron, René. *Le Corps mystique de l'antéchrist*. Montréal: Fides, 1941.

Bertley, Leo. "L'histoire du Québec vue par un Québécois noir." In *Qui est Québécois?*. Edited by R. Vachon and J. Langlais. Coll. Rencontre des cultures, 1. Montréal: Fides, 1979.

Betcherman, R. *The Swastika and the Maple Leaf: Fascist Movements in Canada in the Thirties*. Toronto: Fitzhenry and Whiteside, 1975.

Bibeau, Gilles. *Les Bérets blancs, essai d'interpretation d'un mouvement québécois marginal*. Montréal: Editions Parti pris, 1976.

Boileau, Ethel. *When Yellow Leaves*. Toronto: Ryerson, 1935.

Bourassa, Henri. "Impressions d'Europe." *Le Devoir*, July 1938.

Brodey, Arthur. "Political and Civil Status of the Jews in Canada." M.H.L. thesis, N.Y. Jewish Institute on Religion, 1933.

Brown, Michael. *Jew or Juif? Jews, French Canadians and Anglo-Canadians, 1759-1914*. Philadelphia: Jewish Publication Society, 1987.

——————. "Jewish Foundations in Canada: The Jewish the French and the English, to 1914." Dissertation, State University of New York, Buffalo, 1976.

Bruce, Robert A. *Address on Gentile-Jewish Relationships*. Toronto: N.p., 1934.

Brunelle, Dorval. *Les trois colombes, essai*. Montréal: VLB Editeur, 1985.

Bureau, Margeurite Bourgeoys. *Un lis fleurit entre les épines*. Montréal: N.p., 1928.

Caux, Réal. "Le parti national social chrétien. Adrien Arcand, ses idées, son oeuvre et son influence." M.A. thesis, Université Laval, 1958.

Cherniack, J. A. *The Case for Refugees*. Winnipeg: Conference of National Groups for Refugees, 1939.

Cohon, S. S. *Saint Thomas et les Juifs, réponse au R.P. Benoît Mailloux*. Montréal: Congres juif canadien, 1937.

Cohon, Samuel. "Why Do the Heathen Rage? Exposing the Deliberate Falsifications of the Bible, Talmud, and Other Sacred Literature." *Canadian Jewish Chronicle* [Montreal], 1937.

Concile oecuménique Vatican II. Constitutions, décrets, déclarations, messages. Paris: Editions du Centurion, 1967.

Cresthol, L. D. "The Jewish School Problem in the Province of Quebec from Its Origins to the Present Day: History and Facts." *The Eagle* [Montreal], 1926.

Dansereau, Gilbert et al. *Politiciens et juifs, discours prononcés par Pierre Dansereau, Gilbert Manseau, Pierre Dagenais, René Monette et André Laurendeau.* Montréal: Cahiers des Jeunes Canada, 1933.

De Maupassant, Jean. *Un grand armateur de Bordeaux, Abraham Gradis.* Bordeaux: Féret et fils, 1917.

De Sola, Bram. "The Jewish School Question," *University Magazine*, 8, 4 (December 1909), 556.

Delaplanche, J. F. O. *Le Pèlerin de terre sainte.* Canadian edition prepared by J. N. Duquet. Quebec: N. S. Hardy, 1887.

Douville, Raymond. *Aaron Hart, récit historique.* Trois Rivières: Editions du bien public, 1938.

Drumont, E. *La Dernière bataille.* Paris: Dentre, 1890.

Dupuis, J.-F. *Rome et Jérusalem.* Québec: Léger Brousseau, 1894.

Edmondson, Edward. *The Greatest War in History Now On: International Jewish System against National Patriotism.* New York: N.p., 1937.

Emard, Joseph. *Souvenirs d'un voyage en terre sainte.* Montréal: Chapleau, 1884.

Even, Louis. *Salvation Island: An Illustrated Parable for Young and Old.* Montreal: Institute of Political Action, 1957.

Faribault, Yves M. "A Propos de la question juive." *Revue dominicaine* (June 1935).

_____. "Le Sionisme." *Revue dominicaine* (May 1935), 327-45.

Farley, L. C. *Rapport du Congrès de la jeunesse à Québec, 23-26 juin 1908.* Montreal: Le Semeur, 1909.

Farley, P. A. *La terre sainte.* 2nd ed. Joliette: Action populaire, 1926.

Figler, Bernard. *Sam Jacobs: Member of Parliament.* Ottawa, 1970.

Filion, Fernand G. "La communauté séfarade de Montréal: une analyse ethno-historique des structures communautaires." M. A. thesis, Université Laval, 1978.

Forest, Ceslas. "La question juive au Canada." *Revue dominicaine* (November, December 1935), 247-77, 329-45.

Forsythe, J. Bell. *A Few Months in the East by a Canadian.* Quebec: Lovell, 1861.

Fournier, Marcel. *Communisme et anticommunisme au Québec (1920-1950).* Laval: Editions coopératives Albert Saint-Martin, 1979.

Freed, Josh. *Moonwebs: Journey into the Mind of a Cult.* New York: Virgo Press, 1980.

Freeman, Lawrence. *Don't Fall Off the Rocking Chair.* Toronto: McClelland and Stewart, 1978.

Gaboury, J.-P. "Le nationlisme de Lionel Groulx. Aspects idéologiques." *Cahiers des sciences sociales*, 6. Ottawa: Editions de l'Université d'Ottawa, 1970.

Gingras, Léon. *L'Orient.* Québec: Fréchette, 1848.

Gobeil, S. *La griffe rouge sur l'université de Montréal.* Montréal: Editions du patriote, 1934.

Goesbriand, Louis. *Voyage en Terre Sainte*. Montréal: Librairie St-Joseph, 1884.

Golick, Peter Samuel. *A Tribute to Freedom, 1832-1986: On the 150th Anniversary of the Declaration Granting Equal Rights and Privileges to Persons of the Jewish Religion*. Montreal: Canadian Jewish Congress, 1982.

Groulx, Lionel. *Orientations*. Montréal: Editions du Zodiaque, 1935.

Hamelin, Jean and Nicole Gagnon. *Histoire du catholicisme québécois*. Tome I: *Le XXe siècle, 1898-1940*. Edited by Nive Voisine. Montréal: Boréal Express, 1984.

Hamelin, Jean, ed. *Histoire du Québec*. Montréal: Editions France/Amérique, 1977.

Harpell, I. I. *The New Deal vs the Old System of Exploitation*. Ste-Anne-de-Bellevue: Gardenvale, 1935.

Harrison, C. V. *The Horseman*. Toronto: McClelland and Stewart, 1967.

Harvey, Jean-Charles. *Les demi-civilisés*. Montréal: Editions du Totem, 1934; Editions de l'Homme, 1962.

——————. *Un principe de vie sauvage*. Montréal: Association de l'unité et de bonne entente du Canada, n.d.

Helbronner, Jules. *Rapport de la Commission royal sur les relations entre le travail et le capital*. Annexe O. Ottawa: Imprimeur de la Reine et Contrôleur de la Papeterie, A. Sénécal, surintendant des impressions, 1889.

Howse, E. M. *Two Sermons: I. Christian Canada and the Refugees, and the Refugees-A Policy*. Winnipeg: N.p., 1938.

Huot, J.-Antonio. *La question juive chez nous, avec une lettre d'un lecteur de l'Action catholique à l'auteur*. Québec: Action catholique, 1926.

——————. *Le fléau maçonnique*. Québec: Dussault et Proulx, 1906.

——————. *Le poison maçonnique*. Québec: Action sociale, 1912.

——————. "La Terre Sainte, notes et impressions d'un pèlerin." *La Semaine religieuse de Québec* (July 1928-April 1929).

Indig, Sheldon. "Canadian Jewry and Their Struggle for Exemption in the Federal Lord's Day Act of 1906." M.A. thesis, University of Windsor, 1975.

Jaenen, Cornelius J. "Le Colbertisme." *Revue d'histoire de l'Amérique française*, 18, 1 (June 1964), 64-68, and 18, 2 (September 1964), 252-66.

Jones, Richard. *L'idéologie de l'Action catholique, 1919-39*. Québec: Les Presses de l'Université Laval, 1974.

Jullian, Camille Louis. *Histoire de Bordeaux, depuis les origines jusqu'en 1895*. Marseille: Laffitte, 1980.

Kayfetz, Ben. "The Evolution of the Toronto Jewish Community." In *A People and Its Faith*. Edited by Albert Rose. Toronto: University of Toronto Press, 1959.

Kennaghan, W. P. "Freedom of Religion in the Province of Quebec." Thesis, Duke University, 1966.

La Conquête. No. 16. Montréal: Ligue de l'Achat Chez Nous, 1938.

L'Abbé, G. *La Terre Sainte*. Montréal: L. Perrault, 1841.

Labrecque, Cyrille. *Consultation théologique*. 2nd ed. Québec: Librairie de l'Action Catholique, 1946.

Lacasse, Zacharie. *La quatrième mine*. N.p., 1893.

——————. *Une mine produisante d'or et d'argent*. Québec: Darveave, 1880.

Lalanne, P. E. "Why We Should Oppose the Jews." *Le Patriote* [Montréal], 1935.

Lamarche, M. A. "Notre étude d'ensemble sur la question juive." *Revue dominicaine* (January 1935), 50-54.

Lamonde, Yvan. *Louis-Adolphe Paquet*. Séries Classiques canadiens, 45. Montréal: Fides, 1972.

Langlais, J. and R. Vachon, eds. "The Jewish Community in Quebec." *Interculture*, 96 (July-September 1987).

Langlais, Jacques. *Les Jésuites du Québec en Chine (1919-1955)*. Coll. Travaux du laboratoire d'histoire religieuse de l'Université Laval, 3. Québec: Les Presses de l'Université Laval, 1979.

—————— and Robert Vachon, eds. *Qui est Québécois?* Coll. Rencontre des cultures, 1. Montréal: Fides, 1979.

Langlais, Jacques, Pierre Laplante and Joseph Levy. *Le Québec de demain et les communautés culturelles*. Coll. Vision globale. Montréal: Méridien, 1990.

Laurendeau, André. "Notre nationalisme." *Tracts Jeune Canada*, 5 (1935).

Leduc, André and Jean Hamelin. *Les journaux du Québec, de 1764 à 1964*. Québec: Les Presses de l'Université Laval, 1965.

Léon XIII. Encyclique *Humanum Genum*. Montréal: Les Presses de l'Etandard, 1884.

Lewis, David. *The Good Fight: Political Memoirs 1909-1958*. Toronto: Macmillan of Canada, 1982.

Linteau, P.-A., R. Durocher and J.-C. Robert. *Histoire du Québec contemporain, de la Confédération à la crise, 1867-1929*. Montréal: Boréal Express, 1979.

Lipton, Charles. *Histoire du syndicalisme au Canada et au Québec, 1827-1959*. Translated by Michel van Schendel. Montréal: Editions Parti pris, 1976.

Mailloux, Benoît. "Saint Thomas et les Juifs." *Revue dominicaine* (June 1935). Reprinted as pamphlet by Oeuvre de presse domicaine, Montreal.

——————. "A propos de Saint Thomas et les Juifs." *Revue dominicaine* (November 1936), 123-51.

——————. "Les Juifs et les temps modernes." *Revue dominicaine* (April 1935), 245-64.

Mair, Nathan H. *Quest for Quality in the Protestant Public Schools of Quebec*. Quebec: Conseil superieur de l'éducation, comité protestant, 1980.

Marcus, J. R. *American Jewry, Documents, Eighteenth Century*. Cincinnati: Hebrew Union College Press, 1959.

——————. *Early American Jewry*. Philadephia: Jewish Publication Society, 1951.

Maritain, Jacques. "A propos de la question juive." *Revue dominicaine* (June 1935), 402-10.

Martineau, Raymond-Marie. "Les Juifs et les chrétiens." *Revue dominicaine* (March 1935), 167-85.

Mathieu, Marie. *La Semaine Sainte à Jérusalem*. Montréal: Cook, 1922.

Maugey, Axel. *Poésie et société au Québec, 1937-1970*. Québec: Les Presses de l'Université Laval, 1972.

Memmi, Albert. *Dépendance*. Paris: Gallimard, 1979.

Menard, Joseph. *Enseignement religieux et réveil économique*. Montréal: Editions du Patriote, 1937.

————. *Le clergé et les juifs*. Longueuil: N.p., 1937.

Monière, Denis. *Le développement des idéologies au Québec: des origines à nos jours*. Montréal: Editions Québec/Amérique, 1977.

Montsion, Hollande. "Les grands thèmes du mouvement national social chrétien et d'Adrien Arcand." Thesis, University of Ottawa, 1975.

Neatby, H. Blair. *William Lyon Mackenzie King, 1932-39: The Prism of Unity*. Toronto: University of Toronto Press, 1976.

Novick, Louis. *Meeting the Needs of the Jewish Elderly in Canada*. Jerusalem: Broakdale Institute, 1985.

O'Leary, Dostaler. *Séparatisme, doctrine constructive*. Montréal: Editions des jeunesses patriotiques, 1927.

Ouellette, Jean. "La Palestine au XIXe siècle vue par un voyageur de Québec." *Bulletin du centre de recherches civilisation canadienne-française de l'Université d'Ottawa*, 19 (December 1979), 15-21.

Pagnuelo, Simeon. *Études historiques et légales sur la liberté religieuse au Canada*. Montréal: Beauchemin et Valois, 1872.

Paquet, Msgr. Louis-Adolphe. *Droit publique de l'Église. Principes généraux*. Québec: Imprimerie J.-A. Laflamme, 1916.

————. *Droit publique de l'Église, action religieuse et la loi civile*. Québec: Imprimerie J.-A. Laflamme, 1916.

————. *Études et appréciations, nouveaux mélanges canadiens*. Québec: Imprimerie franciscaine missionaire, 1919.

Parliamentary Debates on the Subject of the Confederation of the BNA Provinces. Quebec, 1865.

Pelletier, A. *La source du mal de l'époque au Canada, par un Catholique*. N.p., 1881.

Perrault, Claude, ed. *Déclaration du Fief et Seigneurie de Montréal, au Papier Terrier du Domaine de Sa Majesté en la Province de Québec en Canada, faite le 3 Février 1781 par Jean Brassier, p.s.s.* Montréal: C. B. Payette, 1969.

Petit, Gérard. *La Vraie France*. Montréal: Editions Fides, 1941.

Pie IX. *Quanta cura et Syllabus. Documents réunis par Jean-Robert Armogathe*. Paris: Jean-Jacques Pauvert, 1967.

Pierrard, Pierre. *Juifs et catholiques français, de Drumont A Jules Isaac, 1886-1945*. Paris: Fayard, 1970.

Plamondon, J.-Edouard. "Le Juif." Conférence donnée au Cercle Charest de l'Association catholique de la jeunesse canadienne, le 30 mars 1910. *L'Action Sociale Catholique*, 1910.

Poliakov, Léon. *Histoire de l'antisémitisme. L'Europe suicidaire, 1870-1933.* Paris: Calmann-Lévy, 1977.

Pouliot, J. F. "La liberté des cultes au Canada." *Rapport de la Société canadienne d'histoire de l'Église catholique* (1933-34), 68-79.

Provancher, Leon. *De Québec à Jérusalem.* Québec: N.p., 1884.

—————— and Frédéric Jonsonne. *Le Chemin de la croix à Jérusalem.* Québec: Typographie de C. Darveau, 1881.

——————. *Pélerinage canadien en Terre Sainte.* Québec: Léger Brosseau, 1883.

Quinn, Magella. "Un prêtre bien de son temps, Zacharie Lacasse." In *Idéologies au Canada français,* Vol. 1: *1850-1900.* Edited by Fernand Dumont et al. Histoire et documentation de la culture. Québec: Les Presses de l'Université Laval, 1971.

Rapport annuel sur les grèves et les lock-outs. Ottawa: Ministère du Travail, 1901-1916.

Rapport de l'Archiviste de la Province du Québec pour 1957-1958 et 1958-59. Correspondance commerciale d'Abraham Gradis pour 1757. Québec: Rédempti Paradis, Imprimeur de sa Majesté la Reine, 1-52.

Rexford, E. I. *The Jewish Population and Protestant Schools.* Montreal: Renouf, 1924.

Rome, David. *The Early Jewish Presence in Canada: A Book Lover's Ramble through Jewish Canadiana.* Montreal: Jewish Public Library, 1971.

——————. "The Many Colours of Canadian Jewish Festivals: An Anthology for Anthropologists." Montreal, 1990. MS.

——————. "The Many Colours of Quebec Jewish Culture." Montreal, 1990. MS.

——————. "Benjamin Hart and 1829." *Canadian Jewish Archives.* New Series, no. 24. Montreal: Canadian Jewish Congress, 1982.

——————. "Clouds in the Thirties, on Anti-Semitism in Canada, 1929-39." *Canadian Jewish Archives.* 13 sections. Montreal: Canadian Jewish Congress, 1977-81.

——————. "Early Anti-semitism, The Imprint of Drumont." *Canadian Jewish Archives.* New Series, no. 35. Montreal: Canadian Jewish Congress, 1985.

——————. "Early Anti-Semitism: The Holy Land; Tardivel." *Canadian Jewish Archives.* New Series, no. 34. Montreal: Canadian Jewish Congress, 1985.

——————. "Early Anti-Semitism: The Voice of the Media, part 1." *Canadian Jewish Archives.* New Series, no. 33. Montreal: Canadian Jewish Congress, 1984.

——————. "Early Anti-Semitism: Threats to Equality." *Canadian Jewish Archives.* New Series, no. 31. Montreal: Canadian Jewish Congress, 1983.

——————. "Inventory Documents on the Jewish School Question, 1903-21." *Canadian Jewish Archives.* New Series, no. 2. Montreal: Canadian Jewish Congress, 1975.

——————. "Men of the Yiddish Press." *Canadian Jewish Archives.* New Series, no. 42. Montreal: Canadian Jewish Congress, 1989.

_____. "On Sunday Observance, 1906." *Canadian Jewish Archives*. New Series, no. 14. Montreal: Canadian Jewish Congress, 1975.

_____. "On the Early Harts." *Canadian Jewish Archives*. New Series, nos. 16, 17, 18. Montreal: Canadian Jewish Congress, 1980.

_____. "On the Jewish School Question in Montreal, 1903-31." *Canadian Jewish Archives*. New Series, no. 3. Montreal: Canadian Jewish Congress, 1975.

_____. "On the Jews of Lower Canada and 1837-38." *Canadian Jewish Archives*, New Series, nos. 28-30. Montreal: Canadian Jewish Congress, 1983.

_____. "Our Forerunners—At Work." *Canadian Jewish Archives*. New Series, nos. 9-10. Montreal: Canadian Jewish Congress, 1978.

_____. "Samuel Bécancour Hart and 1832." *Canadian Jewish Archives*. New Series, no. 3. Montreal: Canadian Jewish Congress, 1975.

_____. "The First Jewish Literary School." *Canadian Jewish Archives*. New Series, no. 41. Montreal: Canadian Jewish Congress, 1988.

_____. "The Immigration Story I—The Jewish Times, etc." *Canadian Jewish Archives*. New Series, no. 36. Montreal: Canadian Jewish Congress, 1986.

_____. "The Immigration Story II—Jacob's Opponents." *Canadian Jewish Archives*. New Series, no. 37. Montreal: Canadian Jewish Congress, 1987.

_____. "The Immigration Story III—The Yiddish Theatre; The Adler." *Canadian Jewish Archives*. New Series, no. 38. Montreal: Canadian Jewish Congress, 1987.

_____. "The Jewish Biography of Henri Bourassa." *Canadian Jewish Archives*. New Series, nos. 39-40. Montreal: Canadian Jewish Congress, 1988.

_____. "The Jewish Times." *Canadian Jewish Archives*. New Series, no. 36. Montreal: Canadian Jewish Congress, 1986.

_____. "The Plamondon Case and S. W. Jacobs." *Canadian Jewish Archives*. New Series, nos. 26-27. Montreal: Canadian Jewish Congress, 1982.

_____, Judy Nefsky and P. Obermeir. *Les Juifs du Québec, bibliographie retrospective annotée*. Québec: Institut québécois de la recherche sur la culture, 1981.

Rosenberg, Louis. *A Statistical Study of the Number and Percentage of Jewish Children in the Protestant Schools of Greater Montreal*. Montreal: Canadian Jewish Congress, 1969.

Rostra, E. M. "Le Monde Chrétien, que doit-il au judaisme?" *Revue dominicaine* (January 1958), col. 68, no. 1.

Royal Canadian Mounted Police. *Law and Order in Canadian Democracy*. Ottawa: E. Cloutier, 1952.

Rumilly, R. *Henri Bourassa, la vie publique d'un grand Canadien*. Montréal: Editions Chantecler, 1969.

Sack, B. G. "History of the Jews in Canada." In *The Jew in Canada*. Edited by Arthur Daniel Hart. Toronto and Montreal: Jewish Publications Limited, 1926.

Secouons le joug. Association Catholique de la Jeunesse Canadienne. N.p., 1923.

Silcox, C. E. *The Challenge of Anti-Semitism to Democracy.* N.p., 1939.

Smith, Cameron. *Unfinished Journey — The Lewis Family.* Toronto: Summerhill Press, 1989.

Saint-Pierre, A. "Le Juifs et les premiers Chrétiens."*Revue dominicaine* (February 1935), 85-97.

Sulte, Benjamin. "Juifs et Chrétiens." *Revue canadienne* 7 (1970).

Talbot, Jeanne. *Ce que femme veut, pour le triomphe de la modestie chrétienne.* Montréal: Oeuvre des tracts, 1927.

Tardivel, J.-P. *Notes de voyage en France, Italie, Espagne, Irlande, Angleterre, Belgique et Hollande.* Montréal: Eusebe Senécal, 1890.

Taschereau, R., and R. C. Kellock, Commissioners. *Report of Royal Commission to Investigate the Facts Relating to the Communication of Secret and Confidential Information to Agents of a Foreign Power.* Ottawa, 1946.

Teboul, Victor. *Mythe et images du Juif au Québec. Essai d'analyse critique.* Montréal: Editions de Lagrave, 1977.

——————. "Antisémitisme, mythe et image du juif au Québec." *Voix et images du pays*, 9 (1975), 87-112.

Torczyner, Jacques. *Client and Community Needs: How They Can Be Better Met.* Montreal: Villa-Maria Social Service Centre, 1974.

Valiquette, Stéphane. *Pour se préparer au dialogue Judéo-chrétien, guide pour Chrétiens.* Montréal: N.p., 1989.

Vaugeois, Denis. *Les Juifs et la Nouvelle France.* Trois Rivières: Editions Boréal Express, 1968.

—————— and J. Lacoursière. *Canada-Québec: synthèse historique.* Montreal: Editions du Renouveau pédagogique, 1978.

Vineberg, Harris. "Zihronie fun alten yiddischen yishuv" (Memories of the Jewish Establishment in Montreal). *Jewish Daily Eagle*, July 8, 1932. Centennial Jubilee Edition (1832-1932). (Yiddish section.)

Wade, Mason. *French Canadian Outlook: A Brief Account of the Unknown North Americans.* New York: Viking Press, 1946.

Weiller, Georgette. *Sarah Bernhardt in Canada.* Québec: Editions Athena, 1973.